Intensional Logic
and
The Metaphysics of Intentionality

Intensional Logic
and
The Metaphysics of Intentionality

Edward N. Zalta

Stanford University

A Bradford Book
The MIT Press
Cambridge, Massachusetts
London, England

This book was typeset in Computer Modern Roman using the LaTeX document preparation system. It was printed and bound in the United States of America.

Library of Congress Cataloging-in-Publication Data

Zalta, Edward N., 1952–
    Intensional logic and the metaphysics of intentionality

    "A Bradford book."
    Bibliography: p.
    Includes index.
    1. Intentionality (Philosophy)   2. Logic, Symbolic and
mathematical.   I. Title
B105.I56Z35   1988   110–dc19   87-32171
ISBN 0-262-24027-0

To Melissa

Contents

III   *Existential* Generalization

IV   Substitutivity and Existential Generalization

Preface

In writing this book, I have had three goals in mind: (1) to develop a
new, expanded conception of intensionality, (2) to explain clearly how
the theory and technical apparatus developed in my first book is sensitive
to this conception, and (3) to extend and apply the theory in new ways.
The expanded conception of intensionality occurred to me while thinking
about the differences among intensional logics. There is a wide variety of
such logics, and some of them have very little in common. Though most
of them were designed to explain apparent failures of the principle of
substitution, each system focuses on a somewhat different body of data.
And each breaks down when faced with intensional data outside its focus.
It seemed important to try to collate and classify the entire range of data
that occasioned the development of these intensional logics. And as a
result of doing this, it became clear that there was a wider group of
inferential principles that appeared to fail in various situations. So the
expanded conception of intensionality is tied essentially to this expanded
set of inferential principles.

My second goal has been to show that the system described in my
first book, *Abstract Objects: An Introduction to Axiomatic Metaphysics*,
can represent the entire range of intensional data. In that book, I developed a theory of abstract objects and tried to construct, by means of
the theory, a progressive explanation of certain sentences that had puzzled metaphysicians and philosophers of language. But there was little
attempt to state explicitly the puzzles that surrounded these sentences.
There was almost no attempt to argue for the theory or compare it with
alternatives. And little mention was made either of the philosophical
presuppositions of the theory or of a host of traditional issues in the
philosophy of language. This situation is rectified in the present work.
But more importantly, the system is reconceptualized in terms of the expanded conception of intensionality. Let me note that familiarity with

my first book is not presupposed, and reference to it has been kept to a minimum.

My third goal has been to expand the theory. Three new areas of application are: (a) the addition of tense operators and the identification of moments of time, (b) the attempt to make some of Husserl's ideas precise, and (c) the inclusion of indexicals and contexts to explain substitutivity failures affecting indexicals. The system described right at the outset includes some of the new additions.

These, then, are the principal goals that have directed this project. I have had one other, more practical, goal. And that is to make the book accessible to philosophers with little training in logic. I have tried to motivate and explain all of the technical material and logical notation. For example, numerous instances of comprehension schemata are constructed, to show how the schemata work. The formal semantics of the system is developed only insofar as it helps one to picture what the theory asserts.

The structure of the book is rather simple. It contains five parts. One of the parts is the Introduction, and another is the Conclusion. The three parts in the middle each deal with one or more of the principles that are used to identify intensional contexts. There is also an Appendix, the only part of the book that focuses entirely on technical definitions. The Appendix contains the most highly evolved incarnation of the system, with all of the new additions and modifications.

The following typographical conventions have been employed. Single quotes are used to mention subsentential words or phrases of English, as well as to mention expressions of the formal language, whether they are terms, formulas, or other symbols. Sometimes, when it is too obvious that I am talking about an expression of the language, the single quotes are omitted. Double quotes are used to mention entire sentences of English. This makes it easier to distinguish them from the surrounding sentences. However, double quotes serve a variety of other purposes. They are used for quotation, as scare-quotes, to give readings of formal expressions in English, and to introduce symbols and abbreviations. The context should make the meaning of the double quotes clear.

There are also conventions concerning typefaces. Italics serve several purposes. Certain symbols and expressions of the formal language (for example, the primitive terms) are always written in italic. Italic is used for emphasis, and for the introduction and definition of new or technical terms. It is also used for most foreign, especially Latin, words. Greek letters, with the exception of λ and ι, are usually used as metalinguistic variables that range over expressions of the object language. The two just mentioned are part of the object language, however. Finally, bold-face is used for one purpose, namely, to identify items associated with the semantics of the object language. The names of interpretations, assignment functions, denotation functions, extension functions, etc., are all written in boldface. When I use boldface variables to range over worlds and times, therefore, I am talking about entities that are primitive in the semantics. But when I use regular italic variables to range over worlds and times, I am talking about entities that are defined in the object language, using only the primitives of the theory.

Finally, let me acknowledge my indebtedness. I am indebted first and foremost to the people at Stanford's Center for the Study of Language and Information (CSLI). The first draft of this work was written while I was a postdoctoral fellow at CSLI. The second draft was also written on the premises, for the Center has supplied me with office space and computer facilities throughout my appointment in the Philosophy Department. The people here create an environment that stimulates like no other that I've encountered. Special thanks go to Chris Menzel, Ken Olson, John Perry, and Dagfinn Føllesdal, whose encouragement and enthusiasm for my work has been a constant source of inspiration. Their observations, criticisms, and insights have led me to improve the manuscript in countless ways. I've also benefitted greatly from discussions with Paul Oppenheimer, Larry Moss, Peter Sells, Mats Rooth, Peter Ludlow, Chris Swoyer, John Etchemendy, Stanley Peters, Jon Barwise, and David Israel. These are just some of the people who have forced me to think more critically about the issues that follow. Also, I would like to thank the kindly and efficient staff members who made it possible for me typeset the book in LaTeX. In particular, Emma Pease and Dikran Karagueuzian often helped me to get around the obstacles I encountered in learning to use this program.

Stanford University
February, 1988

Part I

Introduction

1

Intensionality and Intentionality

1.1 Intensional Logic

Intensional logics are formal systems for representing and explaining the apparent failure of four logical principles. The four principles involved are: *Existential* Generalization, Existential Generalization, Substitutivity, and Strong Extensionality. These principles have played a major role in contemporary philosophical logic and the study of where and why they seem to go wrong is rather intriguing. All four license inferences between certain sentences, yet all seem to be incompatible with ordinary intuitions that we have concerning the validity of some of the inferences so licensed. Intensionality is the property sentences have in virtue of failing to conform to the usual pattern of inference. To represent and explain such failures, an intensional logic should provide a subtle, theoretical conception of the truth conditions of such sentences, one that helps us to understand the sources of failure. Most of the intensional logics that have been developed handle the failures of just one or two of these principles. But the logic described in this book seems to have the capacity to deal naturally with the failures of all four. Thus, the system may provide an insightful link between apparently unconnected puzzles.

In order to make these claims more vivid, let us briefly review the principles in question and examine how they fail. The first principle is *Existential* Generalization. It applies to sentences of natural language that contain denoting expressions. Let S be an English sentence in which there occurs a denoting expression D such as a name or definite description. S has the form "...D...." Now let S' be derived from S by replacing D with the phrase 'something that exists.' So S' is an English sentence of the form "...something that exists...," where this is to be understood as synonymous with "Some existing thing is such

that ... it. ... ." Then the principle of *Existential* Generalization is: from
S, we may infer S'. For example, from "Ronald Reagan married Nancy
Reagan" it seems that we may infer both "Ronald Reagan married something that exists" (or "Some existing thing is such that Ronald Reagan
married it") and "Something that exists married Nancy Reagan." In
order to be true, a simple sentence containing the transitive verb 'married' must have both a subject and a direct object that denote (typically
distinct!) existing objects. The same goes for simple sentences containing such transitive verbs as 'kissed,' 'kicked,' 'met,' etc. But there are
a host of English sentences containing verbs and denoting expressions
for which this is not the case. Consider "Sherlock Holmes still inspires
modern detectives" and "Ponce de Leon searched for the fountain of
youth." We may not infer "Something that exists still inspires modern
detectives" from the former, nor "Ponce de Leon searched for something
that exists" from the latter. The subject of the verb 'inspires' does not
have to denote an existing object for a simple sentence containing it to
be true. Nor does the direct object of the verb 'searched for.' Consequently, *Existential* Generalization fails for these two sentences. An
intensional logic should yield representations that explain these facts.

It is important to distinguish *Existential* Generalization from the related principle of Existential Generalization. The latter derives from the
logical intuition that if a specific object has a property, then something
or other has that property. The former, however, derives both from this
intuition and the intuition that all objects exist. Let S be defined as
in the previous paragraph, and let S' be derived from S by replacing
D with the word 'something.' So S' is of the form "... something... ,"
where this is to be understood as synonymous with "Something is such
that ... it. ... ." Then the principle of Existential Generalization is: from
S, we may infer S'. Clearly, the sentences and verbs that obey *Existential* Generalization also obey Existential Generalization. Both "Muhammad Ali fought something" and "Something fought Joe Frazier" follow
from "Muhammad Ali fought Joe Frazier." But the examples from the
previous paragraph that fail *Existential* Generalization *obey* Existential Generalization. There is at least one reading of "Sherlock Holmes
still inspires real detectives" from which we may validly infer "Something still inspires real detectives" (or "Something is such that it still
inspires real detectives"). For the former sentence to be true, or even
meaningful, 'Sherlock Holmes' must signify something. Similar claims
apply to "Ponce de Leon searched for the fountain of youth." If this
is doubted, consider the fact that if someone had asked de Leon what
he was doing thrashing about in the jungles of Florida exposing himself
and his men to one of the most inhospitable environments imaginable,
he might have responded wryly, "I'm searching for something." We

cannot regard "Ponce de Leon searched for the fountain of youth" as true without also regarding "Ponce de Leon searched for something" as true. Consequently, these inferences do not fail the principle of Existential Generalization. Indeed, it is hard to imagine a meaningful sentence S from which S', as defined above, is not validly inferred by this principle (unless 'nothing' is somehow analyzed as a denoting expression).

However, there are some sentences for which Existential Generalization appears to fail. Consider, for example, the inference from "Ralph believes that the tallest spy is a spy" to "Something is such that Ralph believes it to be a spy." This rather well known example, due to Quine [1956], has been the subject of much dispute. The puzzle is what to say about the situation in which Ralph has no idea who the tallest spy is, though he does believe the apparently trivial claim that the tallest spy is a spy. In such a situation, it seems that we cannot conclude that there is some particular person whom Ralph believes to be a spy. This suggests that we should not accept the inference in question. So it seems that Existential Generalization fails. By representing such inferences, an intensional logic should help us to explain where the inference goes wrong.

The principle of Substitutivity also produces an interesting group of anomalies. This principle derives from the intuition that if two things are identical, anything true concerning one is true concerning the other. If S is any English sentence containing a denoting expression D, and S' is the result of replacing at least one occurrence of D by a different expression D', then Substitutivity may be expressed as follows: from S and "D is identical to D'," we may infer S'. This holds in a wide variety of cases. For example, from "The teacher of Aristotle is a teacher" and "The teacher of Aristotle is Plato," we may validly infer "Plato is a teacher," and from "Mark Twain wrote *Huckleberry Finn*" and "Mark Twain is Samuel Clemens," we may validly infer "Samuel Clemens wrote *Huckleberry Finn*." However, the exceptions to this principle now qualify as some of the most interesting puzzles of contemporary philosophical logic. Consider just the following two. There is at least one reading of "It is necessary that the teacher of Aristotle is a teacher" and "The teacher of Aristotle is Plato" on which "It is necessary that Plato is a teacher" does not follow. And there is at least one reading of "Susie believes that Mark Twain wrote *Huckleberry Finn*" and "Mark Twain is Samuel Clemens" on which "Susie believes that Samuel Clemens wrote *Huckleberry Finn*" is not a consequence. The representations of these failures of Substitutivity are an important aspect of intensional logic. Such representations must assign these sentences truth conditions which not only preserve their intuitive truth value but also explain what it is about the original English sentences that causes the principle to fail.

In what follows, we plan to construe Substitutivity in a rather broad fashion. In particular, we suppose that predicative expressions of English are denoting expressions (they denote properties and relations) and that, consequently, Substitutivity applies to them as well. For example, let S be a sentence in which the predicate 'F' occurs, and let S' be exactly like S except that the predicate 'G' replaces an occurrence of 'F'. Then it would seem that the following broad version of Substitutivity would hold: from S and "Being F is (the same as) being G," we may infer S'. Clearly, "Alan is my male sibling" follows from "Alan is my brother" and "Being a brother is the same thing as being a male sibling." But this inference has its counterexamples as well: "Susie believes that Alan is my male sibling" does not follow from "Susie believes that Alan is my brother" and "Being a brother is the same as being a male sibling." To our knowledge, no intensional logic heretofore has been able to account for these failures.

It is very important to distinguish broad Substitutivity from the principle of Strong Extensionality. To state the latter, let S be an English sentence of the form "Necessarily, all and only F's are G's," and let S' be a sentence of the form "Being an F is the same thing as being a G," where 'F' and 'G' are predicative expressions. Then the principle of Strong Extensionality is simply this: from S, we may infer S'. The principle seems to hold when we substitute certain predicate expressions for 'F' and 'G' in S. Consider again 'brother' and 'male sibling.' It seems to follow from "Necessarily, all and only brothers are male siblings" that "Being a brother is the same thing as being a male sibling." However, there are other expressions for which this inference does not hold. Take, for example, the expressions 'brown and colorless dog' and 'barber who shaves just those who don't shave themselves.' From "Necessarily, all and only brown and colorless dogs are barbers who shave just those who don't shave themselves," we cannot infer "Being a brown and colorless dog is the same thing as being a barber who shaves just those who don't shave themselves." Intuitively, the former sentence is true, since the properties signified by the predicate expressions both necessarily fail to be exemplified; they are properties that no thing could have. Consequently, they are necessarily equivalent, which is what the former sentence asserts. But intuitively, the latter sentence is false, because the properties signified seem to be distinct.

Similar ideas apply to relational predicates and sentences. These expressions signify relations and propositions, respectively. There are versions of Strong Extensionality that offer to identify relations and propositions that are necessarily equivalent. However, such principles fare no better than the original. For example, from "Necessarily, Rover is a brown and colorless dog if and only if Plato is a barber who shaves just those who don't shave themselves," it does not follow that the proposition signified by "Rover is a brown and colorless dog" is identical to the proposition signified by "Plato is a barber who shaves just those who don't shave themselves." This kind of inference fails for lots of other relations, though it is somewhat awkward to give examples in unaffected English. In what follows, Strong Extensionality is understood in its broadest scope, as applying to sentences describing the necessary equivalence and identity of n-place relations, for every n. Note that we shall regard properties and propositions as one-place and zero-place relations, respectively (henceforth, the term "relations" is frequently used to encompass both properties and propositions).

It is now customary to call relations "intensional entities," in virtue of the fact that expressions signifying them occur in sentences failing Strong Extensionality. An intensional logic should provide a way of systematizing these entities. The notion of "logic" intended here is that of a formal system having two basic units—an interpreted, formal language and a deductive apparatus that yields the logical truths of the language as theorems. The language of the intensional logic described here shall serve, in part, as a precise medium for talking about relations. The deductive apparatus associated with this language has a distinguished group of logical axioms and definitions that specify not only very general conditions under which there are relations but also identity conditions for relations. This axiomatization is consistent with the view that necessarily equivalent relations may be distinct.

It is also customary to call the principal verbs and sentential operators that occur in sentences failing one of the above principles "intensional verbs" and "intensional operators." Intensional verbs and operators create "intensional contexts." This profusion of things intensional means that whenever something is identified as "intensional," it is important to know which principles it violates. In some cases, the kind of thing in question makes this clear. But we must remember that a sentence violating one principle does not necessarily violate the others. For example, there are sentences which violate *Existential* Generalization but which *obey* Substitutivity. We cannot infer "Some existing thing is more famous than any real detective" from "Sherlock Holmes is more famous than any real detective," but from the latter together with "Holmes is the central character of the Conan Doyle novels," we may infer "The central character of the Conan Doyle novels is more famous than any real detective." Frequently, it will be clear from the context of the discussion which principle an intensional sentence fails. On other occasions, this must be made explicit.

The conception of intensional logic just outlined differs from the traditional conception that stems from the work of Carnap in [1947]. For one thing, the traditional conception does not require that an intensional logic represent the failures of Strong Extensionality. In fact, there is a striking divergence between the two conceptions regarding the notion of "extension." The divergence is so fundamental that our entire approach to language looks radically different. Carnap took extensions to be associated primarily with linguistic expressions. The extension of a name or description is the individual it typically denotes; the extension of a predicate, or general term, is a set that contains everything to which the predicate truly applies; and the extension of a sentence is a truth value. Moreover, (materially) equivalent expressions have the same extension. For example, the truth of the sentence "All and only F's are G's," semantically implies that the two general terms 'F' and 'G' are equivalent and have the same extension (in our system, the truth of this sentence implies that the *properties denoted* by 'F' and 'G' are equivalent and have the same extension). Consequently, in Carnap's framework, there arises a distinguished class of sentences in which extensionally equivalent expressions can be substituted for one another preserving truth. An example of such as sentence is "Reagan is a human." Truth is preserved when the predicate 'human' is replaced by the extensionally equivalent predicate 'featherless biped.'

Our approach to language is founded on Frege's [1884] notion of an extension. Frege took an extension to be something that is associated primarily with a *concept* (that is, a property or an n-place relation, $n \geq 1$). The extension of a concept is basically the set that contains everything falling under the concept. We shall broaden this notion somewhat, to allow us to say that the extension of a proposition is a truth value (though, this is *not* to say that the denotation of a sentence is a truth value). On our conception, names and descriptions denote objects; predicates, or general terms, denote properties and relations; and sentences denote propositions. The very simplest sentences are true just in case the individual denoted by the name or description is an element of the extension of the property denoted by the predicate. Intuitively, the predicates 'featherless biped' and 'human' denote different properties. If two predicates 'F' and 'G' denote different properties, even properties that happen to have the same extension, then any sentence S containing 'F' intuitively denotes a different proposition from that denoted by the sentence S' which differs from S only by the fact that 'G' replaces 'F.' There is no reason to expect truth to be preserved upon substitution, since the propositions are distinct. The truth-preserving substitution in the case of "Reagan is human" and "Reagan is a featherless biped" is purely fortuitous—the distinct properties the predicates denote just happen to have the same extension. There is no distinguished behavior on the part of the predicates involved.

By focusing attention on such "extensional" predicates, however, Carnap's notion of "intensional" fails to include the really interesting cases. Carnap assigns to each designating expression an intension as well as an extension. He identified the intension of a predicate with the property we take the predicate to denote. A problem arises for Carnap as soon as he takes "Necessarily, all and only F's are G's" to imply that 'F' and 'G' have the same intension. For this essentially identifies necessarily equivalent properties. Such an identification does not square with the intuitions recently described, which suggest that necessarily equivalent properties may be distinct. Thus, Carnap's conception of intensionality does not cover the cases where there are distinct properties that necessarily have the same extension. Neither does the paradigm intensional logic in Carnap's tradition, namely, Montague's [1974] intensional logic, for it also represents relations as entities that are identical if necessarily equivalent. That is one of the reasons why we have formulated a somewhat different conception of intensional logic. Such a logic should yield a representation of relations that is sensitive to the fact that they do not behave this way.

Our conception differs from the traditional conception in another important way. In addition to assigning every designating term both an intension and an extension, traditional intensional logics always explain substitutivity failures of natural language by including terms and contexts in the formal language that fail the formal version of the substitutivity principle. Apparently, the motivation for doing this is the idea that in order to explain the deviant behavior of certain expressions and contexts of natural language, it is necessary to produce a logic having expressions and contexts that exhibit that same deviant behavior. But while this may be necessary for explaining certain features of natural language, it is not necessary for explaining the failures of our four major principles. In what follows, we shall not use the method of intension and extension—the terms of our language receive only denotations, relative to an interpretation of the language and an assignment to the variables. Moreover, Substitutivity is preserved intact in our logic—there are no denoting terms, or contexts, for which it fails. Truth is always preserved when terms having the same denotation are substituted for one another.

This last fact could be a source of confusion, if one were inclined to think of the denotation of a term as corresponding in some way with the extension of a term. For then one could describe our system as *purely extensional*, since not only is truth preserved whenever terms having the same extension (or denotation) are substituted for one another, but also the extension (denotation) of every complex term in our logic is solely a function of the extensions (denotations) of the parts of the term and the way in which they are arranged. However, in what follows, we

shall not equate the denotation of a term with the term's extension. In
fact, no mention of "the extension of a term" will be made, unless it
is for the purpose of comparing our analyses to ones found in a more
traditional logic. But it should be of interest to those who still think of
Montague's intensional logic as a paradigm that a purely denotational
intensional logic such as ours is capable of explaining the failures of the
four principles we've discussed.

1.2 Intentional States

Intentionality is the fascinating property certain cognitive states and
events have in virtue of being *directed*, or *about*, something. Whenever we think, we think about something; whenever we believe, there is
something we believe; whenever we dream, there is something we dream
about. This is true of every episode of such diverse psychological phenomena as learning, imagining, desiring, admiring, searching for, discov-
ering, and remembering. Sometimes, intentional states and events are
trained upon individual things, for instance, when we search for a lost
key, imagine the face of a particular old friend, or admire a painting.
Sometimes, they are directed towards logically more complex objects,
for instance, when we entertain a proposition, or fear a certain state of
affairs, or contemplate a certain depressing situation. But all of these
phenomena are to be contrasted with physical sensations, undirected
feelings of joy, sadness, depression, or anxiety, and with episodes of pain
and discomfort. Sensations, undirected feelings and pains are not about
anything. No other object, state or event is essential to their identity.
Any attempt to specify what such mental states and events are about
simply results in a description of that very same state or event. But
the identity of directed states is inextricably linked to the objects and
propositions upon which they are directed. The identity of a belief is
essentially tied to the identity of the proposition believed; the identity of
a hope is essentially tied to the identity of the state of affairs hoped for;
and so forth. If we discount the possibility of there being cognitive states
which are directed solely at themselves, then it might be useful to say
that a cognitive state is intentional just in case an object or proposition
other than the state itself is essential to its identity.[1]

One of the first things it is important to notice about intentional
states is that often they can be about nonexistent objects, false propositions and states of affairs that don't obtain. For example, someone can
worship Odin even though Odin doesn't exist. Our political leaders may
believe the proposition that the Soviets violated the Salt II treaty, even

---

[1]Compare Searle [1979], p. 182, and Searle [1983], pp. 1–4.

though that proposition may be false. One can fear the state of affairs, there being a Communist takeover of the U.S., even though that state of affairs may never obtain (indeed, the actions of many people can be explained only by referring to their desire that such a state of affairs never obtain). The two most interesting examples of this phenomenon, however, are dreams and proofs by the technique of *reductio ad absurdum*, and it would serve well to consider an example of the latter.

One of the most famous proofs by *reductio* in contemporary logic is Russell's proof that the unrestricted abstraction principle of naive set theory is inconsistent. Russell employed this principle to describe the set of all sets which aren't members of themselves, the being of which implies a contradiction. It is a remarkable fact that when one sets out Russell's proof, one *appears* to be considering an object which turns out, in some sense, to be impossible. One appears to be reasoning about the set of all non-self-membered sets by entertaining propositions that seem to have this object as a constituent. To see this, think about the last line of the proof, namely, that the Russell set is a self-member if and only if *it* is not a self-member.

In what follows, we shall assume that the reader is at least sympathetic to the idea that a genuine understanding of intentionality requires us to take these appearances at face value rather than explain them away. The attempts to explain them away have not been successful. One such strategy has been to suggest that *reductio* is a derived rule and that Russell's proof could be carried out without entertaining any controversial propositions. This strategy just denies the facts. The perfectly rigorous, yet informal rule of *reductio* is in fact the one most often used in the proof. The students of the proof by *reductio* entertain the controversial propositions. Moreover, many logicians, and quite possibly Russell himself, have found *reductio* to be the most natural argument form to employ. As an alternative strategy, one might offer Russell's infamous theory of descriptions as the means of analyzing away the propositions in question. Unfortunately, this theory not only fails to do justice to the apparent logical form of the propositions in question, but more importantly, when applied generally, it fails to preserve the intuitive truth value of a wide range of other propositions. For example, it turns the historical fact that Ponce de Leon searched for the fountain of youth into a falsehood.[2] Results such as this suggest that the theory of descriptions is, at best, not general and, at worst, false.

In order to avoid commitment to nonexistent objects, some philosophers have drawn a distinction between the content and the object of

---

[2]The analysis of this fact becomes: There is a unique thing x that exemplifies being a fountain of youth, and Ponce de Leon searched for x. This is false, if we assume that nothing exemplifies being a fountain of youth.

an intentional state. In the case of Russell's discovery of the set of all non-self-membered sets, they argue that Russell's mental state had a content, or involved a representation of some kind, but that since there is no such set, there is no object his mental state was about. They claim that such states have representational content but no intentional object. The distinction between the content and the object of an intentional state is a useful one, and it will be clarified and employed in this work. But our view is that both intentional objects and representations are always needed (even in a case like the one we're now considering). The reason is that a representation may contain all sorts of inaccurate information that fails to characterize the object represented. For example, the representation one may have of the set of all non-self-membered sets may include information that cannot be deduced from the pure description of this object. Our theory will take this into account, and in such cases, it will yield both representations and nonexistent objects. In recent book [1980], Terence Parsons canvasses other ways of explaining appearances so as to avoid commitment to "impossible" and other nonexistent objects. He argues (successfully, in our opinion) that they are all unsatisfactory. In what follows, we presume some familiarity with, and openness toward, his arguments.[3]

In [1874], Brentano noticed that the capacity for having directed psychological states about objects that need neither exist, be true, nor obtain, is the "mark" of the mental. In other words, it is a feature mental phenomena have that no purely physical phenomenon could have. More importantly, however, is the significance this aspect of intentionality has for a realistic understanding of the world. The traditional view of the realist may be stated as follows: our beliefs, desires, and other directed cognitive states, typically have objects other than the mind itself, unless the psychological state in question is some sort of reflection about the mind (Russell [1904], p. 204). The objects involved are, in some sense, "part" of the world. Since it seems unlikely that worshipping Odin, believing that the Soviets violated Salt II, fearing a Communist takeover, and contemplating the set of all non-self-membered sets are reflective acts about the mind, a realist might come to the conclusion that nonexistent objects, false propositions, and states of affairs that don't obtain, are part of the world. Intellectual pursuit of this last conclusion leads us to study the metaphysics of intentional states.

Some readers, no doubt, will shift uneasily in their seats at the mention of the word "metaphysics." Those who are somewhat hesitant about getting involved in a study of metaphysics, for whatever reason, might

---

[3]See also Parsons [1979] and [1982]. The theory proposed here has, I believe, a wider range of applications than Parsons' theory. Nevertheless, Parsons' work is a must for those who take the data of intentionality seriously.

think of the enterprise by using the following analogy: in the context of producing (a language for) a machine (that is to simulate) having intentional states, metaphysics is something like the *a priori* construction and organization of the ultimate types of abstract data over which all computations are to be performed. We can say, without prejudicing the question of whether a silicon-based machine can in fact have intentional states, that if a machine is at least to simulate having intentional states, it must be given some internal representation of the world to operate upon. But we have to make decisions about the way the world is before we can make decisions about how to represent the world in a machine. The former kinds of decisions are metaphysical ones. Furthermore, those hesitant about doing metaphysics might consider that the evolutionary development of the capacity for having intentional states has tremendous survival value. Survival value is a measure of how well a new development is adapted to (the structure of) the world. So to decide whether the capacity for having intentional states is well adapted, we need to have some idea of what the world is like—not only what things there are, but also how they are structured and related. This is just what a metaphysics should tell us. No purely physical theory of the world, no theory constructed solely in terms of physical objects that exist and what actually is the case, seems able to analyze and explain directedness towards nonexistent objects, false propositions, and states of affairs and situations that don't obtain. At least, that is the way it would seem.

We don't have to look far now to discover the link between intentional states and intensional logic. It is tempting to say that the peculiar objects some mental states are directed upon are the same objects that terms failing Generalization and Substitutivity signify in intensional contexts.[4] But this is somewhat of an oversimplification, and does not exploit to the fullest the ideas reviewed so far. A more clearly articulated link is this: sentences that describe intentional states are intensional. They violate either a Generalization principle or Substitutivity. The sentences that report a particular individual as being the object of thought, admiration, love, search, worship, fascination, and so forth, fail *Existential* Generalization. The sentences that report propositional beliefs, desires, fears, discoveries, concerns, and so forth, have readings that fail either Existential Generalization or Substitutivity. The main verbs in all of these sentences signify types of intentional states and events. So by setting out a formal context for studying the truth conditions and entailments of these sentences, an intensional logic gives us a means for analyzing the logical structure of intentional states.

---

[4]In what follows, the use of 'Generalization' by itself refers to both principles of generalization.

Another link between intensional logic and intentional states is the fact that it is possible to use an intensional logic to formulate theories about the objects involved in intentional states. We've seen that some states are directed towards individual things, some of which exist and some of which don't. A theory is needed about the individuals that don't exist, if we are to take states about them at face value. An intensional logic can provide an environment for expressing such a theory. We've also seen that there are intentional states directed towards propositions that may or may not be true (or states of affairs that may or may not obtain). A theory is needed about such logically complex objects, as well as about the properties and relations they may have as constituents. And again, an intensional logic provides an appropriate environment for constructing such a theory, since propositions, properties, and relations are intensional entities.

The intensional logic we shall investigate successfully forges both of these links to intentionality, once it is coupled with a metaphysical theory about the structure of the world. The metaphysical theory introduces new intentional entities, and these make it possible to analyze hitherto intractable (sentences about) intentional states. The technical foundations for both the logic and the metaphysical theory were formulated in [1983], but little familiarity with this work is presumed. Although this research program will be extended in a variety of ways, the main task of the present work will be to show that the framework is refined enough to explain the puzzles of intensionality and intentionality. In the course of doing this, we produce evidence for thinking that the framework is more refined than others, in the sense that without the choices made available by our logic and theory, philosophers and logicians have been forced to give up natural views concerning the logical or semantic analysis of some uniformity of language. We hope that the reader will come away with an appreciation of the expanded range of choices and alternatives that are made available.

2

An Overview of the Theory

In this chapter, we describe in some detail an enhanced version of the theory developed in [1983]. The modal theory in [1983] is enriched with the expressive power of simple tense logic. The enriched theory has two parts: the foundations and the theory proper. The foundations handle the failures of Strong Extensionality, whereas the theory proper handles the failures of Generalization and Substitutivity. An intensional logic serves as the foundations. In addition to the language, the laws of logic, and the rules of inference, the intensional logic includes distinguished axioms that assert that there is a wide variety of ordinary properties, relations, and propositions (the axioms do not assert that there are any ordinary individuals, for that is a contingent matter). These ordinary relations are represented and described in a way that is consistent with the fact that they fail to be strongly extensional. The theory proper, however, posits *abstract* objects of every kind—abstract individuals, abstract properties and relations, and abstract propositions. Abstract objects serve two basic purposes. They serve as the intentional objects of states directed towards nonexistents. Names and definite descriptions of English that intuitively signify such nonexistents will denote an appropriate abstract object serving in this capacity. This proves to be valuable for the explanation of intensional contexts failing *Existential* Generalization. Abstract objects also serve to characterize and reify the content of mental representations. Such objects are signified by expressions in intensional contexts that fail the principle of Substitutivity.

2.1 The Insight Behind the Theory

At the crux of both the foundations and the theory proper stands the distinction between *exemplifying* and *encoding* a property. The best way to explain this distinction is to motivate it. Consider how the naive interpretation of Meinong's [1904a] theory of intentional, nonexistent objects gets into trouble. This theory seems to require that when we think about the set of non-self-membered sets, the round square, the fountain of youth, or the existent golden mountain, etc., we are thinking about an object that really does exemplify, or instantiate, the described characteristics. On this view, the set of non-self-membered sets really does exemplify being a non-self-membered set; the round square really does have the characteristics of being round and being square; and so forth. But, intuitively, the very being of such objects is inconsistent either with the laws of logic, true non-logical principles, or contingent facts. The set of non-self-membered sets is inconsistent with the laws of logic. The round square is inconsistent with the principle that whatever has or exemplifies the characteristic of being square does not have the characteristic of being round. The existent golden mountain and the fountain of youth are inconsistent with the respective facts that no golden mountains exist and no fountain of youth exists.

One popular way to avoid these results is to reject nonexistent objects and employ complex properties in the analysis of intentional states that are apparently about nonexistents. For example, it has been said that to think about the set of non-self-membered sets is to stand in a certain relation to the property of being a non-self-membered set. And in a similar manner, to search for the fountain of youth is to stand in a certain relation to the property of being a fountain the waters of which confer everlasting life. In analyses such as these, the properties we would be related to, in and of themselves, violate neither the laws of logic, true non-logical principles, nor the facts. Such laws, principles, and facts just force the properties to be unexemplified. However, there is an overriding reason for not following this approach: it does not do justice to certain simple and natural intuitions we have about the logical structure of natural language. To see this, consider the two sentences "Reagan worshipped Bhagwan Rajneesh" and "Augustus Caesar worshipped Jupiter." If we analyze the latter by applying the complex property technique, we face a dilemma in analyzing the former. If we try to be consistent and use the complex property technique to analyze "Reagan worshipped Rajneesh," then we fail to preserve the natural intuition that this sentence should be regarded as a two-place relation between two (existing) individuals. If we don't use the complex property technique for this sentence, then we fail to provide a consistent and general analysis of sentences of the form "D worships D'."

It doesn't really matter whether one is convinced that this is a knockdown reason for finding an alternative analysis. The important thing is to recognize that if we have no pretheoretic prejudice about what kinds of things there are in the world, the simplest explanation of these two sentences leads us back to the view that there are nonexistent, intentional individuals. And that is where the distinction between *exemplifying* and *encoding* a property can be of help. Ernst Mally proposed in [1912] that there is a realm of abstract objects that encode properties. These objects, however, do not have to exemplify the properties they encode.[1] To get an idea of what this distinction amounts to, consider the difference between real and fictional detectives. We can usually talk with, hire, and pay for the services of real detectives. Not so with fictional detectives; they are not the kind of thing we could talk to, or hire, etc. The natural way of explaining this difference is to say that fictional detectives don't have the property of being a detective in quite the same way that real ones do. Real detectives exemplify the property, whereas fictional detectives do not. We shall say that the latter encode the property, however. Things that exemplify the property of being a detective exist, have a location in space and time, are made of flesh and bones, think, solve crimes, and so on, whereas things that just encode the property of being a detective are abstract and do not exemplify any of these characteristics. They might exemplify these properties according to their respective stories, but this is not the same as exemplifying them *simpliciter.*

Consider how this distinction helps us to understand directedness towards "impossible" and other nonexistent objects. Suppose that the set of non-self-membered sets, the round square, the existent golden mountain, and the like, are not objects that exemplify the described characteristics, but rather, are objects that encode those characteristics. An abstract object that encodes being a set of non-self-membered sets doesn't violate the laws of logic, as long as the fact that it encodes such a property doesn't imply that it exemplifies the property. Such an object therefore is not impossible in the usual sense of implying that some contradiction is true, though it is "impossible" in the weak sense that no object *could* exemplify the property it encodes. But since it is not impossible in the strict sense, it may legitimately serve as the object of someone's intentional state. Likewise, if the round square encodes rather than exemplifies the properties of being round and being square, it does not violate the principle that whatever exemplifies being square fails to exemplify being round. Nor are the existent golden mountain

---

[1] 'Exemplify' and 'encode' are technical terms that I have chosen to make Mally's distinction between 'erfüllen' and 'determinieren' vivid to English speakers. See Findlay [1933], pp. 110-112, and pp. 183-184, for an informal description of Mally's views. And see Rapaport [1978] for an informal formulation of Mally's distinction.

and the fountain of youth incompatible with contingent facts. By encoding existence, goldenness and mountainhood, the existent golden mountain is an abstract object that is consistent with the fact that nothing exemplifies these properties. If we define abstractness so that it implies nonexistence, then abstract objects that encode properties prove useful for understanding directedness towards nonexistents. The distinction between encoding and exemplifying a property removes the obstacles the naive Meinongian theory faces with respect to the idea that nonexistent objects are the intentional objects of certain directed states.

Another way of getting your intuitions going about the distinction between exemplifying and encoding a property is to think about your mental representation of Mark Twain. It might involve the property of having a walrus mustache, and maybe the properties of being white-haired and wearing a white suit and bow tie. It might involve a wide variety of facial-feature properties. However, the representation itself doesn't really exemplify these properties. The representation does not have a walrus mustache; the representation is not white-haired; etc. But it does involve these properties in some crucial sense. This sense of 'involve' is what we mean by 'encode.' The properties abstract objects encode characterize them, and so encoding is a kind of predication. An abstract object can be vivid if it encodes visual properties, just as the mental representation of Twain can be a vivid image even though it doesn't exemplify the visual properties involved. By encoding properties of whatever kind, abstract objects have content, and can serve to characterize the content of representations and images. We believe that it is just such objects that are signified by terms in contexts failing the substitutivity principle.

To get some idea of the scope of the domain of abstract objects, you might try to think about the variety of mental representations and images it is possible to have. Be sure to consider the complexity of the representations that can appear in dreams. For each representation with a unique content, there is a unique abstract object that characterizes that content. Unfortunately, however, this method does not give you a good idea of what is in the domain of abstract objects. It is amazingly diverse, and the members that serve as the contents of representations constitute just a small portion of this domain. To get a good idea of what there is in the domain of abstract objects, we need a principle that tells us what conditions have to obtain for an object to be in the domain. Such a "comprehension" principle is one of the basic principles of the theory, and now that we have some feel for the central ideas involved, we can present these principles.

2.2   The Presentation of the Theory

In order to provide a simple and streamlined sketch, we present only
the essential principles, namely, those that describe abstract individuals
and ordinary properties. In Part II of this book, we'll investigate a more
general theory of ordinary relations, and in Part V and in the Appendix,
the most general version of the theory is described. It posits abstract
properties and abstract relations in addition to abstract individuals. But
for the purposes of introduction, the simpler theory presented below is
more appropriate. Seven basic principles are identified. The first three
are part of the theory proper. The next three are part of the foundations.
The final principle is Substitutivity.

Here, then, are the seven basic principles of the theory:

(1) *Ordinary individuals necessarily and always fail to encode proper-*
   ties. (Proper Axiom)

(2) *For every condition on properties, it is necessarily and always the*
   case that there is an abstract individual that encodes just the prop-
   erties satisfying the condition. (Proper Axiom)

(3) *Two individuals are identical if and only if one of the following*
   conditions holds: (a) they are both ordinary individuals and they
   necessarily and always exemplify the same properties, or (b) they
   are both abstract individuals and they necessarily and always en-
   code the same properties. (Definition)

(4) *If it is possibly or sometimes the case that an individual encodes*
   a property, then that individual encodes that property necessarily
   and always. (Logical Axiom)

(5) *For every exemplification condition on individuals that does not in-*
   volve quantification over relations, there is a property which is such
   that, necessarily and always, all and only the individuals satisfying
   the condition exemplify it. (Logical Theorem)

(6) *Two properties are identical just in case it is necessarily and always*
   the case that they are encoded by the same individuals. (Definition)

(7) *If two individuals are identical (or two properties are identical),*
   then anything true about the one is also true about the other.
   (Proper Axiom)

The task of explaining these principles is made easier if we first represent
them formally, for this will exhibit their logical force more clearly. The
first thing we have to do is represent the distinction between exemplifying and encoding a property. Let the variables x_i, y_i, z_i, ... range over

individuals (for every i), and the variables F^n, G^n, H^n, ... range over
n-place relations ($n \geq 1$). To say that $x_1, \ldots, x_n$ *exemplify* F^n, we use
the standard atomic formula: $F^n x_1 \ldots x_n$. To say that x *encodes* F^1, we
use a second kind of atomic formula: xF^1. Consequently, the distinction
between x *exemplifies* F and x *encodes* F is represented by the distinction between the two formulas Fx and xF (when there is no potential
for ambiguity, the superscripts on the relation terms are omitted).

In addition to these basic logical notions, we utilize the standard
complex ones. Here is a list, followed by their symbolic representations:

- *It is not the case that ϕ*: $\sim\phi$

- *If ϕ, then ψ*: $\phi \rightarrow \psi$

- *For every x, ϕ*: $(\forall x)\phi$

- *For every F^n, ϕ*: $(\forall F^n)\phi$

- *Necessarily ϕ*: $\Box\phi$

- *It was always the case that ϕ*: $\mathcal{H}\phi$

- *It will always be the case that ϕ*: $\mathcal{G}\phi$

Conjunction, disjunction, material equivalence, existential quantification, and possibility are all defined and represented in the usual way, by
using the symbols '&,' '∨,' '≡,' '∃,' and '◊,' respectively. Assume that
the modal operators are *S5*-operators, that the tense operators are minimal tense logic operators (of the system K_t), and that the quantifiers
'$\forall x$' and '$\forall F^n$' range over everything whatsoever their respective domains (which are fixed). So the Barcan formulas govern both the modal
and tense operators. We also employ the following standard definitions
from tense logic:

It was once the case that ϕ ("$\mathcal{P}\phi$") $=_{df} \sim\mathcal{H}\sim\phi$

It will once be the case that ϕ ("$\mathcal{F}\phi$") $=_{df} \sim\mathcal{G}\sim\phi$

Always ϕ ("$\blacksquare\phi$") $=_{df} \mathcal{H}\phi$ & ϕ & $\mathcal{G}\phi$

Sometimes ϕ ("$\blacklozenge\phi$") $=_{df} \mathcal{P}\phi \vee \phi \vee \mathcal{F}\phi$

There are complex ways to denote both individuals and properties.
Definite descriptions are complex terms that denote individuals. They
have the form: $(\imath x)\phi$ (read: *the x such that ϕ*). Let these descriptions rigidly denote whatever individual actually now satisfies ϕ. The
λ-expressions are complex terms that denote properties. They have the

form: $[\lambda x \; \phi]$ (read: *being an individual x such that ϕ*). There are some restrictions on the formation of λ-expressions, and these will be discussed below.

Finally, we may define what it is to be ordinary and what it is to be abstract in terms of the one-place predicate '*exists*,' which we represent as: $E!$. By '*exists*,' we mean 'has a location in space.' Intuitively, *ordinary* individuals are the kind of thing that could exist at some time, whereas *abstract* individuals are not the kind of thing that could ever exist. These intuitions are captured by the following definitions:

$$being \; ordinary \; (`O!') =_{df} \; [\lambda x \; \Diamond\blacklozenge E!x]$$

$$being \; abstract \; (`A!') =_{df} \; [\lambda x \; \sim\Diamond\blacklozenge E!x]$$

Note that there is a distinction between '$(\exists x)\phi$' and '$(\exists x)(E!x \; \& \; \phi)$.' We read the first as "There is an x (or, some x is) such that ϕ." We read the second as "There exists an x (or, some existing x is) such that ϕ. Unfortunately, there is a tradition in philosophy of calling '$\exists$' the "the existential quantifier," and many philosophers read the first formula as "There exists an x such that ϕ." In what follows, however, we shall not conform to this tradition. Being and existence are distinguished, and the word 'exists' shall always be used in connection with the latter. The only exception to this concerns the distinction between the principles of Existential Generalization and *Existential* Generalization. The former characterizes the inference from ϕ_α^τ to $(\exists\alpha)\phi$ (where α is any variable and τ any term substitutable for α). The latter characterizes the inference from ϕ_x^τ to $(\exists x)(E!x \; \& \; \phi)$. Consequently, given this way of speaking, Existential Generalization does not yield an *existence* claim—it only yields the conclusion that something satisfies the formula in question. *Existential* Generalization, however, yields a conclusion to the effect that something exists and satisfies the formula in question.

The seven principles stated above can now be represented formally, and the reader should compare the informal statements with the following formal ones:

Principle 1 $(\forall x)(O!x \rightarrow \Box\blacksquare \sim (\exists F)xF)$

Principle 2 *For every formula ϕ in which x doesn't occur free, the following is an axiom:*

$$\Box\blacksquare(\exists x)(A!x \; \& \; (\forall F)(xF \equiv \phi))$$

Principle 3 $x=y \; \equiv_{df}$

$$(O!x \; \& \; O!y \; \& \; \Box\blacksquare(\forall F)(Fx \equiv Fy)) \; \vee \; (A!x \; \& \; A!y \; \& \; \Box\blacksquare(\forall F)(xF \equiv yF))$$

Principle 4 $(\forall x)(\forall F)(\lozenge\blacklozenge xF \rightarrow \square\blacksquare xF)$

Principle 5 *For every formula ϕ in which there are no free F's, no encoding subformulas, and no quantifiers binding relation variables, the following is an axiom:*

$(\exists F)\square\blacksquare(\forall x)(Fx \equiv \phi)$

Principle 6 $F\!=\!G \equiv_{df} \square\blacksquare(\forall x)(xF \equiv xG)$

Principle 7 *For any two formulas $\phi(\alpha, \alpha)$ and $\phi(\alpha, \beta)$, where α and β are both individual variables or both property variables, and $\phi(\alpha, \beta)$ is the result of replacing one or more occurrences of α by β in $\phi(\alpha, \alpha)$, the following is an axiom:*

$\alpha\!=\!\beta \rightarrow (\phi(\alpha, \alpha) \equiv \phi(\alpha, \beta))$

In the ensuing discussion, the expressions 'A-individual' and 'A-object' will abbreviate 'abstract individual.' The words 'object' and 'individual' will be used as synonyms. So properties and relations will not be considered objects in this sense. But remember that later we shall broaden the notion of an abstract object so that it covers abstract properties and abstract relations as well as abstract individuals. In the meantime, no confusion should arise.

Also, in the explanations that follow, we shall derive consequences of these principles. The underlying logic of these derivations is perfectly standard. We use the standard axioms and rules of propositional logic, predicate logic, modal logic ($S5$), and minimal tense logic (K_t), adjusted only for the presence of rigid definite descriptions, some of which might fail to denote. To serve as a reminder, the axioms of K_t are just these: $\mathcal{H}(\phi \rightarrow \psi) \rightarrow (\mathcal{H}\phi \rightarrow \mathcal{H}\psi)$, $\mathcal{G}(\phi \rightarrow \psi) \rightarrow (\mathcal{G}\phi \rightarrow \mathcal{G}\psi)$, $\phi \rightarrow \mathcal{H}\mathcal{F}\phi$, and $\phi \rightarrow \mathcal{G}\mathcal{P}\phi$. K_t also has a rule of inference for each primitive operator that corresponds to the rule of necessitation in $S5$.

2.3   The Explanation of the Theory

Principle 1 should be regarded as a proper axiom. As a representation of the informal sentence (1) that appears at the beginning of Section 2, it seems relatively straightforward. The idea is that since individuals which either exist at some time or might have existed at some time are ordinary, they are not the kind of thing that could encode properties. Principle 2 should also be regarded as a proper axiom schema that represents the informal sentence (2). To see how it works, we need to know what formulas ϕ are permissible and how they represent conditions on properties. First of all, the restriction that ϕ not have free x's is needed to rule out such formulas as '$\sim xF$,' which would produce an immediate contradiction. Those formulas having no free x's but which do have a free 'F' clearly seem to place a condition on properties. Each of the following constitutes a condition that some properties satisfy and others don't: $F = F$ (every property satisfies this), $F \neq F$ (no property satisfies this), $F = E!$ (one property satisfies this), $(\exists x)Fx$ (lots of properties satisfy this), and $\sim(\exists x)Fx$ (lots of properties satisfy this as well). Even sentences, without free variables, constitute conditions on properties—if the sentence is true, every property satisfies it; if it is false, none do. Now Principle 2 asserts that for each of these conditions, it is necessarily and always the case that there is an A-object that encodes just the properties satisfying the condition.

Let us consider a concrete example. "Bhagwan Rajneesh exemplifies being F" is a condition that some properties satisfy. So (2) tells us that necessarily and always, there is an A-object that encodes just those properties Bhagwan Rajneesh exemplifies. The formal representation of (2), namely, Principle 2, has an instance that says just this. Let 'r' denote Rajneesh, and let us formalize the condition on properties as 'Fr.' Then the following is an instance of Principle 2:

(8) $\quad \Box\blacksquare(\exists x)(A!x \ \& \ \forall F)(xF \equiv Fr))$

We can explain the effect the modal and tense operators have by appealing to intuitions about possible worlds and moments of time. Without these operators, this sentence would say that, in fact, there is an A-object that encodes just the properties Rajneesh in fact exemplifies. But let us assume that one and the same individual can exemplify different properties at different possible worlds and times. In addition, let us assume that there is a single domain of individuals, which houses all of the ordinary and abstract individuals. Then, (8) implies that for each world-time pair $\langle \mathbf{w}, \mathbf{t} \rangle$, the domain of individuals contains an A-object that encodes at $\langle \mathbf{w}, \mathbf{t} \rangle$ just the properties that Reagan exemplifies at $\langle \mathbf{w}, \mathbf{t} \rangle$.[2]

Principle 3 should be regarded as a definition. It states a general condition for the identity of objects. The condition is disjunctive; the first disjunct gives identity conditions for ordinary objects, while the second gives identity conditions for abstract objects. Two ordinary objects are identical just in case they necessarily and always exemplify the

---

[2] This reference to worlds and times is designed to exploit some intuitions you may have about modality and tense, to help you picture and understand the effect of the modal and tense operators. They are not primitives of the theory—there are no primitive terms that denote these entities appearing anywhere in the language. Though worlds and times are primitives of the semantics, this is ultimately justified by a construction of worlds and times *in the theory*, out of the primitive notions identified so far. This construction appears in Chapter 4.

same properties. Two abstract objects are identical just in case they necessarily and always encode the same properties. The reason Principle 3 is completely general for arbitrarily chosen objects x and y is that the ordinary and abstract objects exhaust the domain of objects. Principles 2 and 3 together constitute a precise theory of abstract objects. Principle 4 should be regarded as a logical truth about encoding. It says that the properties that an A-object encodes are rigidly encoded. In other words, if an abstract object encodes a property at one world and time, it encodes that property at all worlds and all times. Together, Principles 3 and 4 ensure that the properties an A-object encodes anywhere anytime are all essential to its identity. However, the properties an (ordinary or abstract) object exemplifies may vary from world to world and time to time. In the case of A-objects, these will typically be relational properties that the A-object exemplifies with respect to the ordinary individuals that inhabit the various worlds and times.

To see what effect these new principles have, reconsider (8). Recall that (8) implies, with respect to world-time pair $\langle \mathbf{w}_1, \mathbf{t}_1 \rangle$, that there is an A-object, say a_1, that encodes at $\langle \mathbf{w}_1, \mathbf{t}_1 \rangle$ the properties Rajneesh exemplifies at $\langle \mathbf{w}_1, \mathbf{t}_1 \rangle$. It also implies, with respect to world-time pair $\langle \mathbf{w}_2, \mathbf{t}_2 \rangle$ (where either $\mathbf{w}_1 \neq \mathbf{w}_2$, or $\mathbf{t}_1 \neq \mathbf{t}_2$), that there is an A-object, say a_2, that encodes at $\langle \mathbf{w}_2, \mathbf{t}_2 \rangle$ just the properties Rajneesh exemplifies at $\langle \mathbf{w}_2, \mathbf{t}_2 \rangle$. Principles 3 and 4 now guarantee that $a_1 \neq a_2$. To prove this, note that intuitively, at least one of the properties encoded by a_1 is distinct from those encoded by a_2 (because the properties Rajneesh exemplifies at $\langle \mathbf{w}_1, \mathbf{t}_1 \rangle$ must differ from the ones he exemplifies at $\langle \mathbf{w}_2, \mathbf{t}_2 \rangle$). So to show that $a_1 \neq a_2$, Principle 3 implies that there is a world and time where a_1 and a_2 encode distinct properties. But just choose any world-time pair $\langle \mathbf{w}_i, \mathbf{t}_i \rangle$ you please and look at the properties a_1 and a_2 encode there and then. The rigidity of encoding principle (Principle 4) tells us that if an abstract object encodes a property at any world and time, it encodes that property at every world and time (encoding is, in a certain sense, independent of the worlds and times). So a_1 and a_2 encode at the world-time pair $\langle \mathbf{w}_i, \mathbf{t}_i \rangle$ the same properties they respectively encode at $\langle \mathbf{w}_1, \mathbf{t}_1 \rangle$ and $\langle \mathbf{w}_2, \mathbf{t}_2 \rangle$. Consequently, they encode distinct properties at $\langle \mathbf{w}_i, \mathbf{t}_i \rangle$. Hence, $a_1 \neq a_2$.

Consider, however, the following instance of Principle 2:

(9) $\Box \blacksquare (\exists x)(A!x \ \& \ (\forall F)(xF \equiv F = R \lor F = S))$

If we let 'R' denote the property of being round, and 'S' denote the property of being square, then (9) asserts that, necessarily and always, there is an A-individual that encodes just the two properties of being round and being square. That is because the condition '$F = R \lor F = S$' is satisfied by only two properties, roundness and squareness. The modal and tense operators imply that for every world-time pair $\langle \mathbf{w}, \mathbf{t} \rangle$, there is an abstract individual that encodes at $\langle \mathbf{w}, \mathbf{t} \rangle$ just roundness and squareness. But note the difference between (8) and (9). (9) implies, with respect to arbitrary world-time pairs $\langle \mathbf{w}_1, \mathbf{t}_1 \rangle$ and $\langle \mathbf{w}_2, \mathbf{t}_2 \rangle$, both that there is an A-object, say b_1, that encodes at $\langle \mathbf{w}_1, \mathbf{t}_1 \rangle$ just roundness and squareness, and that there is an A-object, say b_2, that encodes at $\langle \mathbf{w}_2, \mathbf{t}_2 \rangle$ just roundness and squareness. But Principles 3 and 4 now guarantee that $b_1 = b_2$. They guarantee, for an arbitrarily chosen world-time pair $\langle \mathbf{w}_i, \mathbf{t}_i \rangle$, that b_1 and b_2 encode the same two properties at $\langle \mathbf{w}_i, \mathbf{t}_i \rangle$. So they are identical.

If given an arbitrary condition ϕ, it should be clear that, for each world-time pair $\langle \mathbf{w}, \mathbf{t} \rangle$, there is a unique A-object that encodes at $\langle \mathbf{w}, \mathbf{t} \rangle$ just the properties satisfying ϕ at $\langle \mathbf{w}, \mathbf{t} \rangle$. If we use the standard abbreviation '$(\exists! x)\phi$' for '$(\exists x)(\forall y)(\phi_x^y \equiv y = x)$,'[3] then the following theorem schema is deducible using the principles of $S5$ modal logic and K_t tense logic:

Derived Principle *For every formula ϕ in which x doesn't occur free, the following is an axiom:*

$$\Box \blacksquare (\exists! x)(A!x \ \& \ (\forall F)(xF \equiv \phi))$$

The proof is left as a straightforward exercise. As a consequence of this theorem, a formal description of the form '$(\imath x)(\forall F)(xF \equiv \phi)$' is guaranteed to have a denotation, no matter what condition ϕ (having no free x's) is supplied. Such a description denotes the A-object that rigidly encodes just the properties satisfying ϕ now at the actual world.

These formal descriptions make it possible to analyze English descriptions that appear in sentences failing the principle of *Existential Generalization*. Consider the true sentence "Russell thought about the round square," which fails this principle (but obeys Existential Generalization). It appears to have the form '$Tr(\imath x)\phi$,' where 'T' denotes the *thought about* relation, 'r' denotes Bertrand Russell, and '$(\imath x)\phi$' provides a reading of the English description. But we cannot use the formal description '$(\imath x)(Rx \ \& \ Sx)$' to translate the English description, because this description fails to denote anything. Were we to use the formal sentence '$Tr(\imath x)(Rx \ \& \ Sx)$' to represent the English sentence, then it would be a mystery both as to why the English sentence is true and why it obeys Existential Generalization. But we can use the formal description '$(\imath x)(\forall F)(xF \equiv F = R \ \vee \ F = S)$' to represent 'the round square.' The formal sentence '$Tr(\imath x)(\forall F)(xF \equiv F = R \ \vee \ F = S)$' is a good representation of the English. The formal claim is true just in

---

[3] ϕ_x^y is the result of substituting y for every free occurrence of x in ϕ.

case the objects denoted by 'r' and the formal description exemplify the relation denoted by 'T.' Such a representation explains why the English sentence fails *Existential* Generalization, but obeys Existential Generalization. We cannot deduce from it that $(\exists x)(E!x \,\&\, Trx)$, though we can deduce that $(\exists x)Trx$. This explains the facts concerning generalization.

This example shows how the theory makes it possible to produce an intensional reading for English definite descriptions. Such a reading helps us to explain directedness to nonexistent and "impossible" objects. One can, in fact, produce other intensional readings for English definite descriptions. Let '$G \Rightarrow F$' abbreviate '$\square\blacksquare(\forall x)(Gx \rightarrow Fx)$.' Now consider the following consequence of the Derived Principle:

(10) $(\exists! x)(A!x \,\&\, (\forall F)(xF \equiv [\lambda y \; Sy \,\&\, (\forall z)(z \in y \equiv z \notin z)] \Rightarrow F))$

If we let 'S' denote the property of being a set, (10) implies that there is in fact a unique A-object that encodes (at the actual world) every property necessarily-always implied by being a set of non-self-membered sets. This is the object we are directed towards when considering the *reductio* proof of the inconsistency of naive set theory. Clearly, the conclusion of the *reductio*, "The set of non-self-membered sets is a member of itself if and only if it isn't," seems to be true. By using the intensional reading of the English description, and taking the English copula 'is' to mean 'encodes,' we can produce a formal reading of this conclusion that reveals why it appears to be true. To make this reading easier to read and grasp, let us abbreviate the formal description derivable from (10) as '$(\imath x)\psi_1$,' and abbreviate the λ-expression '$[\lambda y \; y \in y \equiv y \notin y]$' as '$[\lambda y \; \chi_1]$.' Then, the formal reading of the *reductio* conclusion is: $(\imath x)\psi_1[\lambda y \; \chi_1]$. This is an atomic predication with a complex subject and complex predicate, which is what the English sentence appears to be. It also happens to be true, since the property of being a self-member iff not a self-member is necessarily-always implied by the property of being a set of all non-self-membered sets.

The theory also produces A-objects that can serve as fictional characters, mythical beings, and the like. We shall not go into the details here, but it should be clear that given any story s and character y, Principle 2 guarantees that there is an A-object that encodes just the properties F that y exemplifies according to s. Names and descriptions such as 'Sherlock Holmes,' 'Jupiter,' 'Odin,' 'the fountain of youth,' 'the lost land of Shangri-La,' and so forth, can all be regarded as expressions that denote. We can therefore produce simple and analogous analyses for "Reagan worshipped Rajneesh" and "Caesar worshipped Jupiter," since all of the names involved denote individuals of some kind. Here, too, the representations explain why *Existential* Generalization fails but Existential Generalization doesn't. Examples such as this, as well as the ones from the preceding discussion, should give you some idea of what the theory proper asserts and how it can be applied to explain the failures of *Existential* Generalization. The study of such intensional contexts is the special focus of Part III.

Principle 5 should be regarded as a logical theorem schema. It is a comprehension schema that attempts to circumscribe the domain of properties. Despite its appearance, it is easy to understand. The important thing to know is what formulas can be used with the principle. The restriction that ϕ not have free F's simply rules out such formulas as '$\sim Fx$,' which would produce an immediate contradiction. The restriction that ϕ not contain any encoding subformulas nor any quantifers binding relation variables means that only those formulas having a structure essentially similar to formulas found in the standard first order modal predicate calculus are acceptable.[4] Any formula ϕ that is constructed entirely out of exemplification subformulas and the logical operators, and that may or may not contain a free variable x, constitutes a condition on individuals. Here are some examples, in which 'c' denotes some particular individual, 'P' and 'Q' denote particular properties, and 'R' denotes some particular relation: (a) x bears R to c: Rxc; (b) x fails to exemplify P: $\sim Px$; (c) x exemplifies both P and Q: $Px \,\&\, Qx$; (d) x exemplifies either P or Q: $Px \vee Qx$; (e) necessarily-always, if x exists, x exemplifies P: $\Box\blacksquare(E!x \rightarrow Px)$; and (f) x bears R to something: $(\exists y)Rxy$. For each one of these conditions, Principle 5 asserts that there is a property F which is such that, necessarily-always, all and only the individuals satisfying the condition exemplify F.

Here are the instances of Principle 5 that correspond to (a) – (f) in the preceding paragraph:

(11) $(\exists F)\Box\blacksquare(\forall x)(Fx \equiv Rxc)$

(12) $(\exists F)\Box\blacksquare(\forall x)(Fx \equiv \sim Px)$

(13) $(\exists F)\Box\blacksquare(\forall x)(Fx \equiv Px \,\&\, Qx)$

(14) $(\exists F)\Box\blacksquare(\forall x)(Fx \equiv Px \vee Qx)$

---

[4]Of these two restrictions, the "no encoding subformulas" restriction is more important. It serves to prevent an important paradox. Without the restriction, the comprehension schema for A-objects would generate an object that encoded just the property $[\lambda x \,(\exists F)(xF \,\&\, \sim Fx)]$. Either this object exemplifies $[\lambda x \,(\forall F)(xF \rightarrow Fx)]$ or it doesn't. But both disjuncts lead to a contradiction. For complete details, see [1983], pp. 158–160. The "no relation quantifiers" restriction may not be necessary. It is included because there is no convenient way to semantically interpret λ-expressions containing such quantifiers, given our conception of relations as primitive, structured entities. But see the first section of the present Appendix (§A.1) for a way of working around this restriction.

(15) $(\exists F)\square\blacksquare(\forall x)(Fx \equiv \square\blacksquare(E!x \rightarrow Px))$

(16) $(\exists F)\square\blacksquare(\forall x)(Fx \equiv (\exists y)Rxy)$

These examples should make it clear that the complex properties produced by the comprehension schema are ordinary ones.

It cannot be emphasized enough that the properties that make these sentences true are not mathematical functions from possible worlds to sets of individuals. Our conception of properties is based on two semantic intuitions: (1) that they are primitive, structured entities that have gaps into which objects can be plugged, and (2) that they have exemplification extensions that vary from world-time pair to world-time pair. For example, take the two-place relation R and plug the individual c into its second place. The result is a one-place property that an individual x exemplifies at world-time pair $\langle \mathbf{w}, \mathbf{t} \rangle$ iff x bears R to c at $\langle \mathbf{w}, \mathbf{t} \rangle$. That there is such a property is semantically implied by (11). (12) semantically implies that there is a property, call it K, which is such that, for any world-time pair $\langle \mathbf{w}, \mathbf{t} \rangle$, all and only the individuals that fail to exemplify P at $\langle \mathbf{w}, \mathbf{t} \rangle$ exemplify K at $\langle \mathbf{w}, \mathbf{t} \rangle$. The exemplification extension of K at $\langle \mathbf{w}, \mathbf{t} \rangle$ contains all of the individuals that fail to be in the exemplification extension of P at $\langle \mathbf{w}, \mathbf{t} \rangle$, for any $\mathbf{w}$ and $\mathbf{t}$. Property K is a negation of the property P, and we may suppose that it is constructed by applying to P a logical operation corresponding to the negation sign. For each primitive logical connective, quantifier or sentential operator in our language, there is a corresponding logical operation that can harness properties (and relations) together to produce complex properties (and relations). The properties so constructed will be the kinds of entities that make quantified claims like (11) – (16) true.

Such properties also serve as the denotations of complex predicates (the λ-expressions). The restrictions described for Principle 5 apply to the formation of these complex terms. If ϕ contains no encoding subformulas and no quantified relation variables, then $[\lambda x \ \phi]$ is a legitimate λ-expression. We have already seen a couple of such expressions; for example, the predicate expression that occurs in the last line of Russell's proof: being a self-member if and only if not a self-member ($[\lambda y \ y \in y \equiv y \notin y]$). That there is such a property is guaranteed by Principle 5, and the reader should be able to verify this by producing the relevant instance.[5] Consider two other properties that are of interest to this discussion: being a brown and colorless dog, and being a barber that shaves

---

[5] Actually, there are several such properties. The logical operations we mentioned earlier yield several ways to construct a property with the appropriate structure. Consequently, a procedure is needed to select, from among the possibilities, a single property for the λ-expression to denote. Such a procedure may be found in our [1983], pp. 64–65. See also Bealer [1982], and Menzel [1986].

just those who don't shave themselves. These can be represented by the following λ-expressions:

(a) $[\lambda x\ Dx\ \&\ Bx\ \&\ \sim Cx]$

(b) $[\lambda x\ Bx\ \&\ (\forall y)(Py \rightarrow (Sxy \equiv \sim Syy))]$

Let us abbreviate these expressions as $[\lambda x\ \psi_2]$ and $[\lambda x\ \chi_2]$, respectively.

In order to answer the question of whether these two properties are identical, we have to ask what it means to say that they are. Principle 6 should be regarded as the definition that does just that. It tells us that properties P and Q are identical just in case, necessarily, and always, P and Q are encoded by the same individuals. This definition makes it possible to represent the failures of Strong Extensionality. Recall, for example, that (18) does not follow from (17):

(17) Necessarily-always, all and only brown and colorless dogs are barbers that shave just those who shave themselves.

(18) Being a brown and colorless dog is the same thing as being a barber that shaves just those that don't shave themselves.

It is straightforward to represent these two sentences as (19) and (20), respectively:

(19) $\Box\blacksquare(\forall y)([\lambda x\ \psi_2]y \equiv [\lambda x\ \chi_2]y)$

(20) $[\lambda x\ \psi_2]=[\lambda x\ \chi_2]$

In our system, (20) does not follow from (19), and this explains why the principle of strong extensionality fails with respect to (17) and (18). We may consistently conjoin (19) with the hypothesis that $[\lambda x\ \psi_2] \neq [\lambda x\ \chi_2]$. However, if two properties P and Q are necessarily-always encoded by the same individuals, it follows that they are necessarily-always exemplified by the same individuals—from $\Box\blacksquare(\forall x)(xP \equiv xQ)$, it follows that $P=Q$, by Principle 6, and so by substituting 'Q' for 'P' into the logical truth that $\Box\blacksquare(\forall x)(Px \equiv Px)$, which we will be allowed to do by Principle 7 (see below), we get $\Box\blacksquare(\forall x)(Px \equiv Qx)$.

There is an intuitive (semantic) way to understand Principle 6. Since encoding is a kind of predication, we may regard properties as having a second kind of extension. In addition to having an exemplification extension, which consists of just those individuals that exemplify the property, they also have an encoding extension, which consists of just those individuals that encode the property. So Principle 6 implies that P and Q are identical just in case, for every world-time pair $\langle \mathbf{w}, \mathbf{t} \rangle$, the encoding extension of P at $\langle \mathbf{w}, \mathbf{t} \rangle$ and the encoding extension of Q at

$\langle \mathbf{w}, \mathbf{t} \rangle$ are the same. While the exemplification extension of a property may vary from world-time to world-time, the encoding extension of a property does not. This is in virtue of Principle 4. Actually, the modal and tense operators in Principle 6 are unnecessary, since they can be derived using Principle 4. But we have included them anyway, since we want to *define* the identity of properties to be a modal and tensed notion. It is interesting that, in our system, there is a way to preserve the idea that properties are strongly extensional! There are now two senses of necessary equivalence: necessary equivalence with respect to exemplification and necessary equivalence with respect to encoding. Properties are not strongly extensional whenever necessarily equivalent in the former sense, but they are strongly extensional whenever necessarily equivalent in the latter sense. In what follows, we always use 'necessarily equivalent' in the former sense (the usual sense), and we employ the traditional understanding of strong extensionality on which properties are not strongly extensional.

We take the definition of property identity to constitute an insight about the nature of properties. Of course, the insight may not be obvious on your first encounter with the theory. That may be due to the fact that you have not yet seen the definition come into play in a variety of ways. As you better understand the consequences of the principles, you get a better idea of the effect this definition has. At the very least, the definition provides a theoretical response to those who find properties mysterious. However, a word of warning is in order. One should not expect this definition to provide a means for 'determining' whether two properties are identical. It is not a "criterion" of property identity. This is not how definitions of identity are to be construed. A definition of identity doesn't specify *how* we know or determine whether the entities in question are identical, other than in terms of the theory. Rather, it specifies *what* it is that we know once we (pretheoretically) determine that the entities are identical or distinct. It is assumed that we have some acquaintance with properties, and on the basis of that acquaintance, can determine whether two properties are identical or distinct. Principle 6 then tells us, from a theoretical point of view, what it is that we know once we have made our determination.

In the context of Principles 5 and 6, a question arises as to what properties A-objects exemplify. Strictly speaking, the theory doesn't say (other than the property of being non-ordinary). For the most part, we can rely upon our intuitions to say, for example, that they exemplify the negations of ordinary properties, such as being non-round, being non-red, etc. A-objects also exemplify intentional properties and relations, such as being thought about (by so and so), being searched for, etc. These intuitions serve well for most purposes, but there may be occasions where we might want to disregard some of them, in return for theoretical benefits. Since the theory is neutral about what properties A-objects exemplify, we are free, from the standpoint of theory, to decide this according to theoretical need.

However, it is important to know that A-objects that necessarily (always) exemplify the same properties need not be identical. There are so many A-objects generated by the theory that the traditional notion of exemplification is incapable of distinguishing them all. Encoding is the only real guide to the identity of A-objects. In particular, for any relation R, it can be shown that there are distinct A-objects a and b for which $[\lambda x Rxa]$ and $[\lambda x Rxb]$ are identical properties.[6] However, this doesn't happen for two ordinary objects—it cannot be shown that $[\lambda x Rxy] = [\lambda x Rxz]$, for distinct ordinary objects y and z! The reason why this happens for A-objects is this: Principle 2, intuitively, tries to correlate the set of A-objects with the power set of the set of properties. Now if for every relation R, Principles 5 and 6 were to generate a new and distinct property $[\lambda x Rxy]$, for every A-object y, then there would be a one-to-one correlation between the set of A-objects and a subset of the set of properties, in violation of Cantor's theorem (no set A which is the power set of a set B can be correlated one-to-one with the members of a subset of B).

These facts simply show that the theory stretches the traditional notion of exemplification past its limits. For the traditional portion of the theory, which concerns just the exemplification of ordinary objects, the theory has only the consequences we expect. It is no fault of the theory that traditional ideas do not not behave in a traditional manner when applied in interesting new ways. In particular, the above facts are not "defects" either of the theory or of A-objects, but rather, insights into the limitations of exemplification.

These insights extend to the traditional notion of identity as well as exemplification. Note that Principles 3 and 6 define the symbol '=' in terms of encoding formulas, for both individuals and properties. This means that there are no properties of the form $[\lambda x \; x = a]$, where a is some arbitrarily chosen individual, since the notation that defines '=' cannot appear in λ-expressions. The reason why this is to be expected stems from the facts outlined in the previous paragraph. Were Principles 5 and 6 to generate a new and distinct property for every A-object so generated, there would be another way of forming a one-to-one correlation between the power set of the set of properties and a subset of the set of properties. That's why it is important to banish the notation defining '=' both from λ-expressions and from Principle 5. Our axioms

---

[6] For the proof of this, see [1983], p. 37.

are too powerful for us to suppose that for each distinct A-object, there is a distinct property of being identical to it. The traditional notions break down in a rich, new context.

However, our intuitions about the traditional notion of identity can be preserved as long as we do not try to apply the notion outside its intended domain of application. The traditional definition of identity, namely, that of necessarily exemplifying the same properties, has standard consequences on the domain of ordinary objects. It is useful to indicate this traditional notion of identity with the symbol '$=_E$.' We treat this symbol as a distinguished primitive two-place relation symbol that is axiomatized by the following principle: $x =_E y \equiv \Diamond\blacklozenge E!x$ & $\Diamond\blacklozenge E!y$ & $\Box\blacksquare(\forall F)(Fx \equiv Fy)$. Since it is a primitive relation symbol, it can appear inside λ-expressions. Frequently, λ-predicates containing this symbol prove to be useful. Such predicates behave just like one expects when used with expressions that denote ordinary objects. If a and b are distinct ordinary objects, then $[\lambda x \; x =_E a] \neq [\lambda x \; x =_E b]$. But we should remember that there are distinct A-objects which cannot be distinguished by identity$_E$. Only someone who thinks that the Russellian universe is the only "normal" universe would think that this last fact is a "defect" of A-objects. Rather, what we have is a case where traditional Russellian and Leibnizian notions do not fare well when the horizons of the world are broadened.

Finally, we turn to Principle 7, which is a totally unrestricted substitutivity principle. It is the formal version of Substitutivity. Now that we have defined identity for individuals (Principle 3) and identity for properties (Principle 6), it makes sense to assert that whenever two things are identical, whatever is true about one is true about the other. This is just what Principle 7 asserts. Note that metavariables α and β are used to state the principle. This means that there will be instances of the following two kinds: $x = y \to (\phi(x, x) \equiv \phi(x, y))$ and $F = G \to (\phi(F, F) \equiv \phi(F, G))$. Consequently, any two terms that denote the same individual or property are substitutable for one another in any context of our language. Note that two other important principles of identity are deducible: (1) $(\forall\alpha)(\alpha = \alpha)$, where α is any variable, and (2) $\alpha = \beta \to \Box(\alpha = \beta)$. The proofs are left as straightforward exercises.

This completes the overview of our enhanced theory. When the theory is technically defined from start to finish, and interpretations for the language of encoding are made precise (in Part II, and in the Appendix), Principles 1, 2, and 7 become non-logical axioms, Principle 4 becomes a logical axiom, Principle 5 becomes a logical theorem, and Principles 3 and 6 become definitions. We'll get a better idea of just how this happens in Chapter 3, where we look at the foundations of the theory in greater detail.

2.4   Some Observations

In these first two chapters, the natural order has been to describe the failures of Generalization and Substitutivity first, and then the failures of Strong Extensionality. However, the natural order of investigation is to begin with the failures of Strong Extensionality. These failures are explained by the foundations of the theory that are couched in the intensional logic, whereas the failures of the other three principles are explained by the theory proper. It is best to begin by acquiring a thorough understanding of the logic. This forms the subject matter of Part II. However, before we begin our investigation, a few observations about the theory are in order. These observations should offer some perspective on the project we are about begin.

The Core Theory: The seven principles that have been formulated and explained constitute only a core theory. Auxiliary hypotheses, assumptions, and axioms have to be added on occasion to supplement the core principles. Some assumptions are required concerning the way English sentences are to be represented by formal sentences. For example, an appeal has already been made to the hypothesis that natural language predication is ambiguous between exemplification and encoding predication. Furthermore, certain applications of the theory require special notions and axioms. For example, when we turn to fiction, the notion of a "story" is needed, and special axioms that govern the operator "according to the story, ... " are added.

Sometimes, it may be helpful to postulate certain properties that are not generated by the comprehension schema. For example, it may be useful to have properties that are constructed with encoding predications. Such properties were banished from the comprehension schema because they sometimes lead to paradox (see footnote 4). But the wholesale banishment of such properties is far too extreme. Many properties constructed with encoding predications are consistent with the theory. Though there will only be a few occasions where we suggest that these properties might be of use, it is important to remember that the theory can be expanded in just such a way.

Analysis: One of the advantages of having a metaphysical system described in an object language that can be given a model theoretic interpretation is that unanalyzed data may be analyzed on three levels: the syntactical, the metaphysical, and the semantical. Take an example from the preceding section, "Augustus Caesar worshipped Jupiter." Pretheoretically, we simply have an English sentence in which there is no explicit mention of linguistic things such as terms or formulas, or of metaphysical things such as objects or relations, or of semantic things such as denotations or extensions. There is, however, a certain understanding, or reading, of the sentence that we want to capture. Once we represent this reading of the unanalyzed English by using a formula of intensional logic, we get an expression that may be systematically resolved in various ways. Consider the following formal representation of this sentence: *Waz*. At the syntactic level, it may be resolved into the primitive terms and the rule which permits their combination into a formula. To some extent, this helps us understand the structural components of the English. The second level of analysis concerns the fact that the formal sentence expresses a certain statement of metaphysics, namely, that the *individual* Augustus Caesar *exemplifies* a certain *relation* to the *individual* Jupiter. Such a statement may be resolved into the primitive notions of the metaphysics (these were italicized), two of which carry ontological commitment to categories of being. This level of analysis directly gives us the truth conditions of the English. The third level of analysis is a semantic one and resolves the truth conditions of the English sentence in terms of semantic notions. In this particular case, the analysis would be: the ordered pair that consists of the denotation of 'Augustus Caesar' and the denotation of 'Jupiter' is an element of the exemplification extension of the denotation of 'worships.'

Once an analysis has been given, the syntactic and semantic analyses, strictly speaking, drop out of the picture. All we should be left with is the sentence of natural language and (the metaphysical understanding of) what the world must be like for the sentence to be true. The formal language of intensional logic and its semantic analysis are both just devices to help us build a metaphysical picture. It would be a mistake to suppose that these devices affected the original data in any way. In particular, it would be a mistake to think that the tests we perform on natural language sentences to determine whether they are intensional can be performed upon sentences of the formal language. No new data can be constructed using the language of intensional logic. Formal sentences are not the kind of thing that exhibit intensionality.[7]

It is important to remember that the formal semantics simply provides a set-theoretic framework in which models of the metaphysical theory may be constructed. The models serve the heuristic purpose of helping us to visualize or picture the theory in a rigorous way. It is extremely important not to confuse the models of the theory with the

---

[7]Consequently, we shall not follow Frege and Church in supposing that the terms of a formal language have senses. Alonzo Church ([1951]) builds a language in which it is possible to construct, for each term in the language, a second term that denotes the sense of the first. In our view, such a project is entirely misguided and unnecessary for the explanation of the behavior of English terms.

world itself. Many theorists today tend to give models of a theory an exalted status that they do not have. They regard model building as the goal of the enterprise of trying to describe the way language works. As far as the present work is concerned, all that the models of a theory do is show that the theory is consistent, that the logic is complete, that the axioms are categorical, and so forth. Moreover, set theory is *not* presupposed as part of our background ontology. No primitive variable ranges over sets, and so there is no quantification over them. And no piece of language is semantically interpreted as signifying a set, unless it is part of the special language of mathematics.

So the goal of our enterprise is not to build a model, but rather to construct a formal theory that correctly mirrors the structure the world may have and, as a result, correctly reflects the entailments among the data. This is the reason why we have not yet spent time to develop the model theoretic definition of truth for the formal language. The truth definition does not yield the ultimate truth conditions for English sentences because the model theory involves all sorts of set-theoretic entities to which the theory is not committed. Rather, the formal object language should be thought of as a direct window to the world. When we represent an English sentence by using a formal sentence of intensional logic, the latter directly identifies the truth conditions of the former in terms of what the world has to be like for the latter to be true. So the only entities there are, from the point of view of our logic, are those over which our primitive variables range.

Artifacts: When an English sentence is translated into a sentence of intensional logic, the most important aspects of the representation are: how the primitives of the theory are related to one another, how they are structured into any definitions used in the representation, how the representations are systematically related to the English, and how the truth value and entailments of English are consistent with and reflected by the representations. But in every analysis, there are artifacts. For example, the particular words used as primitives of the metaphysical theory are to some extent arbitrary. That is because they are all technical terms. We could have coined new expressions to tag the primitives. Of course it is important to choose words such as 'abstract,' 'encode,' 'individual,' 'relation,' etc. that are vivid, to facilitate the reader's understanding. But it is important to remember that the technical senses of these words are not part of the data. It is not a deep objection to the theory to take some formal representation of the data and argue that, on a "natural" understanding of its rendition into English, such a representation could not be true. A more telling objection would be to show that the system cannot adequately represent the truth or entailments of some nontechnical English sentence, either in its own terms or on its own principles.

The bottom line here is that analysis always involves certain artifacts, such as the choice of English words used to identify the primitives, the set theoretic models of the formal language, and so forth. If a theory is constructed properly, the artifacts may be ignored. Such artifacts do not affect the data (they do not give us a new set of things to be explained), nor do they affect the world (they are not to be considered part of the world). If you are tempted to concoct puzzles with artifacts, take a step back from the entire enterprise, think of philosophical explanation as a story, and regard the artifacts as fictional characters. Then, the metaphysical theory may be used at a deeper level to account for the artifacts. This avoids the philosophical rut you can get into over artifactual "puzzles" that arise only in the context of explanation.

Encoding Relations: The reader may wonder why it is that just properties are encoded, rather than relations in general. In fact, the theory may be formulated so that n-place relations, for $n \geq 2$, are encoded. But there are two reasons why we have chosen not to do this. The first is that it would contribute little extra explanatory power. None of the particular applications examined in what follows require that relations be encoded. There may be data that would be explained by encoding relations, and if and when it is identified, we can consider generalizing the notion of encoding to cover relations other than properties.

The second reason for not exploring encoded relations at this time has to do with the conflict between the following two intuitions: (a) in some sense, abstract objects encode information, but (b) n-place relations, in and of themselves, do not constitute information about anything. Of course the *notion* of information is relational in nature; information is always about something. For example, a proposition or state of affairs may bear information about some other proposition or state of affairs. Properties can also constitute information about a thing, and so it seems intuitively reasonable to think that abstract objects encode information. They encode information about other individuals by encoding properties that such individuals exemplify. They can also encode information about the world by encoding propositional properties such as being such that Aquino deposed Marcos, being such that the U.S. violated the ABM treaty, being such that every duck flies south for the winter, etc. Such properties characterize the world. Abstract objects, therefore, encode partial information about individuals and about the world in virtue of encoding ordinary properties and propositional properties, respectively. By doing so, they can serve to represent these things, and this representational role proves to be an important part of the nature of intentionality.

But relations in general, as opposed to properties, do not constitute information about anything. Ask yourself how the relations of *loving*, *meeting*, *admiring*, and so forth, in and of themselves, provide any information about any given thing. They might give us information about *pairs* of things, but this would require us to count such set-theoretic objects as basic constituents of the world. This is something we are expressly trying to avoid. Of course, the relational properties of *loving someone*, *meeting Nixon*, or *admiring Aloysha Karamazov* do give us information about individuals. But there is a real sense in which pure relations do not constitute information. So A-objects that encode relations do not seem to be useful for representing anything. At this stage, this is no reason to reformulate the theory so that relations in general are encoded.

Part II

Strong Extensionality

3

The Basic Theory of Relations

3.1 Taking Relations as Primitive

Some notions are so fundamental and intuitively well-understood that it is better to take them as primitive than to try to define them in terms of other notions. Such is the case with the notion of a relation. Intuitively, we know what they are. In our first logic class, we are taught that such diverse sentences as "John loves Mary," "Schliemann searched for Troy," "One is less than two," and "The null set is a member of the unit set of the null set" signify relationships between things, and that the phrases 'loves,' 'searched for,' 'is less than,' and 'is a member of' are naturally understood as signifying two-place relations. No matter what the subject, no matter what the scheme of individuation, it seems that the simplest thoughts are analyzable in terms of the logical notions of 'object,' 'relation,' and 'exemplification.' This insight set the stage for twentieth-century logic. It is no coincidence that the most basic formal language, the language of the predicate calculus, is centered around the atomic formula $R^n x_1 \ldots x_n$, for all three logical notions are embedded in the intuitive reading of this formula.

The notion of a relation is an important part of the natural semantic conception of truth for "second order" languages. On this conception, an interpretation $\mathbf{I}$ of such a language is modeled as an ordered set with the following components: $< \mathbf{D}, \mathbf{R}, \mathbf{ext_R}, \mathbf{F} >$. These components may be described as follows: $\mathbf{D}$ is the set of individuals; $\mathbf{R}$ is the set of n-place relations with $n \geq 1$; $\mathbf{ext_R}$ is the exemplification extension function that assigns to each $\mathbf{r}^n \in \mathbf{R}$ a set of n-tuples of individuals in $\mathbf{D}$; and $\mathbf{F}$ is the function that anchors each individual constant to a member of $\mathbf{D}$ and each relation constant to member of $\mathbf{R}$. Relative to an interpretation, an assignment function $\mathbf{f}$ to the variables maps each individual variable

to an element of $\mathbf{D}$ and each relation variable to an element of $\mathbf{R}$.[1]
For this simple language, constants and variables are the only terms.
Consequently, the denotation of an arbitrary term τ with respect to an
interpretation $\mathbf{I}$ and assignment $\mathbf{f}$ ("$\mathbf{d}_{\mathbf{I},\mathbf{f}}(\tau)$") is simply this: if τ is either
an individual constant or a relation constant, then $\mathbf{d}_{\mathbf{I},\mathbf{f}}(\tau) = \mathbf{F}(\tau)$, and
if τ is either an individual variable or a relation variable, then $\mathbf{d}_{\mathbf{I},\mathbf{f}}(\tau) =$
$\mathbf{f}(\tau)$.

The natural definition of truth for this language can be developed
as follows. Let an interpretation $\mathbf{I}$ be fixed. If ρ^n is any relation term
(constant or variable), and $o_1, \ldots, o_n$ are any individual terms, then a
variable assignment $\mathbf{f}$ satisfies$_\mathbf{I}$ a formula of the form $\rho^n o_1 \ldots o_n$ if and
only if $\langle \mathbf{d}_{\mathbf{I},\mathbf{f}}(o_1), \ldots, \mathbf{d}_{\mathbf{I},\mathbf{f}}(o_n) \rangle \in \mathbf{ext_R}(\mathbf{d}_{\mathbf{I},\mathbf{f}}(\rho^n))$. This essentially says
that, relative to an interpretation and assignment to the variables, an
atomic formula is true if and only if the n-tuple of individuals denoted
by the individual terms is an element of the exemplification extension of
the relation denoted by the relation term. Intuitively, this is a semantic
principle of predication, and it cashes out the truth of the statement
that individuals stand in a relation in terms of certain set theoretic
conditions. It is routine to extend the definition of satisfaction$_\mathbf{I}$ so that
it applies to formulas of the form '$\sim\phi$,' '$\phi \rightarrow \psi$,' and '$(\forall\alpha)\phi$' (where α
is any variable). And in terms of the general definition of satisfaction$_\mathbf{I}$,
we can define the standard definition of truth-under-an-interpretation
as follows: ϕ is *true$_\mathbf{I}$* iff every $\mathbf{f}$ satisfies$_\mathbf{I}$ ϕ.

The reason this semantic conception of truth for second-order language has not received much attention is that it takes relations to be
primitive. To most logicians, relations have seemed mysterious when
compared to sets, and the notion of exemplification has not seemed as
clear as set membership. The traditional Tarski-style model theory for
this language eliminates relations and exemplification altogether, by employing the set theoretic extensions of relations instead of relations, and
by defining exemplification in terms of set membership. The reason
relations have seemed mysterious when compared to sets is that, until
recently, the *theory* of relations has not been mathematically precise and
well understood, whereas the theory of sets has been. Several good theories that axiomatize the existence and identity conditions of sets have
been proposed. But until recently, there have been no adequate axiom-
atizations of the theory of relations. The main philosophical stumbling
block has been identity conditions, for in a calculus based just on relation exemplification, the only condition available that might serve to
identify relations, namely, being exemplified by the same individuals, is

---

[1]Subscripts on the '$\mathbf{f}$' that relativize it to a particular interpretation have been
suppressed for convenience.

too strong. It identifies relations that are known to be distinct. Coupled with the fact that relations have seemed mysterious when compared to sets, is the fact that the interpretation of the predicate calculus that uses just individuals and sets is adequate for investigating the metatheoretical questions, such as consistency and completeness, that are of interest to pure logicians. In fact, logicians frequently just conceive of relations as sets of ordered sets.

Consequently, the natural semantic conception of truth just outlined never really seemed viable. Similar observations apply to simple, second-order modal languages. By extending the above conception in a simple way, we get a natural conception of truth for such a language.[2] An interpretation $\mathbf{I}$ can be modeled as a set with the following components: $\langle \mathbf{D}, \mathbf{R}, \mathbf{W}, \mathbf{w}_0, \mathbf{ext_w}, \mathbf{F} \rangle$. Here, $\mathbf{D}$ is the set of individuals (that is, the ordinary, possibly existing, individuals); $\mathbf{R}$ is the set of all n-place relations, for every n; $\mathbf{W}$ is the set of possible worlds; $\mathbf{w}_0$ is the distinguished actual world; $\mathbf{ext_w}$ is the function that, for each world $\mathbf{w}$, assigns each n-place relation an exemplification extension at $\mathbf{w}$ (the subscript 'w' on the name of this function indexes the function to world $\mathbf{w}$); and $\mathbf{F}$ anchors each individual and relation constant to some member of the appropriate domain. Again, an assignment function $\mathbf{f}$ relative to $\mathbf{I}$ maps each individual and relation variable to some member of the appropriate domain. Consequently, the denotation of each term τ relative to $\mathbf{I}$ and $\mathbf{f}$ ("$\mathbf{d_{I,f}}(\tau)$") is defined just as it was above (there is no need to relativize denotations to worlds since, in a simple modal language, constants and variables rigidly designate).

The semantic conception of truth for the modal predicate calculus can be made precise by using the following preliminary definition, relativized to interpretations $\mathbf{I}$: an assignment $\mathbf{f}$ satisfies$_\mathbf{I}$ $\rho^n o_1 \ldots o_n$ at world $\mathbf{w}$ if and only if $\langle \mathbf{d_{I,f}}(o_1), \ldots, \mathbf{d_{I,f}}(o_n) \rangle \in \mathbf{ext_w}(\mathbf{d_{I,f}}(\rho^n))$. This essentially says that, relative to an interpretation and a variable assignment, an atomic exemplification formula is true at a given world $\mathbf{w}$ iff the n-tuple of objects denoted by the object terms is a member of the exemplification extension at $\mathbf{w}$ of the relation denoted by the relation term. Again, it is routine to extend the definition of satisfaction$_\mathbf{I}$ so that it applies to molecular and quantified formulas. The clause for modal formulas is: $\mathbf{f}$ satisfies$_\mathbf{I}$ $\Box\phi$ at $\mathbf{w}$ iff for every world $\mathbf{w}'$, $\mathbf{f}$ satisfies$_\mathbf{I}$ ϕ at $\mathbf{w}'$. Finally, we get the notion of truth under an interpretation: ϕ is *true*$_\mathbf{I}$ iff every $\mathbf{f}$ satisfies$_\mathbf{I}$ ϕ at $\mathbf{w}_0$.

This natural semantic conception of truth for basic modal languages has not dominated the traditional semantics of modal logic. The favored conception has been "possible world semantics," in which relations are

---

[2] Compare Kripke [1963].

identified with particular mappings of the **ext_w** function. But though this makes the notion of a relation precise, it perpetuates the mistaken idea that relations are strongly extensional. Our conception differs from standard possible worlds semantics in the following, important way: an essential part of the process of evaluating an atomic formula in a modal context involves finding the relation denoted by the relation term *first* and then considering the extension of that relation at the various possible worlds, in the way specified by the modality in question. On our conception, therefore, relations are rigorously distinguished from their extensions (and from the function that assigns them an exemplification extension at each world). Relations are so fundamental that it just doesn't make sense to try to define them.

There is one other important reason for taking relations as primitive. And that has to do with epistemology and learning. One problem with the possible worlds/set theoretic conception of relations is the mystery of finite representation. Beings with "finite" minds, such as ourselves, clearly know how to use such expressions as 'is red,' or 'is round,' etc. But it becomes a mystery as to how we acquire such knowledge when property denoting expressions signify functions defined on an infinite domain of possible worlds. We do not learn to use such expressions by mastering a function with an infinite number of arguments. By contrast, however, if they denote properties and relations conceived as basic entities, the mystery disappears. For beings such as ourselves could learn to use such expressions by becoming acquainted with these entities. Most of us understand, at some level, what it is to be acquainted with the property of being red, the property of being round, etc. Indeed, it is this acquaintance with relations that accounts for our ability to understand and use predicate expressions in modal discourse. Once acquainted with the property of being red, one could "visit" any possible world and identify the red objects there. Such an ability is without a natural explanation when we eliminate relations in favor of sets and possible worlds.[3]

If relations are not defined in terms of sets, they have to be made precise in some other way. The present course is to axiomatize them, by stating both the conditions under which there are relations as well as the conditions under which relations are identical. We already have some idea of what these will be, since they are generalizations of the ones developed for properties (Principles 5 and 6, Chapter 2). However, in order to have a complete understanding of these principles, we need to develop a natural semantic conception for the language of encoding.

---

[3] We return to this topic in Chapter 12, where our logic is compared with Montague's on this score.

3.2 The Semantic Conception of the Language of Encoding

For simplicity, let us consider a version of the language in Chapter 2 that does not contain any complex terms. So, for the moment, let us ignore the definite descriptions and λ-expressions. Then we can model an interpretation $\mathbf{I}$ of this language as a set having the following components: $\langle \mathbf{D}, \mathbf{R}, (\mathbf{W}, \mathbf{w_0}), (\mathbf{T}, \mathbf{t_0}, <), \mathbf{ext_{w,t}}, \mathbf{ext_A}, \mathbf{F} \rangle$. These components may be described as follows. $\mathbf{D}$ houses all of the individuals—the ordinary and the abstract. $\mathbf{R}$, $\mathbf{W}$, and $\mathbf{w_0}$ are defined exactly like their counterparts in Section 1. The triple $(\mathbf{T}, \mathbf{t_0}, <)$ is the framework for interpreting the tense operators: $\mathbf{T}$ is a non-empty set of times, among which is a distinguished element $\mathbf{t_0}$ (the present moment), and on which $<$ is simply a binary relation. $\mathbf{ext_{w,t}}$ is a function that, for each world-time pair $\langle \mathbf{w}, \mathbf{t} \rangle$, assigns each n-place relation an exemplification extension at $\langle \mathbf{w}, \mathbf{t} \rangle$ (the subscript 'w,t' on the name of this function indexes it to the world-time pair $\langle \mathbf{w}, \mathbf{t} \rangle$). $\mathbf{ext_A}$ is the encoding extension function, which assigns to every $\mathbf{r} \in \mathbf{R_1}$, a set of individuals in $\mathbf{D}$ ($\mathbf{R_1}$ is the subset of $\mathbf{R}$ that contains all of the one-place relations, or properties). The function $\mathbf{F}$ is defined just like its counterpart in Section 1. The definitions of the assignment functions $\mathbf{f}$, and the denotation function $\mathbf{d_{I,f}}(\tau)$ also remain the same.

The semantic concept of truth will be defined in terms of satisfaction, in the usual way. However, since there are two kinds of atomic formulas, the definition of satisfaction has two base clauses—one for exemplification formulas, and one for encoding formulas. Also, the notion of satisfaction is now relativized to world-time pairs. The first clause is: an assignment $\mathbf{f}$ satisfies$_\mathbf{I}$ the formula $\rho^n o_1 \ldots o_n$ at world-time pair $\langle \mathbf{w}, \mathbf{t} \rangle$ if and only if $\langle \mathbf{d_{I,f}}(o_1), \ldots, \mathbf{d_{I,f}}(o_n) \rangle \in \mathbf{ext_{w,t}}(\mathbf{d_{I,f}}(\rho^n))$. This is basically similar to its counterpart in Section 1. The second clause is: if ρ is any one-place predicate, and o any individual term, then $\mathbf{f}$ satisfies$_\mathbf{I}$ the formula $o\rho$ at world-time pair $\langle \mathbf{w}, \mathbf{t} \rangle$ if and only if $\mathbf{d_{I,f}}(o) \in \mathbf{ext_A}(\mathbf{d_{I,f}}(\rho^1))$. This essentially says that, relative to an interpretation and an assignment, an encoding formula is true at a world-time pair iff the individual denoted by the individual term is in the encoding extension of the property denoted by the property term. Note that satisfaction$_\mathbf{I}$ for encoding formulas is defined independently of the worlds and times. The reason is that, on our conception, encoded properties are rigidly encoded, and so this fact is built right into interpretations by making the $\mathbf{ext_A}$ of a property independent of worlds and times. This means that Principle 4 of Chapter 2, which asserts that if an object possibly ever encodes a property, it does so necessarily and always, is a logical truth of the language (that is, it is true$_\mathbf{I}$, for every $\mathbf{I}$).

The recursive clauses for the definition of satisfaction$_I$, which define this notion for formulas containing the ordinary connectives, the quantifier, the modal operator, and the tense operator, are standard. The quantifiers are completely unrestricted, and range over everything whatsoever in their respective domains. As a reminder, the clause for the tense operator '$\mathcal{H}$' is simply: $\mathbf{f}$ satisfies$_I$ $\mathcal{H}\phi$ at $\langle\mathbf{w},\mathbf{t}\rangle$ iff for every time $\mathbf{t}'$, $\mathbf{t}' < \mathbf{t}$, $\mathbf{f}$ satisfies$_I$ ϕ at $\langle\mathbf{w},\mathbf{t}'\rangle$. With this recursive definition of satisfaction, we get the following simple definition of truth under an interpretation: ϕ is $true_I$ iff every $\mathbf{f}$ satisfies$_I$ ϕ at $\langle\mathbf{w}_0,\mathbf{t}_0\rangle$. Notice that this definition of truth for the language of encoding is basically like its counterpart for the modal language of exemplification. No extraordinary arrangements have to be made in order to assimilate encoding formulas into the language of exemplification.

3.3   Conditions Under Which There Are Relations

The semantic conception of truth just outlined should give us an idea of what the truth conditions are for an arbitrarily chosen sentence of the language of encoding. This should facilitate understanding of the comprehension and identity principles for relations formulated in this language in this section and the next, respectively. These principles are generalizations of Principles 5 and 6 of Chapter 2. The generalization of Principle 5 is a comprehension schema for relations:

Relations: *For every formula ϕ in which F^n doesn't occur free, and in which there are neither encoding subformulas nor quantifiers binding relation variables (nor definite descriptions), the following is an axiom:*

$$(\exists F^n)\square\blacksquare(\forall x_1)\ldots(\forall x_n)(F^n x_1 \ldots x_n \equiv \phi)$$

The restrictions on *Relations* are the same as those on Principle 5 in Chapter 2. Since the reasons for these restrictions have already been discussed, it is best to look now at a variety of examples. The following examples demonstrate that the permissible formulas ϕ are just the ones found in a first-order modal language. Consequently, the relations that there are according to *Relations* should be perfectly familiar. In these examples, it is assumed that the constants name particular individuals and relations (also, superscripts have been suppressed):

(1) $(\exists F)\square\blacksquare(\forall x)(\forall y)(Fxy \equiv Sxay)$

(2) $(\exists F)\square\blacksquare(\forall x)(\forall y)(Fxy \equiv \square{\sim}Pxy)$

(3) $(\exists F)\square\blacksquare(\forall x)(\forall y)(Fxy \equiv \mathcal{H}(Q!x \rightarrow E!y))$

(4) $(\exists F)\Box\blacksquare(\forall x)(Fx \equiv \mathcal{G}(E!x \rightarrow Qx))$

(5) $(\exists F)\Box\blacksquare(\forall x)(\forall y)(Fxy \equiv Ryx)$

(6) $(\exists F)\Box\blacksquare(\forall x)(\forall y)(Fxy \equiv (\forall z)Sxyz)$

(7) $(\exists F)\Box\blacksquare(\forall x)(\forall y)(\forall z)(Fxyz \equiv Pxy)$

Intuitively, (1) semantically implies that there is a relation that results by plugging the object denoted by 'a' into the second place of the 3-place relation denoted by 'S.' Necessarily-always, all and only those objects x and y such that x bears S to a and y exemplify this relation. (2) asserts that there is a two-place relation F, which is such that, necessarily-always, F is exemplified by just those objects that necessarily fail to stand in the relation P. (3) gives us the relation that x and y bear to one another just in case y's existence has always depended on x exemplifying Q, whereas (4) gives us the property that x exemplifies iff it will always be the case that x exemplifies Q whenever x exists. The reader should be able to formulate an intuitive reading and understanding of (5) – (7) as well. Note that each of these instances asserts that there is a certain *complex* relation. We know that there are *simple* relations by the principles of ordinary logic. There is no need to formulate an instance of *Relations* in which ϕ is 'Rxy' in order to assert that there is relation with the appropriate extension denoted by 'R.' For one thing, we can derive '$(\exists F)Fab$' from 'Rab' by Existential Generalization. But we can also derive '$(\exists F)\Box\blacksquare(\forall x)(\forall y)(Fxy \equiv Rxy)$' by logic alone. By the rules of modal and tense predicate logic, it is easy to deduce that $\Box\blacksquare(\forall x)(\forall y)(Rxy \equiv Rxy)$. Then by Existential Generalization on the first occurrence of 'R,' we get something that looks just like an instance of *Relations*.

In every interpretation in which *Relations* is true, the domain **R** is forced to have a wide variety of (complex) properties and relations. Since the complex properties and relations that are harnessed together are *logically* complex, it is reasonable to think that *Relations* should be true in every interpretation. In order to ensure that *Relations* is logically true, interpretations can be modified just slightly, so that they include, as a component, a group of logical functions that put together relations into new, complex relations that make instances of this comprehension schema true. So let us suppose that every interpretation **I** has the component **L**, which contains the following group of logical functions: **PLUG**$_i$ (plugging), **NEG** (negation), **COND** (conditionalization), **UNIV**$_i$ (universalization), **REFL**$_{i,j}$ (reflection), **CONV**$_{i,j}$ (conversion), and **VAC**$_i$ (vacuous expansion), **NEC** (necessitation), **WAS** (past omnitemporalization), and **WILL** (future omnitemporalization).

Many of these functions are just the semantic counterparts of the predicate operators Quine developed in [1960], and we shall presume some familiarity with them.[4]

To get some idea of how these functions work, consider how they produce the complex relations that make (1) – (7) true. Fix an interpretation $\mathbf{I}$ and an assignment to the variables $\mathbf{f}$. Then, where "$\mathbf{d}(\tau)$" stands for the denotation of term τ relativized to $\mathbf{I}$ and $\mathbf{f}$, the expressions that follow semantically describe the relations which make (1) – (7) true, respectively:

(a) $\mathbf{PLUG}_2(\mathbf{d}(S), \mathbf{d}(a))$

(b) $\mathbf{NEC}(\mathbf{NEG}(\mathbf{d}(P)))$

(c) $\mathbf{WAS}(\mathbf{COND}(\mathbf{d}(Q), \mathbf{d}(E!)))$

(d) $\mathbf{WILL}(\mathbf{REFL}_{1,2}(\mathbf{COND}(\mathbf{d}(E!), \mathbf{d}(Q))))$

(e) $\mathbf{CONV}_{1,2}(\mathbf{d}(R))$

(f) $\mathbf{UNIV}_3(\mathbf{d}(S))$

(g) $\mathbf{VAC}_3(\mathbf{d}(P))$

Once it is required that the domains $\mathbf{R}$ and $\mathbf{D}$ of every interpretation be closed under these logical functions, it is essential to require that the $\mathbf{ext}_{\mathbf{w},\mathbf{t}}$ function assign extensions to the complex relations that are "in tune" with the extensions of the simpler relations they may have as components. So, for example, the $\mathbf{ext}_{\mathbf{w},\mathbf{t}}$ of relation (a) has as members just those pairs $\langle \mathbf{o}, \mathbf{o}' \rangle$ which are such that the triple $\langle \mathbf{o}, \mathbf{d}(a), \mathbf{o}' \rangle$ is a member of the $\mathbf{ext}_{\mathbf{w},\mathbf{t}}$ of $\mathbf{d}(S)$. And the $\mathbf{ext}_{\mathbf{w},\mathbf{t}}$ of the relation (c) has as members just those pairs $\langle \mathbf{o}, \mathbf{o}' \rangle$ which are such that, for every $\mathbf{t}' < \mathbf{t}$, either $\mathbf{o}$ fails to be a member of $\mathbf{ext}_{\mathbf{w},\mathbf{t}'}(\mathbf{d}(Q))$ or $\mathbf{o}'$ is a member of $\mathbf{ext}_{\mathbf{w},\mathbf{t}'}(\mathbf{d}(E!))$. And so forth. With these examples, and a basic understanding of Quine [1960], one can pretty much guess how the constraints work for the other examples. However, (g) is an interesting case: the $\mathbf{ext}_{\mathbf{w},\mathbf{t}}$ of relation (g) has as members just those triples $\langle \mathbf{o}_1, \mathbf{o}_2, \mathbf{o}_3 \rangle$ such that the pair $\langle \mathbf{o}_1, \mathbf{o}_2 \rangle$ is in the $\mathbf{ext}_{\mathbf{w},\mathbf{t}}$ of $\mathbf{d}(P)$. With the exception of

---

[4]$\mathbf{NEG}$ corresponds to Quine's *Neg*; $\mathbf{COND}$ corresponds to *Conj*, except that it handles the material conditional instead of conjunction; $\mathbf{UNIV}_i$ is similar to Quine's *Der*, except that it handles the universal instead of the "existential" quantifier; $\mathbf{REFL}_{i,j}$ is similar to his *Refl*, and $\mathbf{CONV}_{i,j}$ is similar to his *Inv* and *inv*. Quine did not use anything like $\mathbf{PLUG}_i$, $\mathbf{NEC}$, or $\mathbf{VAC}_i$. $\mathbf{PLUG}_i$ is used for the interpretation of singular terms, which Quine preferred to eliminate from the language. $\mathbf{NEC}$, $\mathbf{WAS}$, and $\mathbf{WILL}$ are used for the interpretation of the operators '$\Box$,' '$\mathcal{H}$,' and '$\mathcal{G}$,' respectively (again, Quine does not employ the modal operator). $\mathbf{VAC}_i$ is used to interpret λ-expressions with variables vacuously bound by the λ.

WAS and **WILL**, the precise definitions of the logical functions and their constraints may be found both in my work [1983] and in the cited works of Bealer and Menzel.[5] But you should now have a pretty good idea of what (complex) relations there are according to our comprehension schema, and of how their extensions correspond to the extensions of the relations they may have as structural components.

By requiring that the domains **R** and **D** be closed under these logical functions, some rather powerful consequences of *Relations* follow. Consider the following three examples, in which '*G*' and '*H*' are variables over relations (and properties):

(8) $(\forall G)(\forall u)(\exists F)\square\blacksquare(\forall x)(\forall y)(Fxy \equiv Gxuy)$

(9) $(\forall G)(\exists F)\square\blacksquare(\forall x)(\forall y)(Fxy \equiv \square\sim Gxy)$

(10) $(\forall G)(\forall H)(\exists F)\square\blacksquare(\forall x)(\forall y)(Fxy \equiv \square(Gx \rightarrow Hy))$

(8) semantically requires that for any 3-place relation G and individual u, there is a 2-place relation that results by plugging u into the second place of G. (8) is a consequence of *Relations* by two applications of universal generalization on the instance in which $\phi = $ '$Gxuy$.' (9) semantically implies that for every 2-place relation, there is another 2-place relation that is the necessitation of its negation. Consequences like this are derivable for every n-place relation. (10) asserts that for any two properties G and H, there is a 2-place relation F that an individual x bears to an individual y just in case, necessarily-always, x's being G necessarily implies y's being H. Other examples can be produced by replacing the relation constants in (1) – (7) by variables and using Existential Generalization.

Before turning to the identity conditions of relations, consider that the system can now accommodate λ-expressions of the form $[\lambda\nu_1\ldots\nu_n\ \phi]$, where $\nu_1,\ldots,\nu_n$ are any individual variables and where ϕ has neither encoding subformulas nor quantified relation variables. That is, such expressions can be assigned denotations. For example, the following λ-expressions denote, relative to **I** and **f**, the relations (a) – (g), respectively: $[\lambda xy\ Sxay]$, $[\lambda xy\ \square\sim Pxy]$, $[\lambda xy\ \mathcal{H}(Q!x \rightarrow E!y)]$, $[\lambda x\ \mathcal{G}(E!x \rightarrow Qx)]$, $[\lambda xy\ Ryx]$, $[\lambda xy\ (\forall z)(Sxyz)]$, and $[\lambda xyz\ Pxy]$. The λ-expressions may have free variables. For example, $[\lambda xy\ Sxzy]$ is a perfectly good λ-expression. The relation that it denotes depends on the object **f** assigns to the variable 'z.' Also, definite descriptions may appear in

---

[5] **WAS** and **WILL** are new, however, and they are developed here for the first time. Here is the definition of **WAS**: **WAS** maps **R** into **R**, subject to the following constraint: $\mathbf{ext_{w,t}(WAS(r^n))} =$
$\{\langle \mathbf{o_1},\ldots,\mathbf{o_n}\rangle \mid (\forall \mathbf{t'})(\mathbf{t' < t} \rightarrow \langle \mathbf{o_1},\ldots,\mathbf{o_n}\rangle \in \mathbf{ext_{w,t'}(r^n)})\}$.

λ-expressions, though if the description fails to denote, so will the λ-expressions containing it (this is discussed further in Chapter 5).

To bring all this about, the definition of denotation has to be extended to cover the λ-predicates. We do not plan to develop the extended definition here, however. Basically, the definition looks at the syntactic structure of a λ-expression, and then determines the denotation of the entire expression in terms of the denotations of the simpler terms appearing in the expression and the way in which those terms are arranged. One can get a good idea of how it works by considering the above examples. However, these examples are rather simple—for each one, the logical functions in **L** can be put together in only one way to produce a relation with the appropriate structure. But there are other expressions, logically more complex than the above, for which there are several ways of constructing a relation with the appropriate structure using the logical functions. For example, there are several ways to combine the logical functions to produce a property that serves as the denotation of the expression '$[\lambda x\ \mathcal{H}(Px \rightarrow\ \sim Skx)]$.' Here are just three of the possibilities:

$$\mathbf{WAS}(\mathbf{REFL}_{1,2}(\mathbf{COND}(\mathbf{d}(P), \mathbf{NEG}(\mathbf{PLUG}_1(\mathbf{d}(S), \mathbf{d}(k))))))$$

$$\mathbf{WAS}(\mathbf{REFL}_{1,2}(\mathbf{COND}(\mathbf{d}(P), \mathbf{PLUG}_1(\mathbf{NEG}(\mathbf{d}(S)), \mathbf{d}(k)))))$$

$$\mathbf{PLUG}_2(\mathbf{WAS}(\mathbf{REFL}_{1,3}(\mathbf{COND}(\mathbf{d}(P), \mathbf{NEG}(S)))))$$

Consequently, to ensure that λ-expressions are well-defined (i.e., have a unique denotation), the definition of $\mathbf{d}_{\mathbf{I},\mathbf{f}}(\tau)$ requires a preliminary definition, which effectively partitions the λ-expressions into equivalence classes. Each cell of the partition contains the expressions that have the same essential syntactic structure. Each cell corresponds to one of the logical functions in **L**, and every expression falls into a unique cell. For example, the partition of the λ-predicates uniquely classifies '$[\lambda x\ \mathcal{H}(Px \rightarrow \sim Skx)]$' as the past omnitemporalization of the expression '$[\lambda x\ (Px \rightarrow \sim Skx)]$.' This expression is in turn uniquely classified as the reflexivization$_{1,2}$ of the expression '$[\lambda xy\ (Px \rightarrow \sim Sky)]$.' The latter is classified as the conditionalization of the expression '$[\lambda x\ Px]$' with '$[\lambda y\ \sim Sky]$.' The former is simple, and so $\mathbf{d}([\lambda x\ Px])$ is just $\mathbf{d}(P)$. The latter is classified as the negation of the expression '$[\lambda y\ Sky]$,' which in turn is classifed as the plugging$_1$ of the simple expression '$[\lambda uy\ Suy]$' by the expression 'k.' In terms of these unique classifications, the denotation of the original λ-expression is the property:
$$\mathbf{WAS}(\mathbf{REFL}_{1,2}(\mathbf{COND}(\mathbf{d}(P), \mathbf{NEG}(\mathbf{PLUG}_1(\mathbf{d}(S), \mathbf{d}(k)))))).$$

The partition uniquely categorizes each λ-expression in this way, and so each one gets assigned a unique denotation. The particular definition for partitioning the λ-expressions that is required for the modal and tense language is just a variant of the one constructed in [1983] (pp. 64–67). Interested readers may look there for the details.[6]

These stipulations turn the most important principle governing λ-expressions, namely λ-*Equivalence*, into a logical truth. This principle asserts that the individuals that exemplify a complex relation stand in just the simple relationships required by the structure of the relation. If we let '$\phi_{\nu_1,\ldots,\nu_n}^{x_1,\ldots,x_n}$' stand for the result of replacing ν_i by x_i everywhere in ϕ $(1 \leq i \leq n)$, then the following captures this idea formally:

λ-**Equivalence:** *For every formula ϕ in which there are neither encoding formulas nor quantifiers binding relation variables (nor definite descriptions), the following is a logical axiom:*

$$(\forall x_1)\ldots(\forall x_n)([\lambda\nu_1\ldots\nu_n\ \phi]x_1\ldots x_n \equiv \phi_{\nu_1,\ldots,\nu_n}^{x_1,\ldots,x_n})$$

Here are two instances:

(11) $(\forall x)(\forall y)([\lambda uw \ \blacksquare \sim Puw]xy \equiv \blacksquare \sim Pxy)$

(12) $(\forall x)(\forall y)([\lambda uw \ Qu \ \& \ Pwu]xy \equiv (Qx \ \& \ Pyx))$

Clearly, this is the kind of logical behavior we should expect from the λ-expressions. What may not be obvious is that *Relations* is deducible from λ-*Equivalence*. To see this, consider the fact that in modal (tense) logic, we can derive modal (tensed) instances of λ-*Equivalence*, by the rule of necessitation (omnitemporalization). Then, since λ-expressions are terms that denote relations, we can use Existential Generalization on these instances of λ-*Equivalence* to produce instances of *Relations*. In other words, for every instance of *Relations*, there is a corresponding instance of λ-*Equivalence* from which it can be derived. Consequently, λ-*Equivalence* is more general. It is the principal logical axiom schema governing relations, whereas *Relations* is a logical theorem schema.

3.4   Identity Conditions for Relations

The key to the identity of relations is the principle of property identity described in Chapter 2 (Principle 6). Recall that two properties F and G are defined to be identical just in case necessarily-always, F and G are encoded by the same objects. Now a definition of relation identity can be constructed in terms of this definition. Here is the basic idea behind the definition. To see whether the 2-place relations F and G are

---

[6]The only modifications required for that definition are clauses for handling λ-expressions with the tense operators '$\mathcal{H}$' and '$\mathcal{G}$.' But these are essentially the same as the one handling λ-expressions with a modal operator.

identical, take an arbitrary object, say x, and plug it into the second
place of F and into the second place of G. Then consider the question
of whether the two properties that result are identical (i.e., consider
whether $[\lambda y \; Fyx]$ and $[\lambda y \; Gyx]$ are necessarily-always encoded by the
same objects). Now take F and G again and plug x into their respective
first places. Consider again the question of whether the two properties
that result are identical (i.e., consider whether $[\lambda y \; Fxy]$ and $[\lambda y \; Gxy]$
are necessarily-always encoded by the same objects). If the answer to
both question is positive, then we shall say that the 2-place relations F
and G are identical.

This definition can be extended for any two n-place relations F and
G, for any $n > 1$. Just take $n - 1$ arbitrarily chosen objects and plug
them into F and G in the same order. The result is a pair of properties.
In fact, for each way of plugging $n-1$ objects into F and G, the result is a
pair of properties. If the members of every pair of properties so produced
are identical (according to the definition of property identity), then the
original n-place relations are identical. In other words, two relations are
identical just in case the members of every pair of relational properties
derivable from them by logical projection are identical. This is just what
the following definition of relation identity requires:

$$F^n = G^n \; \equiv_{df} \quad (\text{where } n > 1)$$

$$(\forall x_1) \dots (\forall x_{n-1})([\lambda y \; F^n y x_1 \dots x_{n-1}] = [\lambda y \; G^n y x_1 \dots x_{n-1}] \; \& $$
$$[\lambda y \; F^n x_1 y x_2 \dots x_{n-1}] = [\lambda y \; G^n x_1 y x_2 \dots x_{n-1}] \; \& \dots \& $$
$$[\lambda y \; F^n x_1 \dots x_{n-1} y] = [\lambda y \; G^n x_1 \dots x_{n-1} y])$$

Remember that the identity sign employed here is defined by Principle 6
in Chapter 2. The resulting definition is consistent with the fact that
necessarily equivalent relations may be distinct. Also, if at any point
it is decided that the system should be expanded to allow n-place relations $(n \geq 2)$ to be encoded by individuals, then this definition can be
simplified to look just like Principle 6 of Chapter 2.

In addition to this definition, there is one logical truth about the
identity of relations that is worthy of discussion. It simply tells us about
the identity of relations denoted by certain kinds of λ-expressions:

λ-**Identity:** *Where ρ^n is any relation term, and $\nu_1, \dots, \nu_n$ are any object variables and $\nu'_1, \dots, \nu'_n$ are any object variables distinct from, and
substitutable for $\nu_1, \dots, \nu_n$, respectively, and ϕ' is the result of substituting all of the ν'_i's for the ν_i's in ϕ, respectively, the following is an
axiom:*

$$[\lambda \nu_1 \dots \nu_n \; \rho^n \nu_1 \dots \nu_n] = \rho^n \; \& \; [\lambda \nu_1 \dots \nu_n \; \phi] = [\lambda \nu'_1 \dots \nu'_n \; \phi']$$

To see that both conjuncts are true in every interpretation, consider two simple examples: $[\lambda x \ Fx] = F$, and $[\lambda x \ Fx] = [\lambda y \ Fy]$. The denotation function is defined so that, in every interpretation, the simple λ-expression on the left side of the identity sign, in each example, denotes "the same" property that the one on the right side denotes. Therefore, in each example, any object that encodes the property denoted by the left expression, encodes the property denoted by the right expression, and vice versa. The reason we say "the same" properties are denoted is that identity is a primitive notion of the semantics, though not a primitive of the object language. Note that our understanding of the semantics rests on a notion for which the theory expressed in the object language provides an analysis.

There are other kinds of logical principles governing the identity of relations that could be added to our theory. For example, one might want to add the principle that if two λ-expressions both have the same structure and their corresponding terms have the same denotations, then they denote the same relation.[7] But since principles like this are not essential for developing the ideas to follow, they are a sideshow. Moreover, some of the principles that one might like to add can not be stated as we now have things set up. For example, we cannot assert: $[\lambda \nu_1 \ldots \nu_n \ \phi] \neq [\lambda \nu'_1 \ldots \nu'_m \ \phi]$, where $n \neq m$. The way identity is defined, the relation terms flanking the identity sign have to be of the same degree. Of course, it is a simple matter to reconstruct things in order to do this—we would have to take identity as a primitive notion, allow relation terms of different degree to flank the identity sign.[8] In such a reconstruction, Principle 6 would become provable, the definition of relation identity would become an axiom, and the principle of non-identity just described would express a logical truth.

However, given our present concerns, there is no reason to do this. It is important to show what can be done without identity as a primitive. The definitions of identity, as they stand, may constitute insights into the nature of properties and relations. No other theory of relations offers identity conditions that are linked to their most distinctive feature, namely, that they can be predicated of other things. Most other theories treat properties and relations as individuals that fall under the

---

[7]See the principles discussed by Bealer ([1982], p. 65) and Menzel ([1986], p. 38). Some of the principles that Bealer and Menzel use would work rather badly in our system. For example, in their systems, the fact that two λ-expressions have terms that denote distinct individuals guarantees that the expressions denote distinct relations. In our system, however, for at least some distinct A-objects a and b, $[\lambda y \ Rya] = [\lambda y \ Ryb]$.

[8]Some restrictions that banish certain kinds of identity claims from λ-expressions and *Relations* would be necessary; see [1983], p. 159.

scope of the individual quantifier '$\forall x$.'[9] For these other theories, the
main principle of identity governing relations is Leibniz's Law—two relations are identical just in case they exemplify the same properties. But
this doesn't link the identity of relations to what we've seen is their most
distinctive feature. It treats relations on a par with non-predicable individuals. This is like defining two sets to be identical just in case they are
members of the same sets. It is much more insightful, and fruitful, to
define two sets to be identical just in case they have the same members.
Such a definition is linked to the most distinctive feature of the sets involved, namely, the fact that they may have members. Our definition of
identity for properties, in contrast to that of other theories, is more like
the second definition of set identity. It defines two properties F and G to
be identical on the basis of their encoding predications. And it ties the
identities of relations and propositions to these encoding predications as
well. So, ultimately, the identity of relations is tied to the fact that they
are predicable entities.

Moreover, unlike most other theories, our theory of relations is not
the only focus of study. It is simply part of the groundwork that is needed
to develop the non-logical part of the theory in a precise way. Our aim
in this work is not so much to produce a maximally powerful theory of
relations as it is to produce one that is precise, insightful, and useful
for explaining the failures of strong extensionality. We hope, by now, to
have demonstrated that it is all three. And as part of a larger theory,
it proves to be useful in a variety of other ways. These applications not
only include the explanation of why English expressions seem to fail the
principles of Generalization and Substitutivity but also the development
of a modal theory of propositions, situations, and possible worlds (to
which we turn in Chapter 4). It remains to be seen whether the other
theories of relations can be applied naturally in these ways. During
the course of the following chapters, we shall sometimes compare these
theories to our own, to see what data each theory naturally handles
best. But for now, the basic theory of relations presented so far should
be clear enough.

Finally, note that our formal principle of Substitutivity (Principle 7,
Chapter 2) can be generalized to cover identical relations. We just stipulate that pairs of relations which are identical according to our definition
behave just the way we would expect identical relations to behave—
anything true about one member of the pair is true about the other,
and vice versa. We regard as true the instances of this principle that
have the following form: $F^n = G^n \rightarrow (\phi(F^n, F^n) \equiv \phi(F^n, G^n))$. Thus,
terms that denote identical relations may be substituted for one another

---

[9]See the cited works of Bealer, Menzel, Cocchiarella, Chierchia, and Turner.

anywhere in any context of our language. It is also straightforward to show that the following is derivable: $(\forall F^n)(F^n = F^n)$. We should note that since identity is a defined notion in our language, Substitutivity is a non-logical principle. It is not true in every permissible interpretation, since it is not true in those interpretations in which "distinct" properties have the same encoding extension. According to our description of interpretations in the previous two sections, there is nothing that excludes such interpretations. So by asserting that Substitutivity is a non-logical axiom, we focus consideration on those interpretations in which relations identical according to our definition behave the way we expect identical relations to behave.

It should be clear that it does not follow from the fact that two relations are necessarily-always equivalent that they are identical. It is consistent with $\square\blacksquare(\forall x_1)\ldots(\forall x_n)(Fx_1 \ldots x_n \equiv Gx_1 \ldots x_n)$, that $F \neq G$. Though, of course, if two relations are identical, then they are necessarily equivalent (by Substitutivity).

4

Propositions, Situations, Worlds, and Times

Our conception of propositions derives from Russell. Intuitively, propositions are structured entities that have constituents and a logical structure based on exemplification. The constituents of a proposition are the relations and objects that it has as parts. These parts can be organized into all sorts of complex logical structures. The metaphysical truth or falsity of these logical complexes is basic. If a proposition is true, there is nothing else that "makes it true." Its being true is just the way things are (arranged). Similarly, if a proposition is false, then there is nothing that makes it false. Its being false is just not the way things are (arranged). The basic, metaphysical truth of propositions should be contrasted with the derivative, semantic truth of sentences. The semantic truth of exemplification sentences depends on the metaphysical truth of propositions they denote—these sentences are the kind of thing that are "made true (false)" by true (false) propositions. The semantic definition of truth for a language is "that which determines the truth conditions" of its sentences. In the case of exemplification predications, whether or not those truth conditions obtain depends ultimately on which propositions are true.

Situations, worlds, and times are intimately related to propositions. A situation is completely characterized by the propositions that are true *in* that situation. A world is completely characterized by the propositions true *at* that world. The same applies to moments of time. Moreover, we state our beliefs about what worlds and times are like in terms of propositions. Intentional states such as belief, desire, and hope are directed towards worlds and times in virtue of being directed upon (modal and tense) propositions. Consequently, an understanding of propositions is extremely important to our understanding of how intentional states are basically organized and structured.

An essential feature of this conception of propositions is that they are not strongly extensional. Necessarily equivalent propositions may be distinct. If the theory of propositions is not fine-grained enough to distinguish necessarily equivalent propositions, the ability to accurately represent belief is lost. Therefore, the theory of propositions is a crucial part of the study of intensionality. It is no accident that the theory of relations developed in the previous chapter can be extended in a simple and natural way to yield a theory of propositions. Intuitively, a proposition is a zero-place relation. The simplest propositions result by plugging objects into all of the places of an n-place relation. All other propositions are logically constructed out of these atomic exemplification propositions.[1]

In order to make this conception of propositions precise, we need to modify slightly the theory developed so far.

4.1   The Basic Theory of Propositions

The object language is modified first. It shall now include simple and complex terms for denoting propositions. This is easily done by allowing the superscript on relation constants and variables to go to zero. So there are constants such as P^0, Q^0, ..., and variables such as F^0, G^0, ..., in the language. We stipulate that all zero-place terms count as exemplification formulas. So the simple zero-place constants and variables count as unstructured, atomic exemplification formulas. Only some of the formulas in the language that results are going to count as complex terms. Essentially, all and only the formulas that satisfy the restrictions on λ-expressions count as complex, zero-place terms. Let us say that a *propositional* formula is any formula in which there are neither encoding subformulas nor quantifiers binding relation variables. Then if ϕ is a propositional formula, $[\lambda\, \phi]$ is a zero-place, complex term (we can read $[\lambda\, \phi]$ as: *that-ϕ*). By stipulation, these terms count as formulas, and for much of what follows, let us abbreviate '$[\lambda\, \phi]$' simply as 'ϕ.'

The intuitive, semantic conception of truth for this language requires only minor modifications. Interpretations are still modeled as structures of the form: $\langle \mathbf{D}, \mathbf{R}, (\mathbf{W}, \mathbf{w}_0), (\mathbf{T}, \mathbf{t}_0, <), \mathbf{L}, \mathbf{ext}_{\mathbf{w},\mathbf{t}}, \mathbf{ext}_{\mathbf{A}}, \mathbf{F} \rangle$. However, $\mathbf{R}$ now houses all of the n-place relations for $n \geq 0$, and the logical functions in $\mathbf{L}$ now produce and operate on zero-place relations. Here are some examples:

---

[1] The truth of encoding formulas does not alter the basic exemplification structure of the world in any way—no new propositions or facts are required for the truth of such formulas.

- Proposition $\mathbf{p}_1$ is produced by plugging an object $\mathbf{o}$ into the only place of property $\mathbf{r}$; i.e., $\mathbf{p}_1 = \mathbf{PLUG}_1(\mathbf{r}, \mathbf{o})$

- Proposition $\mathbf{p}_2$ is produced by universalizing the property $\mathbf{s}$; i.e., $\mathbf{p}_2 = \mathbf{UNIV}_1(\mathbf{s})$

- Propositions $\mathbf{p}_3$ and $\mathbf{p}_4$ are produced by the negation and necessitation of proposition $\mathbf{q}$; i.e., $\mathbf{p}_3 = \mathbf{NEG}(\mathbf{q})$, and $\mathbf{p}_4 = \mathbf{NEC}(\mathbf{q})$

- Proposition $\mathbf{p}_5$ is produced by the conditionalization of the past omnitemporalization of $\mathbf{q}$ and the future omnitemporalization of $\mathbf{v}$; i.e., $\mathbf{p}_5 = \mathbf{COND}(\mathbf{WAS}(\mathbf{q}), \mathbf{WILL}(\mathbf{v}))$.

- Property $\mathbf{u}$ is produced by the vacuous expansion of the proposition $\mathbf{p}_1$; i.e., $\mathbf{u} = \mathbf{VAC}_1(\mathbf{p}_1)$

In addition, the $\mathbf{ext}_{\mathbf{w},\mathbf{t}}$ function has to be extended so that, in addition to assigning to every relation an exemplification extension at each world-time pair, it assigns to every zero-place relation a truth value as well. This function is constrained to work in the appropriate way. Here are some examples of these constraints that are related to the previous examples:

- $\mathbf{ext}_{\mathbf{w},\mathbf{t}}(\mathbf{p}_1) = T$ iff $\mathbf{o} \in \mathbf{ext}_{\mathbf{w},\mathbf{t}}(\mathbf{r})$

- $\mathbf{ext}_{\mathbf{w},\mathbf{t}}(\mathbf{p}_2) = T$ iff for every object $\mathbf{o}$, $\mathbf{o} \in \mathbf{ext}_{\mathbf{w},\mathbf{t}}(\mathbf{s})$

- $\mathbf{ext}_{\mathbf{w},\mathbf{t}}(\mathbf{p}_3) = T$ iff $\mathbf{ext}_{\mathbf{w},\mathbf{t}}(\mathbf{q}) = F$; and $\mathbf{ext}_{\mathbf{w},\mathbf{t}}(\mathbf{p}_4) = T$ iff for every world $\mathbf{w}'$, $\mathbf{ext}_{\mathbf{w}',\mathbf{t}}(\mathbf{q}) = T$

- $\mathbf{ext}_{\mathbf{w},\mathbf{t}}(\mathbf{p}_5) = T$ iff either it is not the case that $(\forall \mathbf{t}' < \mathbf{t})(\mathbf{ext}_{\mathbf{w},\mathbf{t}'}(\mathbf{q}) = T$ or it is the case that $(\forall \mathbf{t}')$(if $\mathbf{t} < \mathbf{t}'$, then $\mathbf{ext}_{\mathbf{w},\mathbf{t}'}(\mathbf{v}) = T$.

- $\mathbf{ext}_{\mathbf{w},\mathbf{t}}(\mathbf{u}) = \{\mathbf{o} \in \mathbf{D} | \mathbf{ext}_{\mathbf{w},\mathbf{t}}(\mathbf{p}_1) = T\}$

Notice that the last item, property $\mathbf{u}$, behaves in the following way: an object $\mathbf{o}$ is in the extension of $\mathbf{u}$ at world-time pair $\langle \mathbf{w}, \mathbf{t} \rangle$ iff $\mathbf{p}_1$ is true at $\langle \mathbf{w}, \mathbf{t} \rangle$. So if $\mathbf{p}_1$ is true at $\langle \mathbf{w}, \mathbf{t} \rangle$, every object exemplifies $\mathbf{u}$ at $\langle \mathbf{w}, \mathbf{t} \rangle$, otherwise no object does.

The final modification of interpretations is that the function $\mathbf{F}$ is extended, so that it maps each of the simple, zero-place constants P_i^0 to a zero-place relation in $\mathbf{R}$.

Next we have to make a few changes in the definitions of the other concepts employed in the definition of truth. Assignments to variables are extended so that the new zero-place variables are assigned propositions in $\mathbf{R}$. The denotation function is modified in two ways. First, it has to cover the new zero-place constants and variables. So, for each simple zero-place term τ, $\mathbf{d_{I,f}}(\tau)$ is either $\mathbf{F}(\tau)$ or $\mathbf{f}(\tau)$, depending on whether τ is a constant or a variable. Second, this function must now assign propositions to the complex zero-place terms. Here are some consequences of this assignment, stated in terms of the examples described two paragraphs back:[2]

- Where $\mathbf{d}(R) = \mathbf{r}$, and $\mathbf{d}(b) = \mathbf{o}$, then $\mathbf{d}(Rb) = \mathbf{p_1}$

- Where $\mathbf{d}(S) = \mathbf{s}$, then $\mathbf{d}((\forall x)Sx) = \mathbf{p_2}$

- Where $\mathbf{d}(Q^0) = \mathbf{q}$, then $\mathbf{d}(\sim Q^0) = \mathbf{p_3}$, and $\mathbf{d}(\Box Q^0) = \mathbf{p_4}$

- Where $\mathbf{d}(V^0) = \mathbf{v}$, then $\mathbf{d}((\mathcal{H}Q^0 \rightarrow \mathcal{G}V^0)) = \mathbf{p_5}$

- Where $\mathbf{d}(R)$ and $\mathbf{d}(b)$ are as above, $\mathbf{d}([\lambda y \, Rb]) = \mathbf{u}$

One minor addition to the definition of satisfaction$_I$ is needed. That's because there is one new kind of atomic formula—the simple zero-place terms. But the clause that dictates the conditions under which they are satisfied is rather simple: if ρ^0 is any simple exemplification formula, then $\mathbf{f}$ satisfies$_I$ ρ^0 at $\langle \mathbf{w}, \mathbf{t} \rangle$ iff $\mathrm{ext}_{\mathbf{w},\mathbf{t}}(\rho^0) = T$. The other clauses in this definition remain the same. Consequently, so does the final definition of truth$_I$: ϕ is *true$_I$* iff every $\mathbf{f}$ satisfies$_I$ ϕ at $\langle \mathbf{w_0}, \mathbf{t_0} \rangle$.

Now that we have a semantic picture for the language of propositions, we can formulate a principle that asserts the conditions under which there are propositions. The following degenerate case of λ-*Equivalence* is true in every interpretation:

λ-**Equivalence:** *Where ϕ is any propositional formula in which no descriptions occur, the following is an axiom:*

$$[\lambda \phi] \equiv \phi$$

We may read this as: *that-ϕ iff ϕ*. Now the following principle is derivable from this degenerate case of λ-*Equivalence*, by first using the rules of necessitation and omnitemporalization, and then Existential Generalization:

Propositions: *Where ϕ is any propositional formula in which no descriptions occur and in which F^0 is not free, the following is a theorem:*

$$(\exists F^0)\Box\blacksquare(F^0 \equiv \phi)$$

---

[2] Readers interested in the exact details may want to look at the definition of denotation the Appendix (§A.2.3).

Because we have set up things so that zero-place variables are both formulas and terms that denote propositions, there is a special way to read the instances of *Propositions*. These readings are based on the following definition, in which we *use* our object language to *define* the metaphysical concept of truth:

$$F^0 \ is \ true =_{df} F^0$$

In other words, we can use our object language to assert that a proposition F^0 is true simply by asserting the proposition. This is part of what we meant when we said at the outset that the truth of propositions is basic. The metaphysical concept of truth is not defined in terms of more basic notions. Consequently, we may read the instances of *Propositions* as follows: there is a proposition F^0 which is such that, necessarily-always, F^0 is true iff ϕ. Here are some instances of *Propositions*:

(1) $(\exists F^0)\Box\blacksquare(F^0 \equiv \sim Rb)$

(2) $(\exists F^0)\Box\blacksquare(F^0 \equiv \Box(\forall x)Sx)$

(3) $(\exists F^0)\Box\blacksquare(F^0 \equiv \Box(\sim Rb \rightarrow (\mathcal{H}Q^0 \rightarrow \mathcal{G}V^0)))$

In every interpretation, there are propositions that make sentences (1) – (3) true. We shall always find propositions that have the following structure, described in terms of previous examples:

(a) **NEG($\mathbf{p_1}$)**

(b) **NEC($\mathbf{p_2}$)**

(c) **NEC(COND(NEG($\mathbf{p_1}$),$\mathbf{p_5}$))**

To complete the theory of propositions, identity conditions must be defined. These should be consistent with the fact that propositions are not strongly extensional. The basic insight behind our definition is that the identity of propositions is tied to the identity of the propositional properties constructed out of them. A propositional property F is one such that there is some proposition G^0 such that $F = [\lambda y \ G^0]$ (we may read $[\lambda y \ G^0]$ as: *being such that* G^0).[3] The following consequence of *Relations* guarantees that for every proposition, there is a corresponding propositional property:

(4) $(\forall G^0)(\exists F)\Box\blacksquare(Fx \equiv G^0)$

Another fact about propositional properties is that, necessarily-always, every object x exemplifies $[\lambda y \ G^0]$ iff G^0 is true. This is required by the following instance of λ-*Equivalence*:

---

[3] Recall that $\mathbf{d}([\lambda y \ G^0]) = \mathbf{VAC}_1(\mathbf{d}(G^0))$.

(5) $(\forall x)([\lambda y\ G^0]x \equiv G^0)$.

So everything whatsoever exemplifies a propositional property derived from a true proposition. Nothing exemplifies one constructed out of a false proposition.

With this understanding of propositional properties, we may define identity conditions for propositions: two propositions F^0 and G^0 are identical just in case, necessarily-always, the properties $[\lambda y\ F^0]$ and $[\lambda y\ G^0]$ are encoded by exactly the same objects:

$$F^0 = G^0 \ =_{df}\ [\lambda y\ F^0] = [\lambda y\ G^0]$$

On this definition, it is consistent with $\Box(F^0 \equiv G^0)$ that $F^0 \neq G^0$. However, from $F^0 = G^0$, it follows that F^0 and G^0 are necessarily equivalent. This is easy to prove, once we stipulate that the Principle of Substitutivity has instances of the following form: $F^0 = G^0 \rightarrow (\phi(F^0, F^0) \equiv \phi(F^0, G^0))$.

In the next section, we shall indicate how this definition of propositional identity is useful. It plays a crucial role in a central theorem that establishes the correctness of the theory of possible worlds. But what is just as important, the definition serves as the final piece to the puzzle of the identity of relations. A unified conception of the identity of relations emerges from our definitions—their identity is linked to the notion of encoding predication.

4.2   Situations, Worlds, and Times

Now that we have a theory of propositions that accounts for the fact that they fail Strong Extensionality, we can investigate situations, worlds, and times. The study of such entities will take us beyond pure intensional logic to the metaphysical theory of objects. The essential nature of a situation, what makes it that situation and not some other, is defined by the propositions that are true in that situation. The same applies to worlds and times—the essential nature of a world (or time), what makes it that world (time) and not some other, is defined by the propositions true at that world (time). Change the truth value of a single proposition true in (at) a given situation, world, or time and you have a different situation, world, or time. Propositions are, in some sense, essential components of these entities. Furthermore, there is a sense in which propositions are abstract. This is not the sense of 'abstract' we defined for individuals. Rather, a proposition has a kind of abstractness that comes from having properties and relations as constituents. Relations are "abstract" in virtue of being universal, repeatable, and predicable entities. By having relations as constituents, propositions have abstract parts. And since propositions are essential components of situations, worlds, and times, there is reason to suppose that these latter entities are abstract as well.

But what are situations, worlds, and times? In what sense are propositions essential components of them? There are no obvious answers to these questions, but it seems that situations, worlds and times are not just very complex propositions or properties. Complex propositions are either true or false, but situations, worlds, and times are not true or false in the same sense as propositions. Nor do they have the other characteristic features of propositions—they are not assertable, nor are they the kind of thing we can believe or disbelieve. Situations, worlds, and times do not seem to be properties either. Intuitively, they are not predicable of other things. It seems more likely, therefore, that these entities are individuals of some sort.

These intuitions and considerations lead us to believe that situations, worlds, and times are abstract individuals. In fact, the A-objects that encode just propositional properties seem to have many of the essential features that situations, worlds, and times have. First of all there is the fact that the latter can be uniquely characterized in terms of the propositions that are true in them. Propositional properties are ideal for characterizing situations. However, from our perspective, situations, worlds, and times are identified and characterized by the propositional properties they encode, rather than exemplify. Here is why.

The properties that an A-object encodes are essential to its identity— even more essential than the properties it contingently or necessarily exemplifies. To see this, look at some of the properties that A-objects contingently and necessarily exemplify. An A-object like 'the round square' can contingently exemplify the property of being something Russell thought about; an A-object like 'the fountain of youth' can contingently exemplify the property of being something explorers have searched for. There are properties necessarily exemplified by A-objects as well, such as failing to exist, being colorless, being shapeless, being textureless, etc. These contingent and necessary properties cannot always distinguish two distinct A-objects however. Only encoded properties can distinguish such A-objects. Now by identifying worlds and times as situations, and by identifying situations as A-objects that encode only propositional properties, we can distinguish the propositional properties that essentially characterize a given situation from the properties that that situation contingently and necessarily exemplifies. The propositional properties are more crucial to their identity.

Another reason why situations, worlds, and times are better characterized in terms of encoded rather than exemplified propositional properties is that no object can be distinguished by the propositional properties it exemplifies. All objects exemplify the same propositional properties—everything whatsoever exemplifies the property $[\lambda y\ F^0]$, where F^0 is a true proposition. But not every A-object encodes every such property. For every group of propositions, the abstraction principle for A-objects requires that there be a A-object that encodes just the propositional properties constructed out of the propositions in the group. Thus, A-objects may differ with respect to the propositional properties they encode. Moreover, it is mistake to think that situations necessarily exemplify the propositional properties that characterize them. This would force situations to be constructed only out of necessarily true propositions. To see this, suppose a is a situation such that $\Box[\lambda y\ F^0]a$, for some F^0 that characterizes a. By λ-*Equivalence*, we know that $\Box(\forall x)([\lambda y\ F^0]x \equiv F^0)$. It follows that $\Box F^0$. So this idea would entail that there are no situations involving contingent propositions, something that is patently false.

No such objections attend to the following definition, however:

$$Situation(x) =_{df} (\forall F)(xF \rightarrow (\exists F^0)(F=[\lambda y\ F^0]))$$

That is, a situation is an abstract object which is such that every property it encodes is a property constructed out of a proposition (that is, every property it encodes is a propositional property). Let 's' be a restricted variable ranging over situations. Then, we may define the notion of *truth in* a situation in terms of *truth*:

$$F^0\ is\ true\ in\ s =_{df} s[\lambda y\ F^0]$$

Note that the definiens can serve as a reading of English sentences of the form "The situation s is such that …," where the ellipsis is filled in with another sentence. The English predicate phrase 'is such that …' denotes the property constructed out of the proposition denoted by the sentence filling in the ellipsis. The English sentence is regarded as an encoding predication. We again make use of the hypothesis that predication in natural language is ambiguous between exemplification and encoding.

It is easy to identify the actual situations—an actual situation is one such that all of the propositions true in that situation are true:

$$Actual(s) =_{df} (\forall F^0)(s[\lambda y\ F^0] \rightarrow F^0)$$

Clearly, this definition is consistent with the fact that some situations are actual and some are not. If the proposition that Carter defeated Reagan is true in a situation s, then s is not actual. We can also account for the fact that some situations are possible and some are not:

$$Possible(s) =_{df} \Diamond Actual(s)$$

So a possible situation is one such that it is possible for all the propositions true in it to be true (together). Possible situations are consistent, in the sense that no incompatible propositions are true in possible situations:

$$Consistent(s) =_{df}$$

$$\sim(\exists F^0)(\exists G^0)(\sim\Diamond(F^0 \& G^0) \& s[\lambda y\ F^0] \& s[\lambda y\ G^0])$$

Another important notion in situation theory is the notion of maximality. A situation is maximal just in case every proposition or its negation is true in it:

$$Maximal(s) =_{df} (\forall F^0)(s[\lambda y\ F^0] \lor s[\lambda y\ \sim F^0])$$

The most important notion of situation theory is the notion of a world:

$$World(s) =_{df} \Diamond(\forall F^0)(s[\lambda y\ F^0] \equiv F^0)$$

A world, therefore, is any situation s such that it is possible that all and only the true propositions are true in s. This definition of worlds in terms of situations makes it possible to use the definition of truth-in-a-situation to define truth-at-a-world:

$$F^0 \text{ is true at } w =_{df} w[\lambda y\ F^0]$$

To see that these definitions are correct, note that the following are consequences of the above definitions:

Theorem 4.1 *Every world is maximal.*

Theorem 4.2 *Every world is possible and consistent.*

Theorem 4.3 *Every proposition necessarily implied by a proposition true at a world is also true at that world.*

Theorem 4.4 *There is a unique world that is actual.*

Theorem 4.5 *A proposition is necessarily true iff it is true at all possible worlds.*

Theorem 4.6 *A proposition is possibly true iff there is some possible world at which it is true.*

The proofs of these can be constructed by using your favorite *S5* deductive system and the principles discussed so far. Many of the proofs require an appeal to the rigidity of encoding. Theorem 4.4 involves a crucial application of the definition of proposition identity formulated in the previous section. Other than this, the theorems may be proved in a relatively straightforward way.[4]

These theorems of world theory have counterparts in the theory of times. On our view, a time is a maximal situation having those features that are the tense-theoretic counterparts of the modal features that worlds have. Here are the definitions of these counterpart notions:

$$Present(s) =_{df} (\forall F^0)(s[\lambda y \; F^0] \rightarrow F^0)$$

$$Historical(s) =_{df} \blacklozenge(Present(s))$$

$$Temporally\text{-}Consistent(s) =_{df}$$

$$\sim(\exists F^0)(\exists G^0)(\sim\blacklozenge(F^0 \; \& \; G^0) \; \& \; s[\lambda y \; F^0] \; \& \; s[\lambda y \; G^0])$$

Intuitively, a present situation is one such that every proposition true in that situation is [present tense] true. A historical situation s is such that either it was once the case that s is a present situation, or s is a present situation, or it will once be the case that s is a present situation. And, two propositions that are never true together are not true in temporally consistent situations. These definitions prepare us for the following definitions of a time and truth at a time:[5]

$$Time(s) =_{df} \blacklozenge(\forall F^0)(s[\lambda y \; F^0] \equiv F^0)$$

$$F^0 \text{ is true at } t =_{df} t[\lambda y \; F^0]$$

A structural similarity between worlds and times clearly emerges from the consideration of the following theses, all of which follow from the foregoing series of definitions:

Theorem 4.7 *Every time is maximal.*

Theorem 4.8 *Every time is both historical and temporally consistent.*

Theorem 4.9 *Every proposition always implied by a proposition true at a time is also true at that time.*

Theorem 4.10 *There is a unique time that is present.*

Theorem 4.11 *A proposition is always true iff it is true at all times.*

Theorem 4.12 *A proposition is once true iff it is true at some time.*

---

[4]Proofs of some of these theorems may be found in [1983], pp. 78–84.

[5]Most of the definitions and theorems that follow were described in [1987].

Again, the proofs of these theorems can be constructed using the minimal tense logic K_t, standard predicate logic, and the metaphysical and logical principles described so far.

These consequences give us insight into the intrinsic features of individual times. The theorems are compatible with a variety of suppositions about the structure of time in general. That's because we've adopted only a minimal tense logic that can be interpreted by structures on which the relation $<$ between individuals times may or may not be transitive, linear, dense, infinite in some direction, etc. Although it seems plausible to suppose that time may indeed have a structure that is transitive, linear, dense, and without beginning or end, these are not questions to be decided by the logic of time alone, for these are interesting metaphysical questions. If one so desires, proper, *a priori* metaphysical axioms may be added to our theory of abstract objects to ensure that the (intended) models of the theory exhibit the structure that philosophical investigation shows time to have.

One other interesting consequence of these definitions should be mentioned. The theory now predicts that the unique present moment is identical with the unique actual world. To see why, note that the truth of a sentence is evaluated in our language at both the base world and base time of the interpretation. As a consequence, the situations that are actual are also present situations, and vice versa. This makes it easy to see that the actual world encodes the same propositions that are encoded by the present moment. This is the kind of new prediction that is characteristic of progressive research programs (see Lakatos [1973]), and a few moments' reflection upon this result should leave one with the impression that this theoretical identification is an insight.

To see why, ask the question, what does it mean to say that the actual world has an identity through time? Moreover, what does it mean to say that the present moment has an identity through worlds? The notions of "identity through time" and "identity through worlds" stand in need of analysis. On the present theory, these notions amount to the following. By encoding all and only the propositions that are [present tense] true, the actual world encodes all such tense-theoretic propositions. This is the sense in which the actual world has an identity through time—it encodes the past and the future in terms of the presently true tense theoretic propositions (it also encodes the possibilities and necessities in terms of the presently true modal truths). Something similar can be said about the present moment. The identification of the present moment essentially depends on which particular modal and tense theoretic propositions are [present tense] true. Thus, the propositions true now at other possible worlds and true now at past and future times are all represented in the present moment in terms of the modal and tense theoretic truths it encodes. A reflection on these facts, we suggest, should help one to overcome any lingering doubts about the theoretical identification of the actual world with the present moment. Both objects are essentially identified by using the same class of modal and tense theoretic truths.

Besides preserving important structural similarities between worlds and times, the theory preserves their other similarities as well. The notions of truth at a world and truth at a time are defined in terms of truth (*simpliciter*). The definitions are structurally the same. Theorems 4.5, 4.6, 4.11, and 4.12 validate the insights that underlie the semantic interpretation of the modal and tense operators as quantifiers over worlds and times, respectively. However, unlike the notions involved in traditional possible world semantics, our notions of world and time are not primitive.

The theory also provides a parallel treatment of possible, but nonactual objects, on the one hand, and objects that have existed or will exist but which don't presently exist, on the other. It offers symmetrical answers to the modal and tense theoretic questions concerning objects that exist only at other possible worlds or that exist at past and future times (though not at present). The step taken in accepting possible but nonactual objects is not different in kind from the step in accepting past and future existents that don't presently exist. However, possible but nonactual objects have been the subject of controversy ever since it was realized that the natural interpretation of modal logic seems, in principle, to be committed to such things. Some philosophers find the very idea of such objects repugnant. These "actualists" are prepared to go to great lengths to reanalyze modal logic in order to avoid commitment to possible but unactual objects. We, however, find the idea of possible, but nonactual objects perfectly intelligible. The definition is straightforward: x is a possible but nonactual object iff $\Diamond E!x$ & $\sim E!x$.

Moreover, the hypothesis that there are such objects affords the simplest interpretation of modal sentences in natural language. Though actualists have proposed treatments of such sentences that do not require that there be possible but nonactual objects, it has been shown recently that there is a group of sentences that cannot be explained naturally from the actualist point of view. Alan McMichael shows in [1983a] that sentences with iterated modal operators cause a problem for actualism. Actualists have no convenient way to analyze sentences like "Kennedy might have had a second son who might have been an astronaut." The embedded modality 'might have been an astronaut' most naturally appears to denote a property exemplified by Kennedy's possible, but non-actual second son. Actualists do not have a natural alternative to this explanation, for though they accept that there are worlds where the proposition that Kennedy has a second son is true, they do not accept that such a proposition involves a possible, but non-actual object (see McMichael's [1983a] for the details).

It would seem that actualists ought to face a similar problem with respect to objects that have existed, or will exist, but which presently don't exist. For example, the sentence "My brother will have a third daughter who will become president" may in fact be true. The embedded tensed phrase 'will become president' most naturally appears to denote a property exemplified by my brother's future, but presently nonexistent, daughter. The notion of a future existent that doesn't in fact exist is a coherent one: x is a future existent that doesn't exist iff $\mathcal{F}E!x$ & $\sim E!x$. The truth of the sentence in question appears to require that there are such objects (assume that the sentence implies that my brother doesn't in fact have a third daughter and that the property of being a daughter is an existence entailing property). Actualists have no alternative understanding of such sentences, for though they accept that there will be a time at which the proposition that my brother has a third daughter is true, they do not accept that such a proposition involves a future existent that doesn't exist. The actualist analysis of such sentences remains a mystery, however, and we prefer the simple analysis that falls naturally out of the theory.

Since the quantifiers range over everything whatsoever, we may not only conclude $(\exists x)\Diamond\phi$ from $\Diamond(\exists x)\phi$, but we may also conclude $(\exists x)\mathcal{P}\phi$ from $\mathcal{P}(\exists x)\phi$ (this inference holds for '$\mathcal{F}$' and '$\blacklozenge$' as well). Our treatment of modality and tense, therefore, provides analogous answers to the questions concerning quantification and nonexistence. The nonexistence of an object doesn't diminish its status as an object over which we may quantify.

4.3   Other Theories of Worlds and Times

To our knowledge, no other system offers such a straightforward theory of situations, worlds, and times. Few authors offer a parallel treatment of worlds and times. There are other world theories, but these systems typically bog down on Theorems 4.4 – 4.6. There are three main views to consider: those of Lewis, the related views of Prior, Fine, Adams, Chisholm, Plantinga, and Pollock, and the views of Barwise and Perry.[6] We shall try to state briefly what we take to be the advantages of our approach, as compared to these others. These are not meant to be knockdown arguments against the other approaches but rather a sketch

---

[6]I'm not sure what to say about Stalnaker's view in [1976], since he explicitly says that the conception of worlds that he defends is not a metaphysical conception ([1985], p. 57).

of some of the problems these other approaches have that ours does not.

Lewis Worlds

In [1986], David Lewis has to stipulate something similar to Theorem 4.6. On his view, it appears to be axiomatic that "every way that a world might be is a way that some world is" ([1986], p. 2 and p. 86). We say "appears to be" because Lewis does not clearly identify all of his basic principles. On our theory, it is clear that this principle is a theorem rather than an axiom. Moreover, it is a critical theorem—every time we add to the system our intuitive judgment that $\Diamond F^0$, the theory ensures that there is a possible world where F^0 is true.

On Lewis' view, the actual world seems to be defined in terms of contingent things. His suggests that the phrase 'the actual world' is an indexical. Whenever beings at a world utter the phrase 'the actual world,' they are referring to the world of which they are a part. So when we use the phrase 'the actual world,' we refer to the world of which we are a part. Does this analysis of 'the actual world' make an essential appeal to the contingent utterances of contingent beings? It may, but more importantly, Lewis appears to stipulate not only that there is a world of which we are a part, but also that we are a part of just one world (on his view, everything is world-bound). By way of contrast, our notion of an actual world is clearly not defined in terms of contingent objects. Nor is it stipulated that there is such a world, or that such a world is unique. These notions and consequences are defined and derived from more general notions and principles. The thesis that there is a unique actual world does not rest on the question of whether or not individuals are world-bound individuals (on our theory, individuals are not world-bound).

There are other interesting points of comparison. Lewis identifies worlds as maximal mereological sums of spatio-temporally interrelated things. In his words, this "makes no provision for an absolutely empty world," and "makes it necessary that there is something" ([1986], p. 73). More precisely, on Lewis' view, it is necessary that there is something that is spatio-temporal. Contrast this situation with our theory. It is a consequence of the theory that necessarily-always there is some individual thing. By the rules of necessitation and omnitemporalization, the instances of the abstraction principle for A-objects are necessarily and always true. Therefore, it is derivable that $\Box\blacksquare(\exists x)(\exists y)y = x$. But it is not derivable that $\Box\blacksquare(\exists x)E!x$. There may be worlds and times where nothing is located in space. The theory does not assert that there are any ordinary objects, though it is certainly true that it is possible that there are objects that exist. In fact, even the theorem that there is a unique actual world does not imply either that something exists or that there are ordinary objects. That is an important reason for thinking that worlds are abstract, for otherwise this wouldn't be a consequence.

Our worlds remove one other mystery that affects Lewis' conception. Lewis says that possible worlds, including the ones of which we're not a part, are "concrete particulars" ([1979], p. 148). This seems to require that possible worlds be concrete in some sense, and Lewis goes to great length to explain that however the abstract/concrete distinction is drawn, worlds are concrete ([1986], pp. 81–86). We find the notion of a "concrete possible object" to be rather mysterious. How could a possible thing be concrete? By way of contrast, we identify the property of being concrete as just the same property as having a location in space ($E!$). Abstract individuals are not the kind of thing that could ever be concrete. Therefore, the actual world and the other possible worlds are not concrete objects—they are not the kind of thing that could ever have a location in space. It is not the worlds themselves but rather the objects that exist at a world that (possibly) have a location in space. The actual world is (encodes) all that is the case, and the totality of all that is the case is not something that has a location. As A-objects, our worlds are distinguished from the objects that exist as well as from the objects that possibly exist. The latter objects are possibly concrete, not concrete possibles. If an object possibly exists but does not in fact exist, then, by definition, it fails to be concrete.

Our conception of worlds may have an additional advantage over Lewis' conception once times are brought into the picture. We may view times as abstract objects on a par with worlds. But on Lewis' conception, one must face the problem of how to account for two natural intuitions: (1) moments of time are not possible objects, and (2) the present moment is not a concrete individual. Since Lewis thinks that other possible worlds are possible objects and that the actual world is a concrete object, it seems that no analogy, either between other worlds and past/future times or between the actual world and the present moment, can be constructed using his views.

Prior, Fine, Adams, Chisholm, Plantinga, and Pollock

It should be mentioned at the outset that none of the views we are about to discuss is supported with a complete theory of finely grained propositions or states of affairs. Few of these philosophers offer a condition that comprehends the domain of propositions (states of affairs). And fewer still offer identity conditions that are consistent with the idea that propositions (states of affairs) are not strongly extensional. Those that do, unfortunately, define these conditions in terms of notions that are neither defined nor axiomatized. In [1976], Chisholm tries both to define states of affairs and assign them identity conditions in terms of an epistemological primitive. On his view, states of affairs are the kind of thing that someone might accept, believe, etc.; two states are identical just in case they imply each other and it is impossible to accept (believe) one without accepting (believing) the other. On this view, however, the foundations of metaphysics involve notions borrowed from epistemology, something which our view does not require. More important, however, is the fact that the basic principles of belief are not given. There is no principled way to understand precisely just what propositions there are or when any two are identical.

This has unfortunate repercussions. One is that when worlds are identified as propositions or states of affairs of a certain sort, it becomes difficult to show that there are any possible worlds. And, finally, it is even more difficult to show that there is a unique world that is actual. To prove such theses, it is essential that one be given comprehension and identity conditions for propositions. This will be discussed in some detail in what follows. Problems such as these affect most of the views described below.

Prior, Fine, and Adams: Fine's view in [1977] is based on the work of A. Prior, who was one of the first philosophers to think about the similarities between modal and tense logic. The principle advantage our theory has over the Fine/Prior view of [1977] is that necessity is analyzed as a quantification over a single domain of possible worlds. Fine's rather austere brand of actualism forces him to give up this simple analysis of modality. On Fine's view, propositions fail to have any kind of being in those worlds where their constituents fail to exist. Thus, the quantifiers that range over propositions do not commute with their respective modal operators, and so the Barcan formulas do not hold for propositions. Consequently, not all occurrences of the modal operators can be eliminated in favor of a quantifier over possible worlds (see McMichael [1983a], p. 66). Presumably, this defect would be inherited in any attempt to define the notion of a time in Fine's theory. If propositions were contingently existing entities, and failed to exist at those times when their constituents fail to exist, then the quantifiers ranging over propositions would not commute with the tense operators. The tense-theoretic Barcan formulas would not hold for propositions. The theory of times that results would not have the ability to analyze all occurrences of the tense operators as quantifiers over a single domain of times.

To show that there is a unique actual world, Fine must add the hypothesis that there is a unique proposition that implies all and only the true propositions. On Fine's view, a world is a proposition p such that $\Diamond(p \ \& \ (\forall q)(q \to \Box(p \to q)))$ ([1977], p. 119). As it stands, his theory of propositions does not guarantee that one of these worlds uniquely implies all the truths. Adams' view in [1974] does not have this particular problem, since he takes worlds to be maximal, consistent sets of propositions. If one supposes that there are sets of propositions, then there is a unique set that has all and only the true propositions as members, and this set is the unique actual world.

Adams' view is open to the objection that worlds are not sets. But there are two, more important, disadvantages to his theory. The first is that since Adams is an austere actualist, his view suffers from the problems associated with contingently existing propositions. He is forced to distinguish *two* notions of truth, truth *in* a world and truth *at* a world, in order to derive theorems like the ones in the previous section. Whether this is a real metaphysical distinction or just a technical device to preserve some semblance of a world theory is a question that is still open to debate. Presumably, a distinction between truth *in* a time and truth *at* a time will also have to be made, since Adams has no truck with future existents that don't (presently) exist (see Adams [1986]). Secondly, Adams' theory involves notions and proper axioms of mathematics as part of his metaphysical foundations. By contrast, our theory does not involve such notions and axioms. Our worlds are not sets of propositions, nor do we rely on the axioms of set theory to prove that worlds have the features they are known to have. We cannot draw these contrasts with Adams' theory with any certainty, however, since he does not offer comprehension and identity conditions for propositions.

Chisholm, Plantinga, and Pollock: The views in Chisholm [1976], Plantinga [1976], and Pollock [1984] are rather similar. Their definition of a world is similar to the Fine/Prior definition, except it is cast in terms of states of affairs instead of propositions. Chisholm, Plantinga, and Pollock believe that a world is a possible state of affairs p such that for all states of affairs q, either p necessarily implies q or p necessarily implies the negation of q. On their view, a world is actual iff it obtains. Since they offer no comprehension condition for states of affairs, these authors cannot address either the question of whether there are any worlds or the question of whether there is a unique actual world. The notable exception is Pollock, who addresses the first, but not the second question ([1984], p. 58). Pollock asserts that there are infinite conjunctions of states of affairs which are themselves states of affairs. With this as an axiom, he can demonstrate that the infinite conjunction of all the states of affairs that obtain is a possible world. To define these infinite conjunctions, Pollock has to incorporate notions from set theory. But setting this aside, his views involve two important omissions. The first concerns the definition of infinite conjunctions. He says, "given a set X of states of affairs, *X's being such that every state of affairs in it obtains*, is a perfectly good state of affairs" ([1984], p. 58). But how do we know that? Upon what theory of states of affairs can Pollock support this claim? Can we take any expression 'X's being such that S,' write it in italics, and be assured that it denotes a state of affairs? What is the semantics of these italicized phrases? These questions are unfortunately left unanswered, and we raise them because answers to them constitute the most important details of the supporting theory of states of affairs.

The other important omission in Pollock's account concerns the second question that arises for the view that worlds are states of affairs; namely, is there a unique actual world? In the absence of a theory of states of affairs, we just don't know. Nothing in the theories offered by Pollock, Chisholm, or Plantinga guarantees that a single state of affairs will satisfy the definition of being an actual world. In fact, the claim that there is a unique actual world seems to be incompatible with any theory that identifies possible worlds as structured states of affairs, structured propositions, or structured properties that are fine-grained enough to fail strong extensionality. In such theories, there will typically be more than one entity that satisfies the definition of an actual world. Let 'p' range ambiguously over states of affairs, propositions, or properties. Then, typically, these theories distinguish between p and the conjunction $p \& q$ (where q is distinct from p). Intuitively, the two entities have different structures. But if a given state of affairs satisfies the definition of an actual world, so will its conjunction with a distinct truth of logic. For example, let p be an actual world, as it is defined by Chisholm, Plantinga, or Pollock. Then, $p' = (p \& (q \vee \sim q))$ must be an actual world as well, for any proposition q one chooses. For if p implies a state of affairs r, so does $(p \& (q \vee \sim q))$. So if p is a world, so is p'. And if p obtains, so does p'. Consequently, if p is an actual world, so is p'. Yet $p \neq p'$.

On our theory, the hypothesis that the proposition P^0 is distinct from the proposition $(P^0 \& (Q^0 \vee \sim Q^0))$ is consistent with Theorem 5.4. The actual world encodes all and only the propositional properties constructed out of true propositions. There couldn't be two actual worlds, for otherwise suppose that w_1 and w_2 were distinct such worlds. Since they are distinct abstract objects, they have to differ by at least one of the properties they encode. Since they are worlds, any such distinguishing property is a propositional property, so without loss of generality, suppose that, for some proposition R^0, w_1 encodes $[\lambda y\ R^0]$ and w_2 fails to encode $[\lambda y\ R^0]$. Since w_2 is a world, it is maximal, and so it encodes $[\lambda y\ \sim R^0]$. But both w_1 and w_2 are, by hypothesis, actual worlds.

So they encode only propositional properties constructed out of true propositions. But then, both R^0 and $\sim R^0$ would be true, which is a contradiction.

These remarks comparing our theory with the views of Chisholm, Plantinga, and Pollock apply to any attempt to extend their framework to account for times. Until these authors develop more precise views on the nature of states of affairs, they will not be able to prove that theorems similar to Theorems 4.7 – 4.12 are consequences of their theory. And in particular, something similar to Theorem 4.10 will be especially problematic.

Barwise and Perry

Finally, we turn to the recent work of Barwise and Perry. Before we compare our respective theory of situations, we should note that many of the intuitions upon which our theory is based are similar to those that motivated the development of situation semantics (as described in Barwise and Perry [1983]). It is a central intuition of both theories that it is a mistake to suppose that the denotation of a sentence is a truth value. Both theories reject the reconstruction of properties (relations) and propositions as set-theoretic functions from possible worlds to sets (of n-tuples) of individuals or truth values. Both agree that complexes of properties (relations) and individuals are part of the very structure of the world. Consequently, both theories reject the identity and substitutivity of necessarily equivalent properties, relations, and propositions. Finally, we should note that our emphasis, like the recent emphasis in situation theory, has always been to axiomatize directly the structure of the world, as opposed to trying to model it.

However, unlike Barwise and Perry, we think of situations as abstract objects. Our reasons for thinking so were described at the beginning of previous section. But perhaps the best reasons for thinking that they are abstract objects is that Theorems 4.1 – 4.12 are consequences of our view. Compare these theorems with the recent developments in situation theory. In Barwise [1985], we find as a corollary to the theory of situations that there is no largest situation. According to Barwise, this seems to show that reality is not a situation (p. 15). By contrast, Theorems 4.1, 4.4, 4.7, and 4.10 force both the actual world and the present moment to be maximal situations. Our theory, unlike Barwise and Perry's, doesn't abandon worlds in favor of situations. The two are developed together. We can preserve the insights that necessary truth is truth at all possible worlds and that eternal truth is truth at all times.

In fact, unlike their theory, ours preserves, and even justifies, much of the tradition in modal and tense logic. "Possible world semantics" is rehabilitated instead of tossed aside. The semantic interpretation of the modal and tense operators as quantifers over worlds and times is still a useful picture. It is also useful to picture relations and propositions as having exemplification extensions that vary from world to world and time to time. But what justifies this picture is the metaphysical theory itself. Theorems 4.5, 4.6, 4.11, and 4.12 are the metaphysical justifications for semantically interpreting the modal and tense operators as quantifiers over worlds and times. The intensional logic of encoding and the $S5$ and K_t axioms for the primitive modal and temporal notions make it possible to *derive* the insights that have played such a major role in the development of the semantics of modal and tense logic.

4.4   The Challenge for Other Logics

Recently, numerous philosophers have put forward logics for properties, relations, and propositions. Some of the notable papers on "property theory" include Cocchiarella [1978], Bealer [1982], McMichael [1983b], Chierchia and Turner [1985], Menzel [1986], and Turner [1987]. Each of these systems formulates the general logic of relations in a new and interesting way. What is most interesting about them is that, with the exception of McMichael's theory, they are untyped. By being untyped, these logics appear to have somewhat greater expressive power than typed theories, since one can predicate relations of themselves and talk about relations as if they were individuals. Properties of properties are not "higher order."

Though this is not an appropriate place for a systematic comparison of these systems, it would serve well to make a few remarks by way of general comparison. We wholeheartedly endorse the investigation of alternative theories of relations. There may in fact be genuine data that require us to think of relations as individuals. However, much of this data is controversial. The sentences "All properties are individuals" and "The property of being self-identical exemplifies itself" do not count as genuine data, at least when read using the technical meanings of their terms. The genuine data are ordinary, non-technical sentences of English that (behave in ways that) are philosophically puzzling. For example, consider the following three sentences: "John is fun," "Running is fun," and "Helping is fun."[7] Should we think of the predicate 'is fun' as denoting the same property in each case? Should all three subject expressions, therefore, be construed as denoting individuals? What about the following pair of sentences: "Bill loves Mary" and "Bill loves wisdom"? Does 'love' denote the same relation in both cases, in the way

---

[7]The first two are sentences that figure in Chierchia [1984].

that 'searched for' denotes the same relation in "Bill searched for the Eiffel Tower" and "Bill searched for the Tower of Babel"? And finally, what about the following belief sentences: "Bill believes John" and "Bill believes that Bhagwan is a holy man"? Should we construe the proposition denoted by "Bhagwan is a holy man" on a logical par with the individual denoted by 'John'?

These are hard questions, and it is unclear what the answers are. It should be said, however, that if the answers are all "Yes!," then there is still a means available in our theory for approximating the idea that relations are individuals. Every property in our system has an individual correlated with it, namely, the A-individual that encodes just that property and no other. Every proposition can be correlated with the individual that encodes just the propositional property constructed out of it. As far as relations go, we could do a couple of things. We could generalize encoding formulas so that relations are encoded by individuals, and then correlate every relation with the A-object that encodes just it and no other. Or we could logically project every relation onto a property and consider the A-object that encodes the result. For example, we could project the two-place relation of *helping* onto the property of *helping someone*, and correlate this property with the individual that encodes it and no other property. These maneuvers may make it possible to represent the alleged data described above. For example, "John is fun," "Running is fun," and "Helping (someone) is fun" could all be represented as exemplification predications: the property of being fun is predicated of three different individuals—John, the individual correlate of the property of running, and the individual correlate of the property of helping someone. Something similar could be done to analyze belief as a relation between two individuals.

These representations should go some way towards satisfying those who take the alleged data to be genuine. However, if there are good arguments for thinking that the above sentences require the relations themselves to be individuals, then there is no alternative but to find a better theory of relations than the one presented here. But note one fact about the other theories of relations. They are all stated in language in which exemplification is the only form of predication. There seems to be no reason why we cannot annex the logic of encoding to one of these variants of exemplification logic. In fact, we would argue that such an annexation is necessary, for as it stands, the alternative theories do not offer a theory of worlds and times.

As yet, Bealer is the only theorist to address directly the special questions posed by worlds and times. However, he gives up the traditional analysis of necessity ([1982], p. 58ff), and wants nothing whatsoever to do with possible worlds (p. 210). It seems that part of the reason Bealer eschews possible worlds is that they are mysterious (p. 206). But, even if he were sympathetic to worlds, they are bound to be mysterious to him. There seems to be no way to reconstruct worlds using just his theory of relations. The only option he has available is to identify worlds as propositions or properties of some sort. But then, he would face the same dilemma faced by Chisholm, Plantinga, and Pollock. To prove that there is a unique actual world, propositions (or properties) would have to be strongly extensional. Otherwise, numerous propositions (or properties) would satisfy the definition of an actual world.[8] Furthermore, there is a real mystery about his analysis of necessity. Bealer suggests: necessarily ϕ iff the proposition that-ϕ is identical to a trivial necessary truth (p. 58). It is difficult to grasp the insight this gives into the conditions under which a proposition is necessarily the case.

Consequently, the principal challenge for the other logics of relations is to develop a theory of worlds and times that preserves the insight that necessary truth is truth in all worlds (and the insight that eternal truth is truth at all times). There seems to be no simpler way to get theorems like those in Section 2 other than the logic of encoding. A second challenge for these other logics is to develop identity conditions for relations that are related to their most distinctive feature, namely, the fact that they are predicable entities. Recall the remarks in Chapter 3 (pp. 53–54), in which we noted that the identity conditions offered by these other frameworks leave something to be desired on this score. Finally, in what follows, we hope to extend these challenges by offering analyses of sentences that remain problematic from the point of view of the alternative theories of relations. These analyses depend crucially on the presence of A-objects and A-relations (relations that encode properties of relations), and without the logic of encoding, there is no way to preserve the natural explanations that are available to us in virtue of postulating such entities. Consequently, the reader is encouraged to compare the analyses found in the remainder of this book with those available in the alternative logics.

---

[8] In his book, Bealer describes a circularity in the theory of worlds. Our theory is not subject to this circularity, however, and interested readers may determine this for themselves by referring to p. 206 of his book [1982].

5

Definite Descriptions

5.1   A Simple View of Descriptions

In preparation for some of the issues discussed in Part III, we consider next the topic of definite descriptions. The question of how to treat definite descriptions has no simple answer. Lots of different treatments have been proposed. Most are compatible with the logic and theory developed so far. Russell preferred to define descriptions contextually, in a way which most of us are familiar with. But we prefer not to use Russell's treatment. The main reason has to do with the fact that Russell's theory analyzes truths as falsehoods. We've mentioned before that the true sentence "Ponce de Leon searched for the fountain of youth" turns out to be false on Russell's theory. The English is represented as '$Sp(\imath x)Fx$,' where this formal notation *abbreviates* the formula: $(\exists x)((\forall y)(Fy \equiv y = x) \mathrel{\&} Spx)$. On the plausible assumption that nothing exemplifies being a fountain of youth, this formula is false. Therefore, if the truth value of the English is to be preserved, Russell's treatment of descriptions cannot be used as it stands.

We plan to regard descriptions as primitive syntactic units. Where ϕ is any formula, '$(\imath x)\phi$' shall be a complex term. These terms cannot be eliminated from the language in favor of more primitive notation. Intuitively, '$\imath$' is a variable binding, term-forming operator, just like 'λ.' It represents the primitive logical notion 'the.'

To interpret these primitive descriptions, there are two questions to address: (a) what are the truth conditions of formulas in which descriptions occur?, and (b) if a sentence containing a description denotes a proposition, what is the contribution of the description? Consider the following simple case of an atomic formula with a 2-place relation constant, an individual constant, and a description: $Ra(\imath x)Gx$. Let $\mathbf{I}$ and $\mathbf{f}$ be fixed, and $\mathbf{d}(\tau)$ be the denotation of τ relative to $\mathbf{I}$ and $\mathbf{f}$. For this atomic case, the answer to our first question will be rather straightforward: '$Ra(\imath x)Gx$' is true iff there is a unique object that satisfies the description and the denotation of 'a' bears the relation denoted by 'R' to that object.

The second question is not quite so easy. Since '$Ra(\imath x)Gx$' is a propositional formula, it will denote a proposition as long as the description denotes. But what is the structure of the proposition denoted? The simple view is that the proposition in question, or $\mathbf{d}(Ra(\imath x)Gx)$, is the result of plugging the denotations of 'a' and '$(\imath x)Gx$' into the two places of the relation denoted by 'R.' The semantic description of this proposition is: $\mathbf{PLUG}_1(\mathbf{PLUG}_2(\mathbf{d}(R), \mathbf{d}((\imath x)Gx), \mathbf{d}(a)))$. In this proposition, the contribution made by the description is the unique object that satisfies the description, namely, $\mathbf{d}((\imath x)Gx)$ (for now, let us assume that there is one). The essential structure of the proposition mirrors the essential atomic structure of the formula. Moreover, the denotation of the entire formula is a function of the denotations of its terms and the way in which they are arranged.

In what follows, we plan to defend this simple treatment against certain standard objections. However, before we outline them, consider two alternative treatments of primitive descriptions that prove to be unsatisfactory. One alternative is to let the description contribute some other kind of semantic value—a value that preserves, in some way, the denotations of the expressions in the body of the description. This alternative is explored by Salmon, who assigns descriptions an "information value" in his [1986] (p. 21). Unfortunately, however, this is hard to square with a Russellian conception of propositions. That's because on a Russellian conception, the non-logical constituents of propositions are entities that are part of the world (or part of the background ontology). Information values, as Salmon and others construe them, do not seem to be part of the world. Were such information values constituents of propositions, we would have to abandon the view that the truth of propositions is basic, for propositions with such constituents are not true or false. Rather, they have to be "evaluated" to determine whether the structure they embody compares favorably to what the world is like. But this evaluation process still forces us back to Russellian propositions, for these are ultimately required to classify what the world is like. So unless there are objects in the ontology that serve somehow as the information values of descriptions, we do not want information values to be constituents of Russellian propositions.

A second alternative is to develop a new semantic function to interpret terms containing descriptions. For example, let the function $\mathbf{THE}_i$ map an n-place relation $\mathbf{r}^n$ and a property $\mathbf{r}^1$ to the $n-1$-place relation $\mathbf{THE}_i(\mathbf{r}^n, \mathbf{r}^1)$. Intuitively, this new relation $\mathbf{THE}_i(\mathbf{r}^n, \mathbf{r}^1)$ will have in its extension all and only those $n-1$-tuples of the form $\langle o_1, \ldots, o_{i-1}, o_{i+1}, \ldots, o_n \rangle$ such that: there is a unique object o in the extension of r^1 and some object o' is both in the extension of r^1 and such that $\langle o_1, \ldots, o_{i-1}, o', o_{i+1}, \ldots, o_n \rangle$ is in the extension of r^n. Unfortunately, the use of $\mathbf{THE}_i$ to interpret formulas containing descriptions introduces numerous complications. We can no longer suppose that a description contributes its denotation to the proposition denoted by a formula in which it occurs. For example, the denotation of '$Ra(\imath x)Gx$' would be the proposition $\mathbf{PLUG}_1(\mathbf{THE}_2(\mathbf{d}(R), \mathbf{d}(G)), \mathbf{d}(a))$. The use of $\mathbf{THE}_i$ makes it difficult to assign denotations to terms in a general way. It may force us to abandon the simple semantic conception of truth. We may no longer be able to say that the formula '$Ra(\imath x)Gx$' is true$_I$ iff the denotations of all of the terms are related in the appropriate way.

Since these alternatives to the simple treatment are unappealing, we are led to reconsider the objections raised against the simple treatment. These typically appeal to the behavior of descriptions in intensional contexts. One standard argument goes something like this. If the sentences "The F is P" and "The G is P" denote the same proposition when 'The F' and 'The G' denote the same object, then we may validly infer "Sharon believes that the G is P" from "Sharon believes that the F is P." But, the argument concludes, there are numerous counterexamples to this inference. This argument goes back to Frege [1892], in which he asserts, in effect, that the sentences "The F is P" and "The G is P" cannot have the same reference, because they express different "thoughts." In recent times, a related objection involving descriptions in modal contexts has been raised (this objection is discussed in Part V). Though a complete response to these objections will be reserved for the last two parts of the book, here is a brief outline of what we plan to say.

A sentence like "The F is P" will receive a second reading in propositional attitude and modal contexts. Inside attitude contexts, 'the F' and 'the G' have a secondary significance. This is their information value. We shall employ A-objects to encode this information value of English descriptions. The A-object that encodes the property of being the F is distinct from the A-object that encodes the property of being the G. And since these A-objects are part of the background ontology, they can appear as constituents in Russellian propositions. We will be able to generate new propositions that serve as the intermediate propositional objects of belief. These have the same structure as ordinary propositions, but have as constituents the A-objects that encode the information values of names and descriptions. So "The F is P" and "The G is P" will secondarily signify distinct propositions, and this explains why Sharon can believe the one and not the other. In Part IV, this analysis is described in detail. In Part V, the interaction of modality and descriptions is analyzed along these lines as well. For now, it should be clear that the theory will undermine the principle objections raised against the simple treatment of descriptions.

In the remainder of this chapter, we examine the logical machinery required to capture the simple interpretation of descriptions. For the most part, we are going to suppose that descriptions rigidly designate. That is, even when they appear inside the scope of modal and tense operators, they will denote the unique object that satisfies the description at the actual world and present moment, should there be such an object. Rigid descriptions and the logic of encoding are all that is needed to analyze the data of intensionality. Moreover, this machinery even offers a way to understand occurrences of English descriptions that seem to be non-rigid. But there are tradeoffs involved, and so we shall look at the changes necessary to incorporate non-rigid descriptions into the system, should one wish to do so. To simplify the following discussion, only the modal portion of the language will be considered. Since the treatments of modality and tense are parallel, tense may be ignored without loss of generality.

5.2   The Semantics of Rigid Descriptions

Some English descriptions clearly seem to designate rigidly. Consider, for example, the description involved in the true sentence, "The inventor of bifocals might not have invented bifocals." If we let 'I' represent 'x invented bifocals,' then it is natural to represent this sentence as: $\Diamond \sim I(\imath x)Ix$. If the description were non-rigid, then this formula would be true just in case in some possible world **w**, it fails to be the case that the unique object that invented bifocals at **w** invents bifocals at **w**. Clearly, this isn't a good analysis of the English. But suppose, however, that the formal description rigidly designates the person who in fact invented bifocals (let us assume that this is Ben Franklin). Then, the formal representation is true just in case in some possible world **w**, Franklin fails to invent bifocals at **w**. These conditions not only obtain, but also seem to capture what is expressed by the original sentence.

Rigid descriptions have not been widely investigated. They fit in nicely with the semantic conception of language outlined in this book. That's because the denotation function, even for modal languages, assigns every term a denotation relative only to interpretations and assignments. Denotations are not relativized to worlds. Consequently, every term of the modal language we've defined rigidly designates what it denotes—no term changes its denotation from world to world. To incorporate non-rigid descriptions, we would have to redefine the denotation function so that terms are assigned denotations relative to each world. But with rigid descriptions, we can keep the denotation function as it is.

A clause has to be added to the definition of the denotation function in order to interpret rigid descriptions. This clause is unlike the clauses that assign denotations to simple terms and λ-expressions. Recall that if τ is a simple term, then $\mathbf{d}_{\mathbf{I},\mathbf{f}}(\tau)$ is either $\mathbf{F}(\tau)$ or $\mathbf{f}(\tau)$, depending on whether τ is either a constant or variable, respectively. If τ is a λ-expression (or propositional formula), then $\mathbf{d}_{\mathbf{I},\mathbf{f}}(\tau)$ is a relation (proposition) that has a structure that corresponds to the structure of the λ-expression (propositional formula). The denotation of a λ-expression is defined by recursion on the complexity of the formula appearing in the term. However, the denotation of $(\imath x)\phi$ does not have to be defined by recursion on the complexity of ϕ. There is a simpler way. If τ is the description $(\imath x)\phi$, then $\mathbf{d}_{\mathbf{I},\mathbf{f}}(\tau)$ can be defined in terms of whether ϕ is uniquely satisfied by some object in the domain $\mathbf{D}$. Since the notion of satisfaction$_\mathbf{I}$ is defined recursively on the complexity of formulas, we can take advantage of that recursion. Consequently, if we define by simultaneous recursion both the denotation function and satisfaction, only a single clause is needed to assign denotations to descriptions.

Consider the following clause, in which '$\mathbf{f}' \overset{x}{=} \mathbf{f}$' means that $\mathbf{f}'$ is an assignment function just like $\mathbf{f}$ except perhaps for what it assigns to x:

Where τ is any description $(\imath x)\phi$, then

$$
\mathbf{d}_{\mathbf{I},\mathbf{f}}(\tau) = \begin{cases} \mathbf{o} \text{ iff } (\exists \mathbf{f}')(\mathbf{f}' \overset{x}{=} \mathbf{f} \ \& \ \mathbf{f}'(x) = \mathbf{o} \ \& \ \mathbf{f}' \text{ satisfies}_\mathbf{I} \ \phi \\ \quad \text{at } \mathbf{w}_0 \ \& \ (\forall \mathbf{f}'')(\mathbf{f}'' \overset{x}{=} \mathbf{f}' \ \& \ \mathbf{f}'' \text{ satisfies}_\mathbf{I} \ \phi \text{ at} \\ \quad \mathbf{w}_0 \rightarrow \mathbf{f}'' = \mathbf{f}')) \\ \text{undefined, otherwise} \end{cases}
$$

Note how Russell's analysis of descriptions is packed into this clause. Intuitively, we want to say that the denotation$_{\mathbf{I},\mathbf{f}}$ of the description is just that unique object $\mathbf{o}$ satisfying ϕ at the actual world, should there be one. However, logically speaking, what guarantees that there is such an object is the fact that there is a certain assignment function $\mathbf{f}'$ that uniquely satisfies ϕ at the actual world. And to assert that $\mathbf{f}'$ is unique, one must use Russell's analysis of uniqueness, and quantify over other possible assignment functions.

There are two other important features of this definition worth mentioning. The first is that no matter what context a description appears in, its denotation is defined in terms of the object "satisfying" the description at the actual world. This is true even for descriptions inside modal contexts. Secondly, the denotation of a description may be undefined. If there is no unique assignment function with the right features, then the description will fail to denote. Consequently, any term containing such a description inherits the failure to denote. The denotation of that term will be undefined. Thus, the denotation of any λ-expression, propositional formula, or description that contains a non-denoting description will be undefined.

However, we cannot allow such undefined terms to undermine the definition of satisfaction. A minor alteration must be made, therefore, to the two base clauses in the definition of satisfaction to ensure that they won't be undefined for formulas containing descriptions that fail to denote. Without such an alteration, the general definition of truth would not have consequences for formulas containing non-denoting descriptions. Essentially, we want the definition of satisfaction to say that, relative to $\mathbf{I}$ and $\mathbf{f}$, atomic exemplification and encoding formulas are true just in case all of their terms have a denotation and the denotations stand in the right semantic relationships. This is what the following base clauses for satisfaction ensure:

1. Where ϕ is a formula of the form $\rho^n o_1 \ldots o_n$, $\mathbf{f}$ satisfies$_\mathbf{I}$ ϕ at $\mathbf{w}$ iff $(\exists \mathbf{o}_1) \ldots (\exists \mathbf{o}_n)(\exists \mathbf{r}^n)(\mathbf{o}_1 = \mathbf{d}_{\mathbf{I},\mathbf{f}}(o_1)$ & $\ldots$ & $\mathbf{o}_n = \mathbf{d}_{\mathbf{I},\mathbf{f}}(o_n)$ & $\mathbf{r}^n = \mathbf{d}_{\mathbf{I},\mathbf{f}}(\rho^n)$ & $\langle \mathbf{o}_1, \ldots, \mathbf{o}_n \rangle \in \mathbf{ext}_\mathbf{w}(\mathbf{r}^n))$

2. Where ϕ is a formula of the form $o\rho^1$, $\mathbf{f}$ satisfies$_\mathbf{I}$ ϕ at $\mathbf{w}$ iff $(\exists \mathbf{o})(\exists \mathbf{r}^1)(\mathbf{o} = \mathbf{d}_{\mathbf{I},\mathbf{f}}(o)$ & $\mathbf{r}^1 = \mathbf{d}_{\mathbf{I},\mathbf{f}}(\rho^1)$ & $\mathbf{o} \in \mathbf{ext}_A(\mathbf{r}^1))$

With these two base clauses, the recursive clauses of the definition need not be altered. Consequently, the definition of truth$_\mathbf{I}$ remains the same.

5.3   Descriptions, Propositions, and Relations

One of the most fascinating consequences concerning these definitions is that atomic exemplification predications involving non-denoting descriptions have truth conditions *even though they don't denote propositions!* For example, even if the description in '$P(\imath x)Qx$' fails to denote, the sentence has well-defined truth conditions. It is true just in case there is a unique object $\mathbf{o}$ in the extension$_{\mathbf{w}_0}$ of Q at the actual world and $\mathbf{o}$ is in the extension$_{\mathbf{w}_0}$ of P. But the sentence doesn't denote a proposition. Note that the logic is still two-valued, despite the fact such sentences don't denote. The sentential logic derives from the definition of satisfaction and truth, and the truth conditions associated with every sentence either obtain or they don't.

This treatment directly addresses a concern that Russell had in his famous [1905a] article "On Denoting." Russell was especially concerned with sentences like "The King of France is bald," where the description is understood to be non-denoting. We are in a position to see clearly just what Russell was worried about. He says, regarding this sentence:

By parity of reasoning, this also ought to be about the denotation of the phrase 'the King of France.' But this phrase,
though it has a meaning, has certainly no denotation, at
least in any obvious sense. Hence one would suppose that
'the King of France is bald' ought to be nonsense; but it is
not nonsense, for it is plainly false. ([1905a], ¶13)

Russell here does not have the distinction between the proposition a
sentence denotes and the truth conditions of the sentence. By saying
that the sentence in question "ought to be nonsense" (since the description fails), Russell must have thought that if a sentence fails to denote
a proposition, it is meaningless. But on the above treatment, this does
not follow. Let 'B' denotes baldness, 'K' denote the relation x bears to
y just in case x is king of y, and let 'f' denote France. Then '$B(\imath x)Kxf$'
clearly says something, and is meaningful, even though it fails to denote a proposition. The fact that it says something, or is meaningful, is
represented by the fact that the sentence has truth conditions.[1]

We've therefore removed one of Russell's primary motivations for
appealing to his theory of descriptions, since he thought that for "The
present King of France is bald" to have a meaning, it had to be assigned
a complex logical form in which every term has a denotation. There
is another puzzle in Russell's [1905a] that our treatment can explain
rather nicely. Before we describe the puzzle, note that the way things
are now set up, there are lots of non-equivalent sentences which, at first
sight, appear to be equivalent. For example, consider '$\sim P(\imath x)Qx$' and
'$[\lambda y \sim Py](\imath x)Qx$.' Consider what happens to these sentences under an
interpretation in which the description fails to denote. Neither formula
denotes a proposition, but whereas the second is false, the first is true.
The second formula is false because it is an atomic formula (albeit with
complex terms), and for such a formula to be true, the description must
denote. But the first formula is true because the truth conditions of
'$P(\imath x)Qx$' fail to obtain. Now since two formulas ϕ and ψ are *logically
equivalent* just in case for every interpretation $\mathbf{I}$, ϕ is true$_\mathbf{I}$ iff ψ is true$_\mathbf{I}$,
these two formulas are not equivalent.

Now reconsider the puzzle concerning the law of excluded middle
that Russell used to test his own theory of descriptions. Russell says:

By the law of excluded middle, either 'A is B' or 'A is not
B' must be true. Hence, either 'the present King of France

---

[1] When this English sentence appears in a belief report, the *de re* reading of the
report is false. The *de re* reading is false because there is no singular proposition
to be believed. Nevertheless, there is a proposition, constructed out of the sense
of the description and, possibly, the sense of the predicate, that can account for
the cognitive significance of this sentence inside propositional attitude contexts.
This will be discussed in Part IV.

is bald' or 'the present King of France is not bald' must be
true. Yet if we enumerate the things that are bald, and then
the things that are not bald, we should not find the present
King of France in either list. ([1905a], ¶17)

The idea here is that by the law of excluded middle, either (1) or (2)
must be true:

(1) The King of France is bald

(2) The King of France is not bald

But if either sentence is true, it is true because the description denotes
an object that exemplifies the property in question. But the puzzle is
that since the description fails to denote, neither (1) nor (2) is true, and
so it is a mystery how their disjunction (and, hence, the law of exluded
middle) could be true.

   Russell's solution to the puzzle is well known. Not only does he
represent (1) as (3), but he makes it plausible to suppose that (2) has
the two readings (4) and (5):

(3) $(\exists x)((\forall y)(Kxf \equiv y = x) \ \& \ Bx)$

(4) $(\exists x)((\forall y)(Kxf \equiv y = x) \ \& \ \sim Bx)$

(5) $\sim (\exists x)((\forall y)(Kxf \equiv y = x) \ \& \ Bx)$

Russell plausibly suggests that (2) is ambiguous. He uses the theory of
descriptions to eliminate the ambiguity. The existence and uniqueness
claims that analyze away the description in (2) can be given wider scope
than the negation sign, as in (4), or given narrower scope than the
negation sign, as in (5). Using these representations, he then argues
that the disjunction of (3) with (4) is not an instance of the law of
excluded middle. Such a disjunction is false, since there must be a
present King of France for it to be true. So the disjunction of (3) with
(4) doesn't represent the true instance of excluded middle that appears
to be expressed by the disjunction of (1) with (2). Rather, the instance
of excluded middle expressed by the disjunction of (1) with (2) is best
captured by the disjunction of (3) with (5). The disjunction of (3) with
(5) is clearly true. So Russell saves the law of excluded middle.

   A simpler maneuver accomplishes the same result with our treatment
of descriptions, however. We use λ-expressions, and take advantage of
the fact that Russell's analysis of 'the' is embedded right into the rules
for assigning denotations to descriptions. This not only allows us to
represent (1) as (6), but also gives us two readings of (2), namely, (7)
and (8):

(6) $B(\imath x)Kxf$

(7) $[\lambda y \sim By](\imath x)Kxf$

(8) $\sim B(\imath x)Kxf$

(6) is false, for the description must denote for the atomic sentence to be true. (7) is an atomic sentence with a complex object term and a complex predicate. It, too, is false, for the same reason as (6). So the disjunction of (6) with (7) is not the reading that preserves the law of excluded middle. But the disjunction of (6) with (8) is such a reading. For (8) is the negation of a false atomic sentence and hence true. So the disjunction of (6) with (8) is true, and this explains why the disjunction of (1) with (2) has a true reading. Russell's puzzle is explained without supposing that sentences with descriptions have a complex logical form. Descriptions can be treated as primitive syntactic units without losing the explanatory power Russell's theory has.

We conclude this section with another interesting example of a pair of non-equivalent sentences that appear to be equivalent. Consider the disjunction '$Ra(\imath x)Qx \lor \sim Ra(\imath x)Qx$' and the atomic formula with a complex term '$[\lambda y \, Ry(\imath x)Qx \lor \sim Ry(\imath x)Qx]a$.' Now take an interpretation in which the description fails to denote. Note that in such an interpretation, neither formula denotes a proposition. But whereas the first one is true, the second is false. The first one is true because either the truth conditions for the left disjunct obtain or they don't. The second formula is false because atomic formulas with non-denoting descriptions are false. This example, and the one in the previous paragraph, indicate that the presence of non-denoting descriptions can interfere with the normal operation of λ-*Equivalence*. That's why descriptions are banished from λ-*Equivalence*—we cannot derive the equivalence of these sentences using this principle. And since *Relations* and *Propositions* are both derived from this principle, definite descriptions may not officially appear in these principles either. However, there is a simple method that allows us to derive instances of these principles which contain denoting descriptions. In the next section, we'll look at such a method and develop the logical principles that justify it.

5.4 The Logic of Descriptions

The traditional rule of universal instantiation permits the substitution of terms into the universally quantified positions in a formula. This rule goes astray when there are terms in the language that fail to denote. If not restricted, the rule permits the inference from '$(\forall x)Px$' to '$P(\imath x)Qx$,' as well as the inference from '$(\forall F)Fa$' to '$[\lambda y \, Ry(\imath x)Qx]a$.'

Such inferences could move us from truth to falsehood in interpretations in which the description fails. A "free logic" is necessary for descriptions, however. The scare quotes give notice that our approach to this subject is different from the traditional one. Many free logicians regard non-denoting descriptions on a logical par with names like 'Pegasus,' 'Odysseus,' and 'Grendel,' which they also regard as non-denoting terms. But from our point of view, this is a mistake. These names denote mythical creatures and they do not behave at all like descriptions that fail to denote. Clearly, the evidence suggests that the use of Existential Generalization on such names is legitimate, though it is not legitimately used on non-denoting descriptions. Moreover, many free logicians fail to distinguish descriptions that denote mythical and fictional creatures from non-denoting descriptions.[2]

In contrast to the views of such free logicians, we regard all meaningful proper names as having a denotation. The descriptions of mythical and fictional objects have a denotation as well. But, of course, some descriptions, especially formal ones, may just fail to denote anything whatsoever. Consequently, by employing a "free logic" for descriptions, we are not accepting the views that many free logicians accept.

In the logic that governs our system, therefore, terms that fail to contain descriptions are automatically substitutable. Terms that contain descriptions are substitutable as long as it is known that the description appears somewhere in a true atomic formula. If this condition obtains, then the description denotes, and so will any term containing it (assuming the other terms it contains denote). The logical axioms that capture these ideas can be stated in terms of two syntactic notions, both of which we describe intuitively. Let us say that a term τ is *substitutable for* a variable α *in* a formula ϕ iff upon substitution, no free variable β in τ gets "captured by" (falls within the scope of) an operator such as '$\forall$,' 'λ,' or '$\imath$' that already binds β in ϕ. Furthermore, let us say that a term τ *contains* a description just in case either τ is a description or a description appears somewhere in τ. Then, where either α and β are both individual variables and τ is an individual term, or α and β are both n-place relation variables and τ is an n-place relation term, the following two logical axioms govern our system:

Logical Axiom 1 $(\forall\alpha)\phi \rightarrow \phi_\alpha^\tau$, *where τ is substitutable for α and contains no descriptions.*

Logical Axiom 2 $(\forall\alpha)\phi \rightarrow (\psi_\beta^\tau \rightarrow \phi_\alpha^\tau)$, *where τ is any term substitutable for both α and β, and ψ is any atomic formula.*

---

[2]See Parsons [1980], p. 113, for a good discussion of the distinction between terms that fail to denote and terms that denote mythical beings.

For example, from $(\forall F)Fa$, we may infer $[\lambda y\ Ry(\imath x)Qx]a$ only if we first assert some atomic formula in which '$(\imath x)Qx$' appears.

Note that although the quantifier '$\exists$' is defined in our system, there are corresponding principles of Existential Generalization that can be derived from each of these axioms. From ϕ_α^τ, we may infer $(\exists\alpha)\phi$, as long as τ contains no descriptions. Otherwise, for the inference to go through, we need to assume that some atomic formula in which τ appears is true. These formal rules of inference really don't place any undesirable restrictions on the informal rule of Existential Generalization! The informal rule is based on the intuition that if a specific object has a property, then something has that property. Both formal rules preserve this intuition, since in the cases in which a description fails to denote, no object is specified. Hence, the conditions for applying either the formal or the informal rules do not obtain.

Note also that the definition of identity for individuals contains atomic formulas in both disjuncts (refer to Principle 3 in Chapter 2). Consequently, by asserting that $(\exists y)y = (\imath x)\phi$, we thereby assert the truth of at least some atomic formula containing '$(\imath x)\phi$.' So by asserting $(\exists y)y = (\imath x)\phi$, we become entitled to substitute the description freely into universal claims.

This logic is very handy for deriving instances of the abstraction principles for relations and propositions that contain descriptions. Consider the following theorems, which have been derived from these principles by universal generalization:

(9) $(\forall x)([\lambda y\ {\sim}Py]x \equiv {\sim}Px)$

(10) $(\forall x)([\lambda y\ Ryx \vee {\sim}Ryx]a \equiv Rax \vee {\sim}Rax)$

(11) $(\forall x)(\exists F)\Box(\forall y)(Fy \equiv Ryx \vee {\sim}Ryx)$

(12) $(\forall G^0)(\exists F^0)\Box(F^0 \equiv G^0 \rightarrow {\sim}Pa)$

(13) $(\forall G^1)(\exists F^0)\Box(F^0 \equiv {\sim}Ga)$

These comply with the restriction that formulas containing descriptions are not allowed in instances of λ-*Equivalence* (and, hence, from any theorems derived from them). However, if we assume the truth of an atomic formula containing '$(\imath x)Qx$,' for example, then in (9) – (11), we may substitute the description for the universally quantified variable 'x,' and in (12) and (13), we may substitute zero-place and one-place terms containing the description for the universally quantified zero-place and one-place variables. Consider the results:

(9') $[\lambda y\ {\sim}Py](\imath x)Qx \equiv {\sim}P(\imath x)Qx$

(10′) $[\lambda y \; Ry(\imath x)Qx \vee \sim Ry(\imath x)Qx]a \equiv Ra(\imath x)Qx \vee \sim Ra(\imath x)Qx$

(11′) $(\exists F)\Box(\forall y)(Fy \equiv Ry(\imath x)Qx \vee \sim Ry(\imath x)Qx)$

(12′) $(\exists F^0)\Box(F^0 \equiv P(\imath x)Qx \rightarrow \sim Pa)$

(13′) $(\exists F^0)\Box(F^0 \equiv \sim[\lambda y \; Ry(\imath x)Qx]a)$

These results show that there is a simple method of deriving instances involving descriptions from the abstraction principles for relations. In particular, (9′) and (10′) show that we cannot derive the equivalence of the sentences discussed at the end of the previous section without first ensuring that the description '$(\imath x)Qx$' denotes an object.

We may even substitute in descriptions involving encoding formulas. Take, for example, '$(\imath x)(\forall F)(xF \equiv F = Q)$.' As long as it is assumed or shown that such descriptions have denotations, they are legitimate candidates for substitution. When they are substituted into the universalized instances of the abstraction schemata such as (9) – (13), the relations generated do *not* have an encoding structure. The only thing that the descriptions contribute to the relations generated are the objects they denote. No extra structure is contributed. This fact makes it possible to allow such descriptions inside λ-expressions. The paradoxes arise only in connection with properties having an encoding structure, and we need not assume that there are such properties to interpret λ-expressions containing descriptions with encoding formulas.[3]

For example, '$[\lambda y \; Ry(\imath x)xQ]$' is a perfectly well-formed λ-expression. It does not violate the "no encoding subformulas" restriction on the formation of λ-expressions. That's because 'xQ' is not a subformula of '$Ry(\imath x)xQ$.' The notion of subformula here is that of a *proper* subformula. It is defined as follows: (i) Every formula ϕ is a subformula of itself, (ii) If ϕ is $\sim\psi$, $\psi \rightarrow \chi$, $(\forall \alpha)\psi$, or $\Box\psi$, then ψ and χ are subformulas of ϕ, and (iii) If χ is a subformula of ψ, and ψ is a subformula of ϕ, then χ is a subformula of ϕ. So on this definition, 'xQ' is not a subformula of '$Ry(\imath x)xQ$,' though it is a component of the expression. The question of whether '$[\lambda y \; Ry(\imath x)xQ]$' has a denotation is determined by whether '$(\imath x)xQ$' has a denotation. If it does, then the property denoted by the λ-expression has the simple form: $\mathbf{PLUG}_2(\mathbf{d}(\mathrm{R}), \mathbf{d}((\imath x)xQ))$.

Finally, to complete our discussion of the logic of decriptions, we present the most important principle that governs them. This is the principle *Descriptions*, which directly captures Russell's analysis of 'the' in the object language. Recall that the formula '$(\exists!x)\phi$' is an abbreviation of the formula '$(\exists x)(\forall y)(\phi_x^y \equiv y = x)$.' The following presentation of *Descriptions* is simplified by this abbreviation:

---

[3]See [1983], Appendix A.

Descriptions: *Where $\psi_y^{(\imath x)\phi}$ is any atomic formula or (defined) object identity formula (or conjunction of such formulas) in which the description '$(\imath x)\phi$' replaces the variable 'y,' the following is an axiom:*

$$\psi_y^{(\imath x)\phi} \equiv (\exists! y)\phi_x^y \ \& \ (\exists y)(\phi_x^y \ \& \ \psi)$$

Some examples make this axiom much more perspicuous:

(14) $(\imath x)Qx\,P \equiv (\exists! y)Qy \ \& \ (\exists y)(Qy \ \& \ yP)$

(15) $a = (\imath x)Qx \equiv (\exists! y)Qy \ \& \ (\exists y)(Qy \ \& \ a = y)$

The first asserts that $(\imath x)Qx$ encodes property P iff there is a unique object that exemplifies Q, and something both exemplifies Q and encodes P. The second asserts that the object a is identical with $(\imath x)Qx$ iff there is a unique object that exemplifies Q and something both exemplifies Q and is identical to a. Clearly, these statements should be true in a proper treatment of the definite article.

Note that the uniqueness claims in *Descriptions* involve a notion of identity that is defined in our system. Although everything still works normally, *Descriptions* is logically true only in the left-to-right direction. In the right-to-left direction, we take it as a proper axiom. Were identity a primitive in our system, it would be logically true in both directions.[4] Note also that *Descriptions* makes it possible to prove an important set of theorems: $\psi_y^{(\imath x)\phi} \rightarrow (\exists u)(u = (\imath x)\phi)$, where ψ is any atomic formula or defined identity formula in which $(\imath x)\phi$ appears. The proof requires two applications of *Descriptions*—once from left to right, to derive $(\exists! y)\phi_x^y$ from $\psi_y^{(\imath x)\phi}$, and once from right to left, to prove that for the unique object a satisfying ϕ, that $a = (\imath x)\phi$. Then, Existential Generalization on 'a' yields $(\exists u)(u = (\imath x)\phi)$.

Descriptions has a special status among our axioms. It is the only axiom that is not a necessary truth. The reason why it is not necessary has to do with the fact that descriptions are rigid. Consider a simple consequence of *Descriptions*: $P(\imath x)Qx \rightarrow (\exists x)Qx$. If this were necessary, then we could distribute the modal operator to the antecedent and consequent, since distributivity preserves truth. The result

---

[4]In [1983], I added a few other logical axioms to govern descriptions. These were needed because the first disjunct in the definition of object identity was defined in terms of the theoretical relation *identity$_E$*. However, in the present formulation (Principle 3, Chapter 2), we did not use this relation to define identity. A result is that *Descriptions* is a logical truth in the left to right direction, for non-standard interpretations in which identity$_E$ is interpreted as something other than an equivalence relation (on the ordinary objects) no longer cause problems. Since *Descriptions* is logically true from left to right, we can now deduce the *L-Descriptions* principles 1, 2, and 3 developed in [1983] (pp. 56–57), and so they are unnecessary.

is: $\Box P(\imath x)Qx \rightarrow \Box(\exists x)Qx$. There are, however, numerous interpretations in which this sentence is false. Consider any interpretation in which there is a unique thing in the exemplification extension of Q at the actual world that is in the exemplification extension of P at every world, but in which there is a world where nothing is in the exemplification extension of Q. In such an interpretation, '$\Box P(\imath x)Qx$' is true, since the object rigidly denoted by the description exemplifies P necessarily. But '$\Box(\exists x)Qx$' is false, since there is a world in which nothing exemplifies Q. So '$P(\imath x)Qx \rightarrow (\exists x)Qx$' is a contingent statement when the description is rigid. Its negation is a metaphysical possibility. For a more complete discussion of this topic of logical truths that aren't necessary, the reader should consult [1988a].

So if *Descriptions* were necessary, we would be able to derive consequences that are false in some interpretations. To prevent such derivations, the logic of rigid descriptions restricts the rule of necessitation. The rule of necessitation, which permits the derivation of $\Box \phi$ from a derivation of ϕ, may not be applied either to instances of *Descriptions* or to any formula derived from an instance of *Descriptions*. No other adjustments have to be made to the ordinary *S5* axioms and rules. Moreover, principles such as λ-*Equivalence* and Substitutivity do not have to be restricted in other ways in a system with rigid descriptions. This is unlike systems with non-rigid descriptions. Systems with non-rigid descriptions have to introduce a variety of restrictions to prevent the derivation of falsehoods. In the concluding section, we take a look at the complications that arise when non-rigid descriptions are introduced into intensionsal logic.

5.5   Non-rigid Descriptions

Some English descriptions appear to be non-rigid. Consider the description in "The man playing the lead role might have been Derek Jacobi." Suppose, that in fact, Ben Kingsley is the man playing the lead role. Clearly, this sentence does not imply that Ben Kingsley might have been Derek Jacobi. Yet, that is what it would imply semantically were the English description interpreted rigidly. In formal terms, the representation '$\Diamond(\imath x)Px =_E j$' does not do justice to the English sentence when '$(\imath x)Px$' rigidly denotes Ben Kingsley. There is no world **w** where the object denoted by the description, namely Kingsley, is identical with Jacobi.[5] These facts seem to require us to use a non-rigid description to represent the English description. What's more, the use of non-rigid

---

[5]It is a theorem that $x \neq y \rightarrow \Box x \neq y$. The proof is straightforward, once it is established that $x = y \rightarrow \Box x = y$.

descriptions requires a restriction on the principle of Substitution. Otherwise, from the truth that $\Diamond(\imath x)Px =_E j$ (assume the description is non-rigid) and the fact that $(\imath x)Px =_E k$, we could derive $\Diamond k =_E j$.

Before we look at the other adjustments that have to be made in order to incorporate non-rigid descriptions, it should be said that there is some reason to think that sentences like the above do not require non-rigid descriptions. One might argue that the phrase 'the man playing the lead' as it occurs in this sentence is not a *definite* description because it doesn't definitely describe any particular thing. It is not about anyone, and in particular, it is not a description that describes Ben Kingsley, at least, not insofar as the interpretation of this sentence goes. For Ben Kingsley plays no role in the truth conditions of the reading we're considering. Nor does the description describe Jacobi, since Jacobi doesn't satisfy the condition 'man playing the lead.' But it is tempting to argue that the sentence as a whole is about Derek Jacobi, and that it asserts of Jacobi, that he exemplifies the following property: being a man who might have played the lead role. That is, the description is eliminated as the subject of the sentence, and reappears embedded in the predicate. In formal terms, the correct analysis of "The man playing the lead might have been Jacobi" would be: $[\lambda x \; \Diamond(\forall y)(Py \equiv y =_E x)]j$.

Still, there are other sentences that seem to force the use of non-rigid descriptions. Consider "The man playing the lead might have been the director of the play." There is certainly one reading of this sentence on which something is being said about the person who is in fact playing the lead, namely, that he might have been the director of the play. But there is a reading of the English on which the sentence is true in worlds **w** where the person playing the lead at **w** is the same person as the one directing the play at **w**. Were '$(\imath x)Px$' and '$(\imath x)Dx$' non-rigid, this reading would be captured by the formula: $\Diamond(\imath x)Px =_E (\imath x)Dx$. There is no simpler way to capture this reading. Note, however, that there is a way to use rigid descriptions and the logic of encoding to represent such a reading. It is not as elegant as the reading using non-rigid decriptions, but it gets the truth conditions right. To simplify the presentation of this reading, let '$(\imath x)\psi$' abbreviate the rigid description: $(\imath x)(\forall F)(xF \equiv F = [\lambda y \; (\forall z)(Pz \equiv z =_E y)])$. So '$(\imath x)\psi$' denotes the A-object that encodes just the property of being the man playing the lead. And, similarly, let '$(\imath x)\chi$' denote the A-object that encodes just the property of being the man directing the play. Then consider the following sentence: $\Diamond(\exists u)(\exists y)[(\forall F)((\imath x)\psi F \rightarrow Fu) \; \& \; (\forall F)((\imath x)\chi F \rightarrow Fy) \; \& \; u =_E y]$. This requires that in some world, some object that exemplifies being the man playing the lead there is the same as the object that exemplifies being the man directing the play there. And this condition obtains iff the English sentence is true (on the reading in question).

Of course, this representation doesn't preserve the apparent logical form of the English. The analytical technique we used treats the English descriptions as signifying objectified individual concepts (these are the A-objects encoding that individual concept). A moment's reflection should reveal that there is something to this—these readings of the English descriptions are not directly about particular persons. Instead, they seem to be about conceptions. The sentence is analyzed as an assertion to the effect that at some world, a single person exemplifies these conceptions. Such an analysis can not be constructed using rigid descriptions and the logic of exemplification alone. Rather, the logic of encoding makes it possible to develop a variety of new rigid descriptions. The advantage this analysis has to offer is that it preserves a simple picture of how language works. In this picture, the truth conditions of a sentence are constructed by going directly to what the words of the sentence mean at the world in which the sentence is uttered. No expression is evaluated by considering what it means in some other possible world. In practical terms, this means that every term of the language is interpreted as a rigid designator. What it denotes at the actual world is what it denotes, period.

Fortunately, our intensional logic and theory of objects is neutral with respect to this picture. But we have used it as a guide because it is simpler than the alternative in which the truth conditions of a modal sentence are linked to what the terms of the sentence denote at other possible worlds. However, other considerations might cause us to abandon our picture. The choice may boil down to whether one prefers the simplicity associated with the non-rigid description analysis of the above sentences or the simplicity associated with the picture of language just described. Each has its advantage and price. To inform our judgment, let us see what changes have to be made to the system in order to accommodate non-rigid descriptions.

Let us distinguish '$(\imath x)\phi$' from '$(\iota x)\phi$.' The former shall be rigid, the latter non-rigid. Let us assume that all simple constants rigidly denote. Then we can leave interpretations exactly as they are. The function $\mathbf{F}$ associated with each interpretation $\mathbf{I}$ assigns each constant of the language to an element of the appropriate domain. Such an assignment need not be indexed to worlds (we're presuming that constants are still rigid). Nor do the variable assignment functions $\mathbf{f}$ have to be indexed to worlds. The first definition that needs to be world-indexed is the definition of denotation. Here, the definiendum is: the denotation$_{\mathbf{I},\mathbf{f}}$ of term τ at world $\mathbf{w}$ ('$\mathbf{d}_{\mathbf{I},\mathbf{f}}(\tau, \mathbf{w})$'). The clauses of this definition that apply to simple constants, variables, and rigid descriptions remain essentially unchanged, except that the objects these terms were assigned before are now assigned to them at every world. So these terms remain rigid, since their denotation doesn't vary from world to world. However, if τ is a non-rigid description, or any term containing a non-rigid description, the new definition of denotation has to relativize its denotation to worlds.

The clause that gets this off the ground assigns world-relative denotations to non-rigid descriptions:

Where τ is any non-rigid description $(\iota x)\phi$,

$$\mathbf{d}_{\mathbf{I},\mathbf{f}}(\tau,\mathbf{w}) = \begin{cases} \mathbf{o} \text{ iff } (\exists\mathbf{f}')(\mathbf{f}' \stackrel{x}{=} \mathbf{f} \ \& \ \mathbf{f}'(x) = \mathbf{o} \ \& \ \mathbf{f}' \text{ satisfies}_{\mathbf{I}} \ \phi \\ \quad \text{at } \mathbf{w} \ \& \ (\forall\mathbf{f}'')(\mathbf{f}'' \stackrel{x}{=} \mathbf{f}' \ \& \ \mathbf{f}'' \text{ satisfies}_{\mathbf{I}} \ \phi \text{ at} \\ \quad \mathbf{w} \rightarrow \mathbf{f}'' = \mathbf{f}')) \\ \text{undefined, otherwise} \end{cases}$$

It is now routine to modify the other clauses so that λ-expressions, propositional formulas, and other non-rigid descriptions are assigned world-relative denotations that vary with any non-rigid description such terms may contain.

The final group of semantic modifications needed to assimilate non-rigid descriptions begin with the definition of satisfaction. Compare the following two base clauses with the ones constructed for rigid descriptions:

1. Where ϕ is a formula of the form $\rho^n o_1 \ldots o_n$, $\mathbf{f}$ satisfies$_{\mathbf{I}}$ ϕ at $\mathbf{w}$ iff $(\exists o_1)\ldots(\exists o_n)(\exists r^n)(o_1 = \mathbf{d}_{\mathbf{I},\mathbf{f}}(o_1,\mathbf{w}) \ \& \ \ldots \ \& \ o_n = \mathbf{d}_{\mathbf{I},\mathbf{f}}(o_n,\mathbf{w}) \ \& \ r^n = \mathbf{d}_{\mathbf{I},\mathbf{f}}(\rho^n,\mathbf{w}) \ \& \ \langle o_1,\ldots,o_n\rangle \in \mathbf{ext}_{\mathbf{w}}(r^n))$

2. Where ϕ is a formula of the form $o\rho^1$, $\mathbf{f}$ satisfies$_{\mathbf{I}}$ ϕ iff $(\exists o)(\exists r^1)(o = \mathbf{d}_{\mathbf{I},\mathbf{f}}(o,\mathbf{w}) \ \& \ r^1 = \mathbf{d}_{\mathbf{I},\mathbf{f}}(\rho^1,\mathbf{w}) \ \& \ o \in \mathbf{ext}_A(r^1))$

The only difference between these two clauses and the ones formulated in Section 2 is that satisfaction$_{\mathbf{I}}$ at $\mathbf{w}$ now depends on what the terms of the given formula denote at $\mathbf{w}$, rather than what they denote *simpliciter*. The new clause has no affect on formulas containing only rigid terms (that is, formulas that fail to contain non-rigid descriptions). The same applies to the definition of truth$_{\mathbf{I}}$: ϕ is *true*$_{\mathbf{I}}$ iff for every $\mathbf{f}$, $\mathbf{f}$ satisfies$_{\mathbf{I}}$ ϕ at $\mathbf{w}_0$. But note that the truth of modal formulas containing non-rigid descriptions depends on what the descriptions denote at other possible worlds.

This standard semantics for non-rigid descriptions forces us to place a host of restrictions on logical and theoretical principles. To begin with, the modified logical axiom of universal instantiation needs a further modification. We may not instantiate $(\forall\alpha)\phi$ to any term τ that has a denotation only at the actual world; instantiation is legitimate only if τ has a denotation at every world. For otherwise, consider what happens under interpretations in which a given non-rigid description '$(\iota x)\psi$'

fails to have a denotation at some worlds. Suppose that '$(\forall x)\Box Px$' is true under this interpretation. Note that the quantifier ranges over everything whatsoever—in particular, the domain of individuals includes objects that exist at possible worlds other than our own, and these fall under the scope of the universal claim. But suppose we were to instantiate this true universal generalization to '$(\iota x)\psi$.' Then, '$\Box P(\iota x)\psi$' should be true. But, in fact, it is false. The formula '$P(\iota x)\psi$' is false at worlds where the description fails to denote. Consequently, it is important to stipulate that non-rigid descriptions cannot be instantiated into universal modal claims unless we assume first that the description has a denotation at every world. The principal way of doing this is to assume the truth of some modal atomic formula in which the description appears. This new restriction on universal instantiation is easily satisfied by assuming that, with respect to a given description $(\iota x)\psi$, the following is true: $\Box(\exists y)(y = (\iota x)\psi)$ (this is, in fact, derivable from the the assumption that a modal atomic formula involving the description is true, by using the version of *Descriptions* that applies to non-rigid descriptions; see below).

It is also essential to banish non-rigid descriptions from instances of Substitutivity and λ-*Equivalence* that contain modal operators. Consider the following cases, the first of which is a variant of the case described at the beginning of this section. Suppose that both $\Box Pa$ and $a = (\iota x)Qx$. Then, if Substitutivity were unrestricted, it would follow that $\Box P(\iota x)Qx$. But there would certainly be interpretations in which: (a) the description has a denotation at every world, (b) a necessarily exemplifies P, (c) a uniquely exemplifies Q at the actual world, and (d) there is a world $\mathbf{w}$ where the thing uniquely exemplifying Q at $\mathbf{w}$ does not exemplify P at $\mathbf{w}$. Under such an interpretation, '$\Box P(\iota x)Qx$' would be false, and so the above inference is invalid. Therefore, we must stipulate that the terms of a contingent identity statement may not be substituted for one another inside modal contexts.

Care must be taken to block the other invalid inferences involving non-rigid descriptions. For example, without further modifying universal instantiation, $\Box P(\iota x)Qx$ could still be derived from $\Box Pa$ and $a = (\iota x)Qx$. To see how, apply universal generalization twice to the following instance of Substitutivity: $x = y \rightarrow (\Box Px \equiv \Box Py)$. Then, instantiate the x and y quantifiers in $(\forall x)(\forall y)(x = y \rightarrow (\Box Px \equiv \Box Py))$ to a and $(\iota x)Qx$, respectively (this is legitimate, because in the case we're considering, let us assume the description has a denotation at every world). This would yield: $a = (\iota x)Qx \rightarrow (\Box Pa \equiv \Box P(\iota x)Qx)$. And thus from $\Box Pa$, one could derive $\Box P(\iota x)Qx$, which may be false.

The best way to block this inference is to place another restriction on universal instantiation: where τ is any non-rigid description

or term containing a non-rigid description, it is impermissible to instantiate τ into any universal claim derivable from the Substitutivity prin-
ciple. This prevents the instantiation of $(\iota x)Qx$ for y in $(\forall y)(a = y \rightarrow (\Box Pa \equiv \Box Py))$, since this latter sentence is derived from the principle
of Substitutivity.[6]

There are also cases involving λ-*Equivalence* that require special attention. Consider the following:

(16) $[\lambda y \ \Box Cy](\iota x)Px \equiv \Box C(\iota x)Px$

Clearly, there are interpretations in which this sentence is false. Consider any interpretation in which: (a) the description has a denotation
at every world, (b) for every world $\mathbf{w}$, the object denoted by the description at $\mathbf{w}$ exemplifies C at $\mathbf{w}$, and (c) the object denoted by the
description at the actual world does not exemplify C at every world.
Under such an interpretation, (16) is false, since the left side of the
biconditional is false while the right side is true. It is just as easy to
construct interpretations in which the left side of (16) is true and the
right side false. Therefore, it is important to ensure that such instances
of λ-Equivalence are not permitted and that the rules for substitution
and instantiation proscribe the derivation of (16) from the following in-
stance of λ-*Equivalence*: $[\lambda y \ \Box Cy]z \equiv \Box Cz$. Non-rigid descriptions may
not be instantiated into modal universal claims that are derivable from
λ-*Equivalence*.[7]

Finally, a version of *Descriptions* that applies to non-rigid descriptions is required. The only difference between this version and the one
formulated already is that the instances of *Descriptions* involving only
non-rigid descriptions may be regarded as necessary. It is necessary, for
example, that $P(\iota x)Qx \equiv (\exists! y)Qy \ \& \ (\exists y)(Qy \ \& \ Py)$. In every possible
world $\mathbf{w}$, if the object that uniquely exemplifies Q at $\mathbf{w}$ exemplifies being
P at $\mathbf{w}$, then there is an object uniquely exemplifying Q at $\mathbf{w}$, and some
object exemplifies both Q and P at $\mathbf{w}$.

---

[6]There is an alternative way to block the inference, but it is needlessly restrictive.
One could reformulate Substitutivity as a schema involving metavariables that
range over all terms (instead of just variables). Then one could restrict Substitutivity by stipulating that the only permissable instances of this schema are ones
in which the terms flanking the identity sign in the antecedent do not stand inside
the scope of a modal operator in ϕ. However, such a procedure prevents us from
deriving: $a = b \rightarrow (\Box Pa \equiv \Box Pb)$, where a and b are names. This is certainly valid,
even when non-rigid descriptions are added to the system.

[7]K. Lambert, in [1983], uses an example similar to (16) to argue that λ-*Equivalence*
is a suspicious principle and ought to be rejected. The work we're doing here proves
to be important when we consider his argument in Chapter 8.

5.6   Final Comments

This concludes our discussion of the changes that are required to incorporate non-rigid descriptions into the system. The decision to simplify the analyses of certain English sentences by using non-rigid descriptions must be weighed against the complications that arise when adding such terms to the language. Whether or not non-rigid descriptions are added, the above definitions still constitute the simplest treatment of primitive descriptions in a modal theory without identity. However, it is not a naive treatment—it need not be abandoned in order to account for certain simple facts about propositional attitudes. The metaphysical theory of abstract objects will help us to account for those facts.

Primitive descriptions, the logic of encoding, and the theory of abstract objects offer a new perspective on the debate about the realm of nonexistent, fictional, and mythical objects. Russell believed that the logic of descriptions alone could sufficiently deal with sentences describing such objects. He suggests:

> The whole realm of nonentities, such as 'the round square,' 'the even prime number other than two,' 'Apollo,' 'Hamlet,' etc., can now be satisfactorily dealt with. All these are denoting phrases which do not denote anything. A proposition about Apollo means what we get by substituting what the classical dictionary tells us is meant by Apollo, say 'the sun-god.' All propositions in which Apollo occurs are to be interpreted by the above rules for denoting phrases. ([1905a], ¶34)

This is clearly a mistake, however. Russell's strategy forces one to equate terms like 'the King of France,' which have readings on which they genuinely fail to denote, with terms like 'Hamlet,' which names a certain fictional character that doesn't exist. Lumping these terms into the same category impedes the investigation of intensional logic, for an important distinction necessary to getting such a investigation off the ground is lost.

Russell's move is plagued by several obvious difficulties, some of which we've already mentioned. For example, it turns the sentence "Some Anglo-Saxons feared Grendel" into a falsehood and trivializes the valid inference from "Hrothgar feared Grendel" to "Hrothgar feared something" (since there are no interpretations under which the premise is true). These are serious problems, and they place constraints on any logic and metaphysics that is to have the capacity to accurately represent the data. Moreover, Russell's strategy should generalize to include all proper names, if names are all to work alike. This would capture what must surely be a significant generalization about the operation of language. If the procedure is not generalizable, sentences with apparently the same logical form, in fact would have to have widely divergent logical forms (for example, "Reagan worshipped Bhagwan Rajneesh" and "Cleanthes worshipped Zeus"). But when Russell's strategy is generalized, it has the unfortunate consequence that even names like 'Reagan' don't contribute their denotations to the proposition denoted by sentences in which they occur. Recent work by such authors as Chisholm [1973] and Parsons [1979] suggests that Russell's strategy of paraphrasing away names and terms denoting non-existents in terms of definite descriptions has unsolvable problems. There is no general procedure for producing a correct paraphrase.

With these considerations in mind, therefore, let us turn to a serious investigation of nonexistent objects, fictional and mythical characters, and dream objects. The key to the intensionality of sentences about these entities lies in such an investigation.

Part III

Existential Generalization

6

The Turn-of-the-Century Debate About Intentionality

Existential Generalization is the inferential principle that licenses the move from an English sentence of the form "...D... ," where D is a name or definite description, to a sentence of the form "...something that exists..." (or "Some existing thing is such that ...it...."). In this part of the book, the focus will be on sentences that invalidate this inference but which obey Existential Generalization. For example, we may not validly infer "Cousteau searched for something that exists" from "Cousteau searched for the lost city of Atlantis," though we may validly infer "Cousteau searched for something." A proper analysis of this inference should also tell us why it is appropriate to use the word 'it' to refer back to the subject term or object term of a sentence, even when the term signifies something that doesn't exist. Consider, for example, "The monster you dreamed about last night doesn't exist, so you need not be frightened by *it*." Such anaphoric uses of 'it' are abundant in everyday speech, and the explanation of this phenomenon is an important aspect of intensional logic.

Clearly, the sentences under consideration intimately describe our psychological life. The mental states involved in searches, dreams, and the like, are intentional mental states. An understanding of these states provides an insight into the intensional logic of the sentences that describe them. Accordingly, we begin our investigation by taking a close look at this kind of intentionality. The best place to start is with the ideas of the turn-of-the-century intentional theorists—Brentano, Meinong, Husserl, and Mally. Traditionally, it was thought that Meinong and Husserl developed opposite approaches to puzzling questions that Brentano faced about the nature of intentional objects. However, the

theory developed here, based on the ideas of Meinong's student Ernst
Mally, provides us with a direct interpretation of the views of both
Meinong and Husserl, and it shows that there is a way to reconcile
their work.

In this chapter, we develop an informal understanding of the issues.
In the subsequent chapters of this part, the issues are recast into our
technical idiom. One of the things we hope to show is that much of the
debate in the recent literature on the proper interpretation of Meinong's
views has been conducted with a restricted set of interpretative options.
However, before embarking on these tasks, it is important to say a few
words about the use of the word 'exists' in what follows.

6.1   Two Kinds of Existence

Recall that in Chapter 2, we decided not only to read formulas of the
form '$(\exists x)\phi$' as "there is an x such that ϕ," but also to reserve "there exists an x such that ϕ" as the reading of formulas of the form '$(\exists x)(E!x$ &
$\phi)$.' There are good reasons for doing things this way, and it is important to say what they are and indicate what the alternatives are before
we discuss the ideas of the early intentional theorists.[1]

Clearly, there are two notions of existence that may be distinguished
in our logic. One is expressed by the predicate 'E!.' The other is expressed by the quantifier '$\exists$,' even though we have used the words 'some'
and 'there is' to read this symbol. Many philosophers insist that this
latter notion is the only correct notion of "existence." Such philosophers
are swayed by the Russellian intuition that if '$(\exists x)\phi$' is true, something
must exist to make ϕ true. Quine goes a step further, by asserting that
there is only one legitimate reading for nonexistence claims of natural
language. He says:

> We have all been prone to say, in our common sense usage
> of 'exist,' that Pegasus does not exist, meaning there is no
> such entity at all. If Pegasus existed, he would indeed be
> in space and time, but only because the word 'Pegasus' has
> spatio-temporal connotations, and not because 'exists' has
> spatio-temporal connotations. ([1948], p. 3)

Quine offers little evidence in support of his view about what is meant
by utterances of "Pegasus does not exist." Since we wish to avoid verbal
disputes, let us simply note that with certain modifications, the theory
developed so far could have been made consistent with Quine's way of
speaking. Here is how.

---

[1]Parsons argues eloquently in [1982] why things should be done this way, and we
refer the reader to this work in support of the ideas that follow.

There are two basic modifications: read the predicate '$E!$' as 'being concrete' instead of 'exists,' and read the quantifier '$\exists$' as 'there exists.' Given this way of speaking, English sentences of the form 'τ exists' should be analyzed as "$(\exists\alpha)\alpha = \tau$.' For then, by saying such things as "Reagan exists" (i.e., $(\exists x)x = r$) and "The property of being a self-shaver exists" (i.e., $(\exists F)F = [\lambda y\ Syy]$), we would imply semantically that the terms 'r' and '$[\lambda y\ Syy]$' have denotations. It would be a theorem that there are no nonexistent individuals and no nonexistent relations, since both $(\forall x)(\exists y)(y = x)$ and $(\forall G)(\exists F)(F = G)$ are derivable. True nonexistence claims would not assert anything about particular individuals or relations. Claims such as $\sim(\exists y)y = b$, $\sim(\exists y)y = (\imath z)\psi$, and $\sim(\exists F)F = [\lambda y Ry(\imath x)\psi]$ would not imply that the entities denoted by 'b,' '$(\imath x)\psi$,' and '$[\lambda y\ Ry(\imath x)\psi]$' fail to exist. Note also that the abstraction schemata employ '$\exists$' to quantify over A-objects, properties, relations, and propositions. With the modifications now under consideration, these axioms would assert that the entities generated exist. Since neither A-objects nor relations of any kind are concrete or have a location in space and time, the theory could be regarded as a kind of Platonism based on first principles. And the resulting theory would even be Russellian in a certain sense, at least to the extent that Russellianism is consistent with the existence of *abstract* entities of all kinds.

However, we cannot emphasize strongly enough that this regimentation of our philosophical language is legitimate only relative to the choice of certain philosophical goals. In particular, it is legitimate only with respect to the goal of rectifying the philosophically naive use of the word 'exists' in natural language. If one's goal, however, is to explain how commonsense (nonexistence) claims of natural language, when taken at their face value, mean what they seem to mean (Quine's idea of what they mean notwithstanding), and have the truth value, logical form, and entailments that they seem to have, one will prefer to speak differently. In particular, one will prefer to distinguish *being* (that is, logical or metaphysical existence) from *existence* (that is, physical existence). And one will prefer to use the quantifier '$\exists$' to represent the former and '$(\exists x)(E!x\ \&\ldots)$' to represent the latter.

There are many advantages to this way of speaking. For one thing, we can represent the claim "there are nonexistent objects" without turning it into a logical falsehood. This is a thesis about which we should be able to disagree, without supposing that philosophers who accept the thesis can be refuted on logical grounds alone. But that is what would happen were we to regiment our use of 'exists' in Quine's manner, since '$(\exists x)\sim(\exists y)(y = x)$' is a logical falsehood. This trivializes the question of whether there are nonexistent objects.

Moreover, it seems intuitively clear that names like 'Pegasus,' 'Zeus,' and 'Hamlet' are names of nonexistent, mythical and fictional creatures. The logic of natural language seems to presuppose that it makes sense to refer to and talk about these creatures. This is suggested by each of the following facts, many of which we've already discussed: (a) Existential Generalization preserves truth when we move from a sentence like "John's paper is about Hamlet" to "John's paper is about something" or "There is something which John's paper is about." If Quine were right when he says that "Hamlet doesn't exist" means '$\sim(\exists x)(x = h)$,' then 'Hamlet' would fail to denote. This would make the inference just described complex and mysterious. (b) In general, the use of anaphoric pronouns is sytematically related to antecedent terms that denote, yet we use such pronouns in conjunction with names and descriptions of mythical and fictional characters. Here is an example similar to the one mentioned in the paragraph opening this chapter: "Most people believe that the Loch Ness monster doesn't exist, but that hasn't prevented teams of scientists from searching for *it*." (c) The analysis of the following argument is simplified by the logic of nonexistent individuals:

> Mythical characters don't exist.
> Jupiter is a mythical character.
> Augustus Caesar worshipped Jupiter.
> Therefore, Caesar worshipped something that doesn't exist.

And, finally, (d) even the language we use to refer to the objects of our dreams behaves like referential language rather than language that fails to refer to anything at all.[2]

Now when these facts are considered in light of the dilemma facing the treatment of such names and descriptions as names of properties rather than individuals (recall Chapter 2, Section 1), a powerful case emerges for thinking that the logic underlying natural language is sensitive to the distinction between being and existence. In each of the above cases, it seems to make sense to talk about individuals that don't exist. Of course, this is not a knockdown argument. Rather, it is a *prima facie* justification for our original way of using the word 'exists.' One final reason in favor of this way of speaking is that this is the way Brentano, Meinong, Husserl, and Mally usually speak. They typically use 'exist' to characterize the concrete objects of physical space. Indeed, the early Russell followed this usage, before he fell under the grip of his theory of descriptions and developed a prejudice in favor the actual. Consequently, our way of speaking will capture more faithfully the views of the early intentionalists.

---

[2]See Parsons [1980], pp. 112–114; and his [1982], pp. 366–367.

6.2   Brentano, Meinong, and Husserl

Many scholars believe that both Meinong and Husserl developed theories to account for a problem Brentano faced regarding intentional objects.[3] Brentano supplemented his thesis of intentionality, that the capacity for having mental states about objects that need not exist is the "mark" of the mental, with the thesis that in every thought, there is always something that we think about, even when we think about things that don't exist. For the cases where we think about nonexistents, however, Brentano faced rather difficult questions concerning the proper characterization of the intentional object. Brentano rejected the suggestion that such intentional objects were mental objects, on the same grounds that Frege and Bolzano rejected this view—when we think about Pegasus, for example, we are not thinking about our idea of Pegasus, just as when we think about the moon, we are not thinking about our idea of the moon (to paraphrase an argument of Frege's).

The option apparently explored by Meinong was to regard the intentional object in these cases as a physical object that does not exist. Brentano, however, could not make any sense of the distinction between being and existence, a distinction that Meinong made use of to defend his view.[4] Like many philosophers studying intentionality, Brentano might have accepted that there are false propositions and states of affairs that don't obtain. But he drew the line at nonexistent objects. The motivation for this stance is a reasonable one, for there is a clear sense in which there really are no winged horses, demons, monsters, etc., not even nonexistent ones. The intuition here has to do with the nature of exemplification—most of us are inclined to believe that no object whatsoever, not even a nonexistent one, really exemplifies the property of being a horse that flies; we are inclined to believe that no object, not even a nonexistent one, really exemplifies the properties of being round and square; and so on. These intuitions were discussed in Chapter 2, Section 1, in connection with the objections Russell raised to the idea that there are entities that exemplify these kinds of properties. So even if one can make sense of the distinction between being and existence, as we did in the previous section, the notion of exemplification still stands in the way of thinking that such nonexistents are involved in intentionality.

To avoid commitments to such objects, Husserl explored a different, more attractive option. Basically, Husserl's [1913] view is that while every intentional state has a "content," not every state has an object. For Husserl, such states as fearing Grendel, admiring Alyosha Karamazov, searching for the golden fleece, and others like them, are not about

---

[3]See the papers in Dreyfus [1982], and in particular, Føllesdal [1982a].

[4]See Føllesdal [1982a], Brentano [1874].

nonexistent objects, because there are no such objects. Instead, these states have contents that are or involve "representations." The representative content of a state is to be distinguished from the object towards which the state may be directed, and in the cases of apparent directedness towards nonexistents, there just are no such objects. Nothing out in the world exemplifies the properties involved in the representative content. Husserl introduces an intermediate entity, the *noema*, as a way of objectifying these intermediate representational contents.[5] So Husserl's view is that even though thoughts about nonexistents have no object, the reason it is true to say that they are about something is the fact that there is an intermediate object, the noema, that structures and directs our minds towards the world. The noema is the representational content of our state.

When it comes time to tie Husserl's views into a philosophy of language, an important question arises. And that is, what is the Husserlian semantic analysis of the sentences "K is thinking about Reagan" and "K is thinking about Pegasus"? A general semantic theory should treat these sentences on a logical par. Consequently, we should rule out the analysis on which the truth conditions of the first involve the denotation of 'Reagan' and the truth conditions of the second involve the noema signified by 'Pegasus.' This analysis is not a general one. On the other hand, if the general analysis of both sentences involves the noemata associated with 'Reagan' and 'Pegasus,' then it fails to preserve the natural intuition that the analysis of the former sentence involves the denotations of 'K' and 'Reagan.' The basic problem here is that on Husserl's view, it appears that even though names of nonexistent objects have cognitive significance in virtue of being systematically related to noemata, they fail to have a denotation. But it is just this idea, that such names have denotations, that can simplify the logic of intensional contexts. It simplifies our understanding of how such sentences have the entailments, anaphoric correlations, etc., that they in fact have.

Actually, Husserl's views are not fundamentally incompatible with the idea that names like 'Pegasus' have denotations. It is possible to develop an intermediate view on which (a) the name 'Pegasus' denotes a fictional object, and (b) intentional states are directed towards such objects in virtue of having noemata as their content. Before we turn to the development of this view, note that the denotation of 'Pegasus' may be an object that has a rather large number of properties associated with it. These are the properties that might be featured in a storytelling of the myth. They include properties that are relevantly entailed (relative

---

[5] *Noemata* are entities that are similar to Frege's Senses and Bolzano's Objective Ideas.

to normal storytellers and listeners) by the propositions described in a storytelling. Even though there is no single uncorrupted version of the myth, a distinction must nevertheless be drawn between Pegasus the mythical character from the content of someone's intentional state "directed towards Pegasus." The noema that is involved when the sentence "K is thinking about Pegasus" is true may involve far fewer properties than those featured in a complete storytelling. Stories may be very long, whereas our minds have only so much cognitive capacity for storing properties of the characters described. Also, a person might get the details of the story wrong, possibly as a result of mishearing the storyteller. Consequently, the state in virtue of which "K is thinking about Pegasus" is true may be characterized by a content involving properties that are not attributed to Pegasus in the myth. Reasons such as these incline us to try to develop a view on which characters of fiction are distinct from the noemata involved in the states directed towards them.

To develop this intermediate view, we need an answer to one other important question concerning Husserlian noemata, namely, what kind of entities are they? For many analytic philosophers, noemata are strange and mysterious entities that desperately need a theoretical treatment. Our best understanding comes from Dagfinn Føllesdal's work in [1982b]. He suggests that the following group of twelve theses fundamentally characterize noemata: (1) The noema is an intensional entity—like Fregean senses, they play a central role in the explanation of the failures involved in intensional contexts; (2) A noema has two components: (a) one component that is common to all acts which have the same object (Husserl called this the "noematic *Sinn*"); and (b) one component that is different for each type of act (i.e., a component that varies depending on whether the act is a perceiving, remembering, imagining, etc.); (3) The noematic Sinn is that in virtue of which consciousness relates to the object; (4) The noema of an act is not the object of the act (i.e., it is not the object toward which the act is directed); (5) To one and the same noema there corresponds only one object; (6) To one and the same object there may correspond several different noematic *Sinne*; (7) Each act has only one noema; (8) Noemata are abstract entities; (9) Noemata are not perceived through our senses; (10) Noemata are known through a special reflection, the phenomenological reflection; (11) The phenomenological reflection can be iterated; and (12) The noema is a complex system of 'determinations' that make a multitude of visual, tactile, and other data be appearances of one object.

Many of these items will become more vivid if they are examined in the context of some ideas of Ernst Mally. Mally's ideas will help us to focus the search for a theoretical treatment of noemata.

6.3   Mally, A-Objects, and Noemata

Ernst Mally's work is not very well known. In the eyes of many philosophers, the fact that he was a student of Meinong makes him guilty by
association. It might come as a surprise that Mally's early work was
well known to Russell. Russell held Mally's work [1904] in high enough
regard to devote several pages to its exegesis. This appeared in Russell's
[1905b] review in *Mind* of the collection of essays produced by the members of the school at Graz (the collection was edited by Meinong under
the [1904b] title *Untersuchungen zur Gegenstandstheorie und Psychologie*). Russell said in the conclusion to [1905b]:

> The book as a whole does the highest credit to the Graz
> school of psychology and philosophy; and its main articles
> contain theories which demand and deserve careful study.
> The second and third articles, by Ameseder and Mally, con-
> tain so many important definitions in quick succession that
> it has been impossible to give an adequate idea of their con-
> tents in the space of a review.

Unfortunately for Mally, however, it was his later work in [1912] that
contained his most exciting, though obscurely described, philosophical
ideas. These ideas contain the seeds from which a clear and coherent response to Russell's objections to Meinongian metaphysics may
be developed. They are produced in his book, *Gegenstandstheoretische
Grundlagen der Logik und Logistik* (Leipzig: Barth, 1912), a work that
was published in what might still be considered an early stage of Mally's
career.[6] But by the time it was published, Russell appears to have been
so deeply entrenched in his new paradigm, that work from the school of
Graz was no longer commanding his attention.

In his book of [1912], Mally did something radically new. He introduced a new primitive notion, that of a property *determining* an
object. He posited a realm of abstract objects that are individuated by
the properties that determine them. Though a given object is determined by a property, it need not satisfy that property. Here is Findlay's
characterization of Mally's views:

---

[6] Before the publication of his book, Mally had made other contributions to Meinongian metaphysics. He developed the Principle of Independence, which states that
a thing need not have being to have a nature or to have properties. Meinong
was influenced by this principle, though Mally later rejected it (we shall discuss
the principle in some detail in Chapter 8, Section 4). Mally also originated the
nuclear/extranuclear distinction, to which Meinong appealed in his defense of 'the
existent golden mountain.' Though the distinction is not among the primitives
upon which our theory is based, Parsons has shown that a rigorous object theory
can be based on this distinction.

On the view of Mally, every determination determines an object, but not every determination is satisfied (*erfüllt*) by an object. The determination 'being two-legged and featherless' *determines* the abstract determinate 'featherless biped,' which is usually called a 'concept,' but it is *satisfied* by nearly every human being. On the other hand, the determination 'being round and square' determines the abstract determinate 'round square,' but it is not satisfied by any object. The object which satisfies a certain determination is really characterized by that determination; ... But the determinate of a certain determination need not really *possess* that determination. The round square is not really round, nor is it a square at all; ... ([1933], p. 111)[7]

In another passage in [1933] describing Mally's views, Findlay says the following:

In apprehending concrete existents, we do so by means of the determinates of certain determinations. We grasp *through* the determinates *at* the object which satisfies a set of determinations. ... the determinate gives us our direction, but the cognitive situation, considered in itself, need not tell us whether we have hit anything at all. We may discover that there is nothing to hit in that direction, in which case only the determinate remains in our hands. (pp. 183–184)

There clearly seems to be a remarkable similarity between Husserl's views as described by Føllesdal and Mally's views as described by Findlay. Note first of all, that Husserl and Mally both take the line that there are no objects that really exemplify the properties attributed to Pegasus in the myth, or being golden and being a mountain, or being round and being square, etc. So they both appear to be in opposition to the Meinongian solution to Brentano's puzzle. Both Husserl and Mally believe that the there are certain abstract entities that give our mental states direction, regardless of whether there exists an object that exemplifies the properties involved. Both believe that these abstract entities are intimately linked to 'determinations,' and that the pattern of determinations is essential to the identity of the abstract entity in question (recall item (12) in Føllesdal's description).

It should be apparent to our readers by now that there is good chance that all of this rather vague talk about "noemata" and "determinations" can be more rigorously understood by looking at the axiomatized realm

---

[7]Findlay cites Mally's [1912], pp. 64, 76 as the source of these ideas.

of A-objects. Clearly, A-objects are designed to do the job Mally's determinations are supposed to do, and more. If we suppose that Mally's
notion of 'determination' corresponds to our notion of 'property,' that
Mally's notion of 'determinate' corresponds to our notion of 'A-object,'
and that our notion of encodes captures the way determinations and
determinates are metaphysically linked, then Mally's views require, at
the very least, that for every (complex) property, there is an A-object
that encodes that (complex) property. Our theory goes even further, by
requiring that for every group of properties (simple or complex), there
is an A-object that encodes just the properties in the group.

The more interesting question to address is whether A-objects can
be used to give a theoretical treatment of noemata. Can they do the
job Husserl's noemata are designed to do? In order to give a comprehensive answer to these questions, aspects of intentionality other than
the problems of nonexistence must be considered. These other aspects
have to do with the propositional attitudes and, in particular, Frege's
ideas about the nature of senses. The reason these other aspects have
to be considered is that A-objects satisfy item (1) in Føllesdal's characterization of noemata. They are the entities that will account for the
intensional behavior of propositional attitude contexts. However, since
this is a topic that is reserved for Part IV, comprehensive answers to
our questions must be postponed. In what immediately follows, we give
only a basic outline of the answers.

The answers depend on an observation and an assumption. The
observation is that an A-object may *be* the content of a state in virtue
of *having* a content that uniquely characterizes that state. A-objects
have content, in virtue of encoding properties. If the properties encoded
are vivid, the A-objects will have a vivid content. Furthermore, we can
say that A-objects *are* the contents of mental states, in virtue of the fact
that the particular group of properties they encode are involved in the
state in some way. By saying some A-object is the content of a mental
state, we do not mean that it is part of anyone's mind. Rather, we are
simply objectifying the principal feature of the state that is responsible
for its having that content and not some other.

The assumption is that though one may have a mental state that is
about, or directed towards, a certain object, the content (noema) of that
state may involve properties that the object doesn't really exemplify. We
have already discussed this on several occasions. Another good example
to consider is the perception of an object in bad light. It may appear
to have a property that it in fact does not exemplify. Our mental state
is, nevertheless, about this object, even though the content of our state
includes properties that do not properly characterize the object of the
state. Consequently, the content of the state itself is not the place to

look to determine philosophically what the state is about. Rather, the place to look is the contextual and historical facts that give rise to the state. The contextual/historical fact that a particular object stands at the source of this perceptual state is what makes it true to say that that state is about, or directed towards, that object.

In light of these considerations, it appears that A-objects have many of the features Husserl ascribes to "noematic *Sinne*." The noematic *Sinn* is the most important feature of noemata. Recall that it is that part of the noema that is common to all acts that have the same object (item (2) in the previous section). To see that A-objects could play this role, consider a situation in which a person has had a single perceptual encounter with an object. Suppose a particular A-object is the content of the person's mental state during that encounter (it may, for example, encode just the perceptual properties available to the observer from a certain visual perspective). Suppose further that the person acquires no new information about the object. It now seems plausible to suggest that future mental states directed towards this object, whether they be rememberings, imaginings, fears, etc., will be mediated by the A-object in question. This is the sense in which the noematic *Sinn* is "that which is common to all acts that have the same object." Of course, if new information about the object is acquired, some other A-object may come to serve as the content of states directed towards this same object.

Consider next items (3) and (4) of Føllesdal's characterization of noemata. It should be clear that there is an sense in which A-objects are "that in virtue of which consciousness relates to objects" (item (3)). By encoding properties, A-objects can direct us toward the world, that is, toward other objects that exemplify (or even encode) those properties. Moreover, in the cases where we are directed towards ordinary objects (such as in perception), A-objects will not be the object of mental states (item (4)). In states directed towards nonexistents, however, two A-objects are typically involved. One serves as the content of the state. It is linked to the cognitive capacities of the person experiencing the state. The other serves as the object of the state and is to be identified with the particular nonexistent (or fictional) character in question. It is linked to the properties involved in the story in which the character originates. We'll discuss this in more detail below, when we consider the relationship between Mally's ideas and Meinong's.

Consider now items (5), (6), and (7) of Føllesdal's characterization of noemata. Given the example described a couple of paragraphs back, in which a person has had a single perceptual encounter with an object and acquires no new information, it should be clear that there is a correspondence set up between the A-object serving as the content of the state and the object of the state. For the person in question, this particular A-object will not serve as the content of states directed towards other objects. This is the sense in which "to one and the same noema there corresponds only one object." As we mentioned before, however, as new information is acquired, a new correspondence may be set up, between a different A-object and the object of the original perceptual state. And it might turn out that the first A-object is subsequently utilized as the content of a state directed towards some other object[8] Furthermore, there should be no obstacle to the idea that "to one and the same object there may correspond several different noematic *Sinne*." Lots of different states, each characterized by a distinct, though unique, A-object, may all be directed towards the same object. Thus, items (6) and (7) in Føllesdal's characterization may be satisfied by A-objects.

The reader may judge items (8) – (12) upon their own merits. It seems plausible to suggest that these items characterize A-objects. Note in particular (8) and (12). Husserl's views about noemata and noematic *Sinne* seem to have a rather straightforward interpretation in the theory of A-objects.

There may be two places where these suggestions may diverge from Husserl's basic ideas. The first concerns the nature of the relationship between noemata and the objects of states. Husserl may have envisioned a rather stringent relationship, as stringent as the relationship between Fregean senses and the denotations of terms with which they are associated. If the noema of a state is supposed to determine the object the state is about, then the particular story we have told is not completely faithful to Husserl's views. However, this doesn't mean that a somewhat different story, in which A-objects are still employed to model noematic *Sinne*, will not shed light on these rather mysterious noemata.

The other point of divergence concerns the analysis of states directed towards nonexistent objects. Recall that the Husserlian analysis of the sentences "Russell thought about George IV" and "Russell thought about the round square" do not allow us to generalize the workings of language. We may agree with Husserl that the relation *thinking about* is a mental state that has a content characterized by a noema. But it is important to preserve the idea that the denotations of 'George IV' and 'the round square' contribute to the truth conditions of the sentences in question. In the final section, we develop this idea and try to reconcile both the Husserlian view that states like *thinking about* have content and the Meinongian view that such states have objects.

---

[8]This could happen if the first A-object encoded properties the ordinary, perceived object doesn't exemplify. It might subsequently serve as the content of a state directed towards a different object that does exemplify the properties in question.

6.4   A-Objects and Meinong

In his [1904a] essay "The Theory of Objects," Meinong asserted "the round square is surely round as it is square."[9] Presumably, he would also accept the sentence, "Pegasus is winged." If by saying "The round square is round" and "Pegasus is winged" Meinong meant "The object exemplifying roundness and squareness exemplifies roundness" and "Pegasus exemplifies being winged," respectively, then what he said, from our point of view, is false. However, Meinong did not use the technical term "exemplify." Rather, he used natural language to express his views. His words, therefore, are open to interpretation and analysis. With the traditional resources of exemplification logic, philosophers have had only one option for interpreting Meinong's use of the predicative copula 'is' and the definite article 'the.' The 'is' of predication just means 'exemplifies,' and a description such as 'the so and so' just means 'the object that exemplifies being so and so.' Consequently, one's first inclination is to suppose that Meinong has made a mistake. Even if there were a nonexistent object that satisfies the description 'the round square,' how could a nonexistent object really exemplify being round? How could a nonexistent object like Pegasus really exemplify being winged? Doesn't the fact that an object exemplifies being round, or being winged, entail that it exists?

These are certainly good questions, and the failure to answer them is bound to leave Meinong's views unintelligible. The resources of encoding logic, however, offer an alternative interpretation of Meinong's assertions, and on this interpretation these questions do not apply. The sentence "The round square is round" might be true if it's truth conditions are "The object that encodes just being round and being square encodes being round." The fact that an object encodes these two properties does not imply that anything jointly exemplifies them. Furthermore, the sentence "Pegasus is winged" might be true if it's truth conditions are "Pegasus encodes being winged." Such truth conditions do not entail that any nonexistent object exemplifies being winged. So the questions that plague the pure exemplification interpretation of Meinong's utterances do not apply to the interpretation available in the logic of encoding.

On the encoding interpretation, Meinong may be regarded as having said something true, though as having used ambiguous language. He correctly insisted that natural language sentences like "The round square is round" and "Pegasus is winged" are true *in some sense*. Even modern philosophers agree with this. David Lewis says in [1978], "...is there not

---

[9]This is taken from Chisholm's [1960] English translation of Meinong's [1904a], p. 82.

some perfectly good sense of 'is' in which Holmes, like Nixon, *is* a real-life person of flesh and blood?" (p. 37). This interpretation even allows us to understand Meinong's view that objects like Pegasus, Grendel, etc., are physical objects! The property of being a physical object is a property these entities exemplify according to their respective myths. Consequently, this is a property that Pegasus and Grendel encode. Now if we were to describe this fact in ambiguous English, we would say something like "Pegasus (Grendel) is a physical object." This is the kind of claim that has made Meinong infamous, but we now have an interpretation for it that represents it as being true.

This eliminates the objections to the intermediate view that incorporates the ideas of both Husserl and Meinong. This intermediate view employs the Meinongian analysis of intentionality to construct analyses of sentences of natural language. The sentences "K is thinking about Reagan" and "K is thinking about Grendel" may have a general analysis. Both are true just in case the objects denoted by the names stand in the relation denoted by 'is thinking about.' This intermediate view also incorporates the Husserlian analysis of intentionality to explain the directedness of mental states in general. In particular, the mental states these sentences describe have a "direction." The direction is represented by an A-object in its role as a noematic *Sinn*. The A-object attaches the properties involved in the cognitive state to a single focal point. Though Husserl would disagree with the view that *thinking about Grendel* has both a content and an object, we have offered reasons why it is important to think that one A-object serves as content, while another serves as object. Other than this discrepancy, we see no reason to think that there is any deep inconsistency between Husserl's views and Meinong's.

This shows that the tradition of opposing Husserl's views to Meinong's views is based on a limited set of interpretative options. Mally's distinction seems to provide a fruitful insight for resolving their differences. Both Husserlian intentional objects and Meinongian intentional objects become somewhat clearer when they are represented as A-objects that encode properties.

This description of the turn-of-the-century debate about intentionality has really been just a sketch. It provides the underlying conception by which we approach the failures of *Existential* Generalization. However, there are a variety of details that require attention. It is important to formulate a rigorous response to Russell's famous objections to Meinong's views. And it is important to systematize the analysis of sentences about stories and fictional characters. To attend to these and other details, we need a formal development of the above ideas. And then once the picture is filled in, we can return to the principles of Generalization.

7

The Analysis of *Existential* Generalization

To understand the puzzles of *Existential* Generalization, it is imperative to have an analysis of sentences about nonexistent and fictional objects, for these sentences figure prominently in the failures of this principle. However, certain traditional obstacles have stood in the way of such an analysis. These are the objections Russell formulated to Meinong's views. Russell was legitimately concerned with the question of whether the essential Meinongian doctrines imply falsehoods. Though we have sketched a way to disarm these objections, it is important to be more rigorous about the matter before moving on to consider the data involved in *Existential* Generalization. So in Sections 1 and 2, we look at Russell's objections in some detail. In Section 3, we use the theory to analyze a wide variety of names and descriptions that appear to denote fictional characters. Finally, in Section 4, we use the formal representations developed in the first three sections to explain the failures of *Existential* Generalization.

7.1 Russell's Objections to Meinong's Views

There are two classic passages in which Russell delivers his most influential objections to Meinong's views.[1] Consider what he says in [1905a]:

---

[1] Smith claims in [1985] that there are eight "major explicit objections Russell brought against Meinong's nonexistent objects" (p. 311). However, some of these "objections" are really just disagreements about the logical form of the data, and about the primitives necessary for metaphysical definitions (see her objections (5), (6), and (3), respectively). Others seem to be just theoretical claims Russell made regarding the efficacy of his own theory (see her objections (7) and (8)). We shall focus on the genuine puzzles that Russell developed for Meinong's theory.

Of the possible theories which admit such constituents the simplest is that of Meinong. This theory regards any grammatically correct denoting phrase as standing for an *object* [Russell's emphasis]. Thus, 'the present King of France', 'the round square', etc., are supposed to be genuine objects. It is admitted that such objects do not *subsist*, but nevertheless they are supposed to be objects. This is in itself a difficult view; but the the chief objection is that such objects, admittedly, are apt to infringe the law of [non]contradiction. It is contended, for example, that the existent present King of France exists, and also does not exist; that the round square is round, and also not round, etc. But this is intolerable; and if any theory can be found to avoid this result, it is surely to be preferred. (¶11)

Secondly, a passage in Russell's [1907] review, published in *Mind*, of Meinong's book *Über die Stellung der Gegenstandstheorie im System der Wissenschaften*, provides what seems to be a fundamentally different kind of objection. He does not argue here simply that there is an incompatiblity with the law of noncontradiction, but argues that Meinong's principles imply that certain things exist which clearly don't. He says:

Meinong's next argument is an answer to my contention that, on his principles, 'the existent round square' exists. To this he replies that it is existent but does not exist. I must confess that I see no difference between existing and being existent; and beyond this I have no more to say on this head. ([1907], ¶7)

At first, it might seem that the objection in this passage is just the same as the objection in the first passage concerning the 'the existent present King of France.' But there seem to be at least two objections that can be distinguish here: (i) that Meinong's principles are inconsistent, and (ii) that Meinong's principles are incompatible with contingent facts.

Russell's first objection may be clarified by examining the following argument, in which statements (1) – (3) are the premises, and (4) is the conclusion:

(1) The round square is round.

(2) The round square is square.

(3) If something is square, then it is not the case that it is round.

(4) (Therefore) It is not the case that the round square is round.

In this argument, premises (1) and (2) are supposed to be justified by Meinongian principles, while premise (3) is a proper axiom governing the properties of being round and being square. The argument appears to be valid—if one accepts the first two premises on the grounds that 'the round square' denotes an object that exemplifies being round and being square, then the acceptance of premise (3) implies the negation of the first premise.

The first question to address concerning this argument is: why is it that Russell believed that premises (1) and (2) are consequences of Meinongian principles? The answer has to do with Meinong's use of language. In view of Meinong's utterances such as "The round square is as surely round as it is square," Russell quite naturally attributed to Meinong the doctrine that every grammatically correct denoting phrase stands for an object ([1905a], ¶11). Actually Russell's objection attributes a stronger principle to Meinong, namely, that every description denotes an object that satisfies the description. The formal representation of this stronger principle captures it as an "unrestricted satisfaction" principle. Consider Principle (A):

(A) $(\exists y)(y = (\imath x)\phi \ \& \ \phi_x^y)$, for any formula ϕ in which x is free

Principle (A) indeed captures the idea that for any condition on objects ϕ, the description '$(\imath x)\phi$' not only denotes an object but also denotes an object that satisfies ϕ. Principle (A) should not be attributed to Meinong, for reasons to be discussed below. However, it does seem to be the natural way to formalize Meinong's use of language, and so let us proceed for the moment as if it were a Meinongian principle.

Before examining how Principle (A) figures into the formalization of Russell's objection, it is important to point out that it is inconsistent. Note that it is equivalent to the conjunction of two claims—that every description has a denotation, and that any entity denoted by a description satisfies the description. These two parts to the principle can be captured in logical notation by the following principles (B) and (C):

(B) $(\exists y)(y = (\imath x)\phi)$, for any formula ϕ

(C) $(\forall y)(y = (\imath x)\phi \rightarrow \phi_x^y)$

Principle (C) is not controversial. It is deducible in any standard logic in which something like *Descriptions* (Chapter 5) is the axiom governing descriptions.[2] But whereas Principle (C) is true, Principle (B) generates

---

[2]To see this, assume the antecedent. The following is an instance of *Descriptions*: $y = (\imath x)\phi \equiv (\exists! u)\phi_x^u \ \&(\exists u)(\phi_x^u \ \& \ y = u)$. So we may infer the right side of this biconditional. Consider its right conjunct. Since there is a u such that $y = u$ and such that u satisfies ϕ, y satisfies ϕ.

a contradiction. Just let ϕ be 'Sx & $\sim Sx$.' Then by (B), it follows that $(\exists y)(y = (\imath x)(Sx$ & $\sim Sx))$. If we call such an object 'b,' we know that $b = (\imath x)(Sx$ & $\sim Sx)$. But by (C), it follows that $b = (\imath x)(Sx$ & $\sim Sx) \to Sb$ & $\sim Sb$, which yields a contradiction by Modus Ponens.

Principle (A), therefore, does indeed infringe upon the law of non-contradiction, since it is equivalent to the conjunction of Principles (B) and (C). Since (C) clearly seems to be true, (B) emerges as the principle that is too strong. Unfortunately, Russell's objection, as it is embodied by statements (1) – (4) above, doesn't really show that (B) is inconsistent. Rather, his objection shows that Principle (B) is inconsistent with the non-logical axiom (3), namely, that if something exemplifies being square then it fails to exemplify being round. Let us look at the objection in some detail.

The subject term of (1) is 'the round square,' and in the standard logic of exemplification, this definite description is analyzed as:

(a) $(\imath x)(Rx$ & $Sx)$

If we abbreviate this description as '$(\imath x)\phi_1$,' then (1) should be represented as (1a):

(1a) $R(\imath x)\phi_1$

Note that there is a non-trivial derivation of (1a) from Principle (B).[3] Analogously, we get (2a) as the representation of (2):

(2a) $S(\imath x)\phi_1$

There is also a non-trivial derivation of (2a) from Principle (B). Finally, (3a) is the straightforward representation of (3):

(3a) $(\forall x)(Sx \to \sim Rx)$

Clearly, (1a), (2a), and (3a) are inconsistent. From these three sentences, we may derive the following, formal representation of (4) using classical principles of logic:

(4a) $\sim R(\imath x)\phi_1$

Russell's objection, therefore, is best construed as a rejection of the principle that yields (1a) and (2a), namely, Principle (B), since it is incompatible with a widely accepted non-logical axiom.

Of course, a slight modification of Russell's example reveals the purely logical inconsistency in (B). The following example generates the formal contradiction we derived from Principle (B) a few paragraphs back:

---

[3]By (B), it follows that there is an object, say c, such that $c = (\imath x)\phi_1$. By Principle (C), we may derive that Rc. Consequently, $R(\imath x)\phi_1$, since we know that the description denotes.

(5) The non-square square is square.

(6) The non-square square is non-square.

Let '$\bar{S}$' abbreviate '$[\lambda y \sim Sy]$.' Now consider the following description:

(b) $(\imath x)(\bar{S}x \ \& \ Sx)$

Using this description, which we'll abbreviate as '$(\imath x)\phi_2$,' Russell could argue that (5a) and (6a) are derivable from Principle (B):

(5a) $S(\imath x)\phi_2$

(6a) $\bar{S}(\imath x)\phi_2$

Clearly, a contradiction is derivable from (5a) and (6a) using the principles of classical logic and λ-*Equivalence*. If '$(\imath x)\phi_2$' denotes an object, then a simple application of λ-*Equivalence* produces the negation of (5a) from (6a). Non-logical axioms are not required.

Consequently, there are really two objections contained in Russell's first attack on Meinong's views. Although he tried to show that Principle (B) is inconsistent with the laws of classical logic, the example he used shows only that it is inconsistent with a widely accepted non-logical law. This constitutes the first objection. However, a simple modification of the example produces a consequence of (B) that does indeed infringe the law of noncontradiction. This constitutes Russell's second objection.

Before looking at a good response to these objections, let us develop Russell's other objection, his "third" objection. The objection seems to be that there are certain accepted facts which have negations that are deducible on Meinongian principles. Consider the following argument, in which (7) is the premise, and (8) is the conclusion:

(7) The existent golden mountain exists, is golden, and is a mountain.

(8) (Therefore) Some golden mountain exists.

Intuitively, if one accepts (7) on the grounds that 'the existent golden mountain' denotes an object that exemplifies existence, goldenness, and mountainhood, then one must accept (8). But (8) is incompatible with the following fact, about which there is little doubt:

(9) No golden mountains exist.

The formal analyses of these statements capture these intuitions. Consider following description:

(c) $(\imath x)(E!x \ \& \ Gx \ \& \ Mx)$

If '$(\imath x)\phi_3$' is used to abbreviate (c), then the following representation of (7) is derivable from Principle (B):

(7a) $E!(\imath x)\phi_3$ & $G(\imath x)\phi_3$ & $M(\imath x)\phi_3$

Moreover, (8a) follows from (7a):

(8a) $(\exists x)(E!x$ & Gx & $Mx)$

Clearly, (8a) contradicts (9a):

(9a) $\sim(\exists x)(E!x$ & Gx & $Mx)$

Therefore, Principle (B) does indeed yield consequences that run contrary to contingent facts.

7.2 A Clear Response to Russell's Objections[4]

Our response to Russell's objections is consistent with all of the laws of classical logic. We reject Principle (B) (and, also, Principle (A)). Our response preserves the following intuitions that most of us share:

- Descriptions (a), (b), and (c) fail to denote.

- Statements (1a), (2a), (5a), (6a), and (7a) are false.

- Statements (3a) and (9a) are true.

Just as importantly, however, our response is sympathetic to Meinong. First of all, it shows that there is some truth to the idea that "every grammatically correct description denotes an object." This would validate Meinong's apparent reliance upon this idea. Secondly, the response provides us with a reading of Meinong's utterances (1), (2), (5), (6), and (7) on which they come out true.

The response depends on two important observations. The first concerns a distinction that reveals why it is a mistake to attribute Principle (B) to Meinong. The claim that "every description denotes something" may be interpreted in two ways. Let us distinguish "every description of natural language denotes something" from "every description of the formal language denotes something." The latter is captured formally by Principle (B). Strictly speaking, however, Meinong is committed only to the former and not the latter claim. It is a mistake to think that to capture the former claim, one must build a formal language in which the latter claim is true! One need not attribute Principle (B) to Meinong to

---

[4]The technical developments that underly the formal representations in this section were first outlined in [1983], Chapter II, Section 2.

represent his view that "every description denotes something." Rather, it is sufficient to produce a formal language that can generate, for every description of natural language, at least one formal, denoting description that can serve as a legitimate reading of the natural language description. By a "legitimate" reading, we mean one that can be used to show why the ordinary statements involving the original description have the truth values and entailments that they intuitively have.

The second observation is that, given (3a), the formal description that represents 'the round square' in exemplification logic fails to denote. Indeed, no formal description in exemplification logic helps us to understand how (1) or (2) might be true. Atomic formulas containing these descriptions are false. In the logic of encoding, however, there is another option. We can represent 'the round square' as the following:[5]

(d) $(\imath x)(\forall F)(xF \equiv F = R \lor F = S)$

Description (d) denotes the unique A-object that encodes just the two properties of being round and being square. That there is a unique such object is guaranteed by the comprehension principle and identity condition for A-objects. These facts prove to be useful for the analysis of (1) and (2). By abbreviating description (d) as '$(\imath x)\psi_1$,' and by employing the hypothesis concerning the ambiguity of the predicative copula 'is,' we get the following readings for (1) and (2):

(1b) $(\imath x)\psi_1 R$

(2b) $(\imath x)\psi_1 S$

These two sentences are not only true, they are consequences of the theory. On the hypothesis that the English predicative copula is ambiguous, (1b) and (2b) become legitimate readings of (1) and (2), respectively. These formalizations disambiguate the English sentences that are essentially like the ones Meinong uttered. Moreover, the fact that the representations are derivable suggest why Meinong considered his utterances to be true *a priori*. Such claims are non-logical theorems of the theory of objects, and as such, can be derived and known *a priori*. But more importantly, (1b) and (2b) are consistent with (3a), consistent with the fact that the descriptions in (1a) and (2a) fail to denote, and consistent with the fact that (1a) and (2a) are false.

In [1983], we generalized this analytical technique to any arbitrary description of English that is used in the way Meinong used descriptions (p. 48). Suppose that 'the $G_1, \ldots, G_n$' is such an arbitrary English

---

[5] Actually, there are lots of other options in the logic of encoding besides the following, but for now, we are going to discuss the simplest that does the job.

description, where the 'G_i' is a predicative adjective, predicative noun, relative clause, etc. Now consider the following formal description:

(e) $(\imath x)(\forall F)(xF \equiv F = G_1 \vee \ldots \vee F = G_n)$

This denotes the unique A-object that encodes just the properties $G_1, \ldots, G_n$. Clearly, any English sentence of the form "The $G_1, \ldots, G_n$ is G_i" ($1 \leq i \leq n$) can be analyzed as a truth by using (e). Where '$(\imath x)\psi_2$' is an abbreviation of (e), the analysis of such a sentence is: $(\imath x)\psi_2 G_i$.

This reading validates Meinong's particular way of using arbitrary definite descriptions as if they had denotations. Though it suggests that he used ambiguous language, there is an interpretation of his words on which his claims turn out to be true. To analyze assertions such as (1) and (2), we do not have to attribute Principle (B) to him. The same is true of the controversial assertions involved in the other Russellian objections. Sentences (5) and (6) seem to be true. To see what truths they express, consider the following description, constructed according to the procedure just described:

(f) $(\imath x)(\forall F)(xF \equiv F = \bar{S} \vee F = S)$

Description (f) has a denotation! It denotes the unique A-object that encodes just the property of being non-square and the property of being square. These facts allow us to formulate true readings of (5) and (6). To simplify these readings, we abbreviate (f) as '$(\imath x)\psi_3$':

(5b) $(\imath x)\psi_3 S$

(6b) $(\imath x)\psi_3 \bar{S}$

(5b) and (6b) are both true. They are derived from the principles of our theory, not from Principle (B). Moreover, they are consistent with the laws of classical logic. No contradictions follow from the fact that an A-object encodes a property and its negation.

Finally, note that statement (7) also receives a true reading. Given the procedure outlined above, we may use the following formal description to interpret 'the existent golden mountain':

(g) $(\imath x)(\forall F)(xF \equiv F = E! \vee F = G \vee F = M)$

Let us abbreviate (g) as '$(\imath x)\psi_4$.' Then the following sentence provides an analyses of (7) that preserve its intuitive truth value and entailments:

(7b) $(\imath x)\psi_4 E!$ & $(\imath x)\psi_4 G$ & $(\imath x)\psi_4 M$

Clearly, (7b) is a theorem, and hence, true. It is consistent with (9a), which asserts that nothing jointly exemplifies existence, goldenness, and mountainhood.[6]

In retrospect, I think fair-minded philosophers will want to say that Russell and Meinong were both defending views that have a great deal of truth to them. The charitable way to read Russell is that he correctly argued against the truth of Principle (B). The charitable way to read Meinong is that he correctly believed that every description of natural language could be used to specify an object which in some sense "has" the properties involved in the description. By viewing the debate in this way, we can see that Russell and Meinong were not all that far apart. In fact, the Russell of [1903] embraced the view that there are objects which have being but which don't exist. But when it became apparent that a basic principle connected with this view predicted logical, non-logical, and contingent falsehoods, Russell was forced to retreat. For without Mally's distinctions in hand, such appearances were practical certainties. It is, of course, a cruel mistake to regard Meinong as a kind of villainous philosophical adversary who committed outrageous fallacies.

7.3   Names, Descriptions, and Fiction[7]

Now that Russell's objections to Meinongian metaphysics have been disarmed, we can focus our attention on the analysis of names and descriptions that are grounded in fiction. Once this analysis is clear, we should be in a good position to explain the failures of *Existential* Generalization.

An important assumption underlying the theory of fiction is that simple English sentences containing proper names or descriptions that fail to denote are not true. In the case of proper names, we take an even stronger view: a simple English sentence containing a proper name that fails to denote is not even meaningful. In our view, if a simple sentence is meaningful, and the denotation of the names in the sentence are traced through the causal/contextual chain of reference, one will find one of two things: (a) that the first use of the name introduced or baptized an ordinary object, or (b) that the first use of the name was connected with a story of some kind, in which the name introduced or

---

[6]Note also that we have a reading for Meinong's cryptic reply to Russell, which was cited in the above passage from Russell's [1907] review in *Mind*. Meinong's reply was, "The existent golden mountain is existent, but doesn't exist." We may read this as: $(\imath x)\psi_4 E!$ & $\sim E!(\imath x)\psi_4$. That is, the existent golden mountain encodes existence, but doesn't exemplify existence. Russell was clearly justified in rejecting Meinong's cryptic reply, but on our interpretation, Meinong said something true.

[7]The material in this section is adapted from and expands upon the material in [1983], Chapter IV, Section 4.

baptized a character in that story. Suppose "...D..." is an English sentence in which 'D' appears to be a name. If 'D' does not denote an ordinary object, and if no story whatsoever is connected with 'D,' there is no reason to think that the sentence in question is even meaningful. Indeed, there is no reason to think that D is even a name.

An example may help. Leverrier used the name 'Vulcan' to refer to the planet that allegedly perturbs Mercury's orbit. It turned out that his theory was incorrect, that such a planet doesn't exist. Nevertheless, the name 'Vulcan' is meaningful. For one thing, it makes sense, or is meaningful, to assert that the object in question doesn't exist. That is, had one of Leverrier's colleagues, for example, gone to him and said "Vulcan doesn't exist," not only would the claim be meaningful, it would have been true. The reason it is true is that 'Vulcan' denotes an object that doesn't exist. When we trace the reference of 'Vulcan' back through the causal/contextual history of its use, we get back to a story, namely, Leverrier's piece of science fiction. In the context of this story, 'Vulcan' names a certain character, namely, the object that, according to the story, perturbs Mercury's orbit. If there is not at least a story to anchor the use of the alleged name, it seems reasonable to suppose that the expression in question is not a name. This would call into question the very meaningfulness of sentences containing the expression.

This view requires us to say something about stories and characters, and indeed, our theory has a lot to say about them. Every story is connected with a group of propositions that are true in the story. For each story s, intuitive judgments of the form "According to s, F^0" are taken as basic. Though we may disagree about which propositions are true in the story, the very concept of a story presupposes that some propositions, and not others, are true in the story. In our theory, stories are identified as situations that have authors, where the notion of authorship is taken to be a reasonably well-understood primitive.[8] Consequently, since situations are technically defined as A-objects that encode just propositional properties of the form $[\lambda y\ F^0]$, we can analyze the judgment "According to story s, F^0" as: $s[\lambda y\ F^0]$. That is, "According to story s, F^0" is taken to mean: s encodes being such that F^0. Let us abbreviate this analysis as: $\Sigma_s F^0$. So a particular story s is identified as the A-object that encodes just the propositional properties $[\lambda y\ F^0]$ such that $\Sigma_s F^0$. We shall assume that the following principle, which involves the notion of relevant entailment ($\overset{R}{\Rightarrow}$) governs the story operator. Any

---

[8]Intuitively, to author a story, one has to delineate a group of propositions and designate them as the truths of the story. The various ways of doing this yield the various kinds of fiction. Note that, unlike worlds, stories are situations that need not be maximal or consistent.

proposition relevantly implied by a proposition true in a story is also true in that story. In formal terms: $[\Sigma_s F^0 \;\&\; (F^0 \overset{R}{\Rightarrow} G^0)] \rightarrow \Sigma_s G^0$.[9]

This identification of stories is essential to the identification of characters, since the notion of a character is story relative. An individual x is a *character* of story s just in case: $(\exists F)(\Sigma_s Fx)$. So a character of a story is any object x such that there is a property x exemplifies in the story. Though this definition permits real individuals to be characters of stories, we are interested in the fictional characters. Fictional characters differ from other characters by the fact that they originate in stories. An individual x *originates in* story s just in case: (i) x is abstract, (ii) x is a character of s, and (iii) x is not a character of any story authored before s.[10] So let us say that x is *fictional* just in case x originates in some story. Now a fictional character x that originates in story s is to be identified with the A-object that encodes just the properties F such that according to s, Fx. This may be captured formally as follows:

$$Originates(x, s) \rightarrow (\forall F)(xF \equiv \Sigma_s Fx)$$

In light of the principle that governs the story operator, this means that a fictional character x encodes not only the properties explicitly attributed to x in the storytelling, but also those that are relevantly implied by these properties, since these are part of the story.

These ideas allow us to represent English names and descriptions grounded in stories as names and descriptions of A-objects. The English sentence "According to *The Iliad*, Hector is a Trojan warrior" has the following simple analysis, where 'i' denotes *The Iliad*, 'h' denotes Hector, and 'W' denotes the property of being a Trojan warrior: $\Sigma_i Wh$. In other words, *The Iliad* encodes the property of being such that Hector is a Trojan warrior. The sentence "Sherlock Holmes inspired Mickey Spillane" has the following simple analysis, where the abbreviations are obvious: $I(h, s)$. If Holmes is the principal character of the Conan Doyle novels, then it follows that the principal character of the Conan Doyle novels inspired Mickey Spillane. This inference has a straightforward reading in our logic. Let 'c' denote the Conan Doyle novels (considered as one very long, possibly inconsistent, story), and let '$(\imath x)Pxc$' represent 'the x such that x is the principal character of c.' The inference in question, therefore, is formally represented as the move from 'Ihs' and '$h = (\imath x)Pxc$' to '$I((\imath x)Pxc, s)$.' This captures the apparent logic of the informal inference.

---

[9]Of course, this principle inherits the obscurity that attaches to the notion of relevant entailment. But it is just this kind of vague notion that seems to govern our judgments about what is true in the story.

[10]Strictly speaking, the notion 'F^0 occurs before G^0' needs to be defined or axiomatized before this definition is completely precise.

A wide variety of descriptions behave in this way, once we suppose that they have a denotational reading. There is no general procedure for producing this reading—theoretical common sense has to be our guide. There are basically three kinds of descriptions that denote nonexistents. The first kind consists of Meinongian descriptions such as 'the round square,' 'the existent golden mountain,' and 'the set of non-self-membered sets,' as well as descriptions such as 'the fountain of youth,' and 'the Loch Ness monster.' In each of these cases, there is a story that grounds the description. This seems to be true even of 'the round square,' 'the existent golden mountain,' and 'the set of non-self-membered sets,' though the story involved may be one that the user of the description has left implicit. Consequently, the descriptions in this group, so grounded, involve only properties exemplified according to the story.

A denotational reading for these descriptions is produced by placing the story operator directly after the description operator. To see some examples, let s_1 and s_2 be the legends that ground 'the fountain of youth' and 'the Loch Ness monster,' respectively. Also, let 'F' denote the property of being a fountain the waters of which confer everlasting life, and let 'M' denote the property of being a monster that inhabits Loch Ness. Then we may formulate the following two descriptions: '$(\imath x)\Sigma_{s_1} Fx$' and '$(\imath x)\Sigma_{s_2} Mx$.'[11] This technique works even for descriptions like 'the round square.' Meinong and Russell both used this description, and they probably grounded it with the same story: the round square is round; the round square is square. Call the A-object that encodes just these two propositions 's_3'. Then, '$(\imath x)\Sigma_{s_3}(Rx \ \& \ Sx)$' denotes the A-object that encodes just roundness and squareness, since those are all and only the properties attributed to the round square in s_3. This is a somewhat more general analysis of 'Meinongian' descriptions than the analysis offered in Section 2.

The second group consists of descriptions like 'Meinong's most controversial impossible object,' 'the principal character of story s' and 'Kafka's most famous character.' These typically do not involve any properties that are attributed to the character in the story. Rather, these descriptions involve philosophical notions such as 'impossible,' 'character' and 'story,' which may be definable in theoretical terms. They also involve properties such as being controversial, being famous, being inspirational, etc., which are exemplified by the objects in question.

Finally, there is a group of descriptions that have mixed character. Some examples are 'the god most venerated by the ancient Greeks,' and

---

[11] A full discussion of how such formal descriptions succeed in picking out the right object may be found in [1983], pp. 97–99.

'the fountain Ponce de Leon searched for.' Some of the properties involved, like being a god and being a fountain, are exemplified in the story, while others, such as being venerated by the ancient Greeks and being searched for by Ponce de Leon, are exemplified *simpliciter*. The formal descriptions that provide denotational readings for these descriptions have to reflect this mixed character.

7.4   The Principles of Generalization

With this brief sketch of the analysis of names and descriptions grounded in fiction, we have looked at a wide enough variety of intensional contexts to reconsider the questions posed by *Existential* Generalization. A central question is, why is it that some sentences seem to obey Existential Generalization yet fail *Existential* Generalization? Ordinary, non-intensional sentences appear to obey both principles. For example, from "Ronald Reagan married Nancy Reagan," we can infer both "Something married something" and "Something that exists married something that exists." It may be best, however, to regard the second inference as an enthymeme, where the suppressed premise is: If something marries something, then the things in question exist. So the logic of the second inference is best represented as the inference (where the abbreviations are obvious) from 'Mrn' and '$(\forall x)(\forall y)(Mxy \rightarrow E!x \ \& \ E!y)$' to '$(\exists x)(\exists y)(E!x \ \& \ E!y \ \& \ Mxy)$.' Of course, the first inference is represented as the move from 'Mrn' to '$(\exists x)(\exists y)Mxy$.'

If this is right, then as far as *Existential* Generalization is concerned, there is nothing special about intensional verbs such as 'inspires,' 'search for,' and 'think about,' since, strictly speaking, all verbs fail this principle. The interesting question becomes why these intensional verbs (which are now to be identified by the fact that they are not governed by non-logical principles requiring their arguments to denote existing objects) obey the principle of Existential Generalization. And this question, of course, is something to which our theory and logic provide an answer. The semantic reason we may infer "Something inspired Mickey Spillane" from "Holmes inspired Mickey Spillane" is the simple fact that the name 'Holmes' denotes something. The logic of this argument is, therefore, very simple: '$(\exists x)Ixs$' follows from 'Ihs' by Existential Generalization. In fact, it has the same logic as the argument whereby "Something inspired Colonel North" is inferred from "Reagan inspired Colonel North." Note also that from "According to the Conan Doyle novels, Holmes is a detective" and "Holmes inspired Mickey Spillane" it follows that "Something which is a detective according to the Conan Doyle novels inspired Mickey Spillane." If 's_4' denotes the Conan Doyle novels, then the logic of this argument is this: from '$\Sigma_{s_4} Dh$' and 'Ihs'

it follows that '$(\exists y)((\Sigma_{s_4} Dy)\ \&\ Iys)$.' Unlike the other treatments proposed for these inferences, our treatment achieves generality through its simplicity. No "special dodges" have been adopted, since none of these arguments have been singled out for special consideration.[12]

This simple analysis extends to somewhat more involved arguments. Recall the following argument:

> Mythical characters don't exist.
> Jupiter is a mythical character.
> Augustus Caesar worshipped Jupiter.
> Therefore, Caesar worshipped something that doesn't exist.

To represent this argument, note that a mythical character is essentially just a fictional character, except that the story in which it originates is a myth. So let us define:[13]

$$Mythological(x) =_{df} (\exists s)(Myth(s)\ \&\ Originates(x,s))$$

We may therefore represent the argument under consideration as follows:

$(\forall x)(Mythological(x) \rightarrow {\sim} E!x)$
$Mythological(j)$
Wcj
Therefore, $(\exists x)({\sim} E!x\ \&\ Wcx)$

Clearly, this argument is valid.

Consider next the use of Existential Generalization on descriptions of nonexistent objects. From "Russell thought about the round square" (which is surely true, given what Russell says in his reviews of Meinong), it follows that "Russell thought about something." With the denotational reading of 'the round square' presented in the previous section, the analysis of this argument is straightforward: from '$Tr(\imath x)\Sigma_{s_3}(Rx\ \&\ Sx)$,' it follows that '$(\exists y)Try$.' Moreover, from the claim that "The round square doesn't exist" (i.e., ${\sim} E!(\imath x)\Sigma_{s_3}(Rx\ \&\ Sx)$), it follows that "Russell thought about something that doesn't exist" (i.e., $(\exists y)({\sim} E!y\ \&\ Try)$). Note that the quantifier in the conclusion has scope over the entire sentence.

There are two final points to make concerning these inferences. The first is that Existential Generalization is legitimate even on names and descriptions that fall under the scope of the story operator. Though we

---

[12] Recall the remark in Lewis [1978] in which he admits that "Meinongian" treatments like the above have the advantage in the analysis of these sentences (p. 38).

[13] Though our logical principles do not automatically guarantee that there are such properties as being mythological and being fictional (the defining conditions contain encoding subformulas), we conjecture that the hypothesis that there are such properties is a safe one.

have already seen one example of this, here is another. From "According to the Beowulf legend, Grendel terrorizes Hrothgar," it follows that "Something is such that, according to the Beowulf legend, it terrorizes Hrothgar." Nothing stands in the way of giving this inference a standard analysis: from '$\Sigma_b T g h$' it follows that '$(\exists x)\Sigma_b T x h$.' The second point is that the anaphoric uses of the pronoun 'it,' in which the antecedent is a name or description of a nonexistent, have a straightforward semantic explanation. Such uses of 'it' simply pick up the denotation of the antecedent. Anaphora involving names and descriptions of nonexistents is no different from anaphora involving names and descriptions of existing objects.

These suggestions unify the quantificational logic of both names and descriptions of nonexistents. The principles of Existential and *Existential* Generalization work in a straightforward way. One can always use Existential Generalization on names and descriptions that refer to nonexistents, though *Existential* Generalization is justified only if the hypothesis that the object in question exists is added. Such hypotheses may implicitly govern non-intensional relations, such as *marry*, *kick*, and *meet*.

By way of comparison, Russell's treatment of these inferences fails rather badly, since it turns non-trivially valid applications of Existential Generalization into trivially valid ones. This is an unfortunate consequence of the theory of descriptions that has received little attention. For example, the inference from "Russell thought about the round square" to "Russell thought about something" is indeed valid on Russell's analysis. Since both the premise and conclusion are represented as existential claims, every interpretation in which the premise is true is an interpretation in which the conclusion is true. But in every interpretation in which 'being round' and 'being square' denote the properties they in fact denote, the premise is false. The inference, therefore, becomes trivially valid.

8

Meinong's Recent Resurrection

In the previous two chapters, we put A-objects to work solving the puzzles about the intentional objects of thought and about the intensional failures of *Existential* Generalization. In so doing, we found a way to reconcile the views of Meinong and Husserl. The special logic associated with A-objects, namely, the logic of encoding, offers new possibilities for interpreting these authors.

However, most of the philosophers reinvestigating Meinong's work have labored within the bounds of traditional exemplification logic. Such philosophers would argue that Meinong intended his metaphysical assertions to be exemplification predications. But it is difficult to determine whether this claim is true, for Meinong did not use formal logic to express his views. Since he expressed his philosophical views only in natural language, his philosophical use of the predicative copula 'is' was probably a considered use. Nevertheless, if the copula has the kind of ambiguity that we've suggested, it is unclear just what kind of weight should be given to Meinong's considered words. From our point of view, Meinong's insistence on questionable metaphysical assertions is better thought of as his recognition that *there is at least some sense* in which those assertions are true.

In this chapter, we would like to show how hard it is to protect Meinong from inconsistency when exemplification logic alone is used as an analytic tool. We shall catalog the prices that have to be paid to square Meinong's views with the principles of classical exemplification logic. The focus will be on those theories that make minor adjustments to classical logic in order to interpret Meinong's views in a consistent way.[1]

---

[1] This means that we shall not consider Richard Routley's [1980] theory of Meinongian objects, since his theory makes radical alterations to classical logic. His

8.1 Parsons' Theory of Meinongian Objects

In the last chapter, we saw that Mally's exemplification/encoding distinction undermines three distinct Russellian objections. However, Mally developed another useful distinction, one that provides a second way to respond to Russell's objections. This is the distinction between nuclear and extranuclear properties. Recently, Terence Parsons employed this distinction to develop a rigorous Meinongian theory that is consistent with classical axioms of propositional logic. He defended Meinong's views by offering a logically clear and coherent response to Russell. The defense is found in his book of [1980], and it is instructive to compare Parsons' defense of Meinong with our own.

Unlike our theory, in which the world is divided up into relations and two basic kinds of objects (ordinary and abstract), Parsons' theory divides the world up into a single kind of object and two kinds of relations (nuclear and extranuclear). The nuclear relations and properties include: being red, being round, being a horse, being winged, loves, kicks, meet, etc. These are rather ordinary when compared to the extranuclear relations, which include: think about, worships, being possible, being mythical, existence, etc. The extranuclear relations include the ontological, intentional, and modal relations. Parsons' logic involves just the notion of exemplification, and his comprehension axiom for objects asserts that for every condition on *nuclear* properties, there is an object that exemplifies just the properties satisfying the condition. In what follows, familiarity with Parsons' views will be presupposed—in particular, we shall suppose that the reader is familiar with the nuclear/extranuclear distinction and with the relationships between the two kinds of relations.[2] In what follows, we shall use the upper case variables F, G, ..., to range over extranuclear relations, and the lower case variables f, g, ..., to range over nuclear relations.

Russell's three objections were based on the belief that Meinong adopted Principle (B) (i.e., that $(\exists y)y = (\imath x)\phi$, for every formula ϕ). Parsons agrees that the unrestricted comprehension schema embodied by Principle (B) is inconsistent. However, he develops readings on which 'the round square,' 'the non-square square,' and 'the existent golden mountain' denote objects. Consider the following description from Parsons' framework:

(a) $(\imath x)(\forall f)(fx \equiv f = r \lor f = s)$

---

theory is based upon "para-consistent logic," which "permits" contradictions but does not permit the derivation of every formula from them.

[2]In Parsons' theory, every extranuclear property is mapped down to a nuclear property that serves as its "watered-down" version. However, distinct extranuclear properties sometimes get mapped to the same nuclear property.

Description (a) denotes the object that *exemplifies* just nuclear roundness ('r') and nuclear squareness ('s'). That there is a unique such object
is guaranteed by Parsons' abstraction and identity principles for objects.
Now reconsider the premises in Russell's first objection: (1) The round
square is round, (2) The round square is square, and (3) If something
is square then it is not the case that it is round. Parsons offers the
following analyses of (1) and (2), where '$(\imath x)\chi_1$' abbreviates description
(a):

(1') $r(\imath x)\chi_1$

(2') $s(\imath x)\chi_1$

Here, (1') asserts that the object that exemplifies nuclear roundness and
nuclear squareness exemplifies nuclear roundness. (2') asserts that this
same object exemplifies nuclear squareness. Clearly, these two readings
analyze (1) and (2) as truths, since on Parsons theory, (1') and (2') are
derivable as theorems.

   However, unlike our theory, the true readings of (1) and (2) are
incompatible with a straightforward understanding of (3). The straightforward translation of (3) into Parsons' system would appear to be (3'):

(3') $(\forall x)(sx \rightarrow \sim rx)$

But if so, then Russell's objection still has its force, for (1'), (2') and (3')
are inconsistent. To avoid this consequence, Parsons argues that (3') is
false. His rather ingenious argument is that (3') is far too broad a claim,
since the quantifier in (3') ranges over both the possible and "impossible"
objects. On Parsons' view, (3') is true only if the quantifier is restricted
to the domain of possible objects. He argues that nonexistent, impossible
objects may indeed exemplify incompatible properties. Parsons' reply
is persuasive from the point of view of his theory, but from our point
of view, he appears to have complicated the traditional understanding
of what it is to exemplify a property. What is it for an object, even
an impossible one, to exemplify being square, if its doing so does not
rule out its being round? In our framework, everything whatsoever that
exemplifies being square fails to exemplify being round.

   To respond to Russell's second objection, Parsons banishes the true
negations of nuclear properties from his system. To see this, let '$\bar{s}$' denote
the nuclear property of being non-square ('$\bar{s}$' abbreviates the nuclear λ-
expression '$[\lambda^N y \sim sy]$'). In Parsons' theory, the following description
denotes the object that exemplifies just the nuclear properties of being
square and being non-square:

(b) $(\imath x)(\forall f)(fx \equiv f = s \vee f = \bar{s})$

Reconsider, then, the premises of Russell's second objection: (5) The non-square square is square, and (6) The non-square square is non-square. Parsons has the following true representations for (5) and (6), where '$(\imath x)\chi_2$' abbreviates description (b):

(5') $s(\imath x)\chi_2$

(6') $\bar{s}(\imath x)\chi_2$

Both (5') and (6') are derivable from Parsons' abstraction and identity principles for objects. However, in contrast to our theory, the true reading given to (6) doesn't involve the genuine negation of the property involved in the true reading given to (5). The following principle can not be an axiom of Parsons' theory:

(D) $(\forall g)(\forall x)([\lambda^N y \ {\sim}gy]x \equiv {\sim}gx)$

Were this principle true, one could derive the negation of (5') from (6'). Therefore, Parsons' must argue that the standard law governing property negation does not apply to the negations of nuclear properties. Instead, they are governed by the following law:

(E) $(\forall x)(E!x \rightarrow ([\lambda^N y \ {\sim}sy]x \equiv {\sim}sx))$

So in Parsons theory, the nuclear negation of a simple nuclear property has in its extension all and only those *existing* objects (i.e., objects exemplifying extranuclear existence) that fail to exemplify the nuclear property. In general, Parsons' theory employs the following λ-abstraction principle for complex nuclear properties ([1980], p. 104):

(F) $(\forall x)(E!x \rightarrow ([\lambda^N y \ \phi]x \equiv \phi_y^x))$

Given this explanation, it appears that Parsons has employed the same strategy to undermine both objections. The strategy seems to be: restrict the range of the quantifier in the relevant laws (the relevant laws being (3') and (D)). But the strategies may differ. Whereas (3') is a non-logical principle, (D) seems to be a principle governing the logical behavior of nuclear properties. If so, then restricting (D) is a much more serious matter than restricting (3'), and it may constitute a different strategy. It appears that in Parsons' system, one cannot explain Russell's second objection and retain the usual understanding of negation. This may be contrasted with our system, where it is an axiom that every property has a genuine negation. Our defense against Russell's second objection doesn't require that restrictions be placed on the negations of any relations.

Parsons' defense against Russell's third objection seems more appealing, since it doesn't involve restricting any principles. His defense centers on the traditionally problematic notion of existence. The defense is that the description 'the existent golden mountain' denotes an object that exemplifies nuclear existence, goldenness, and mountainhood. However, it does not exemplify the most important kind of existence, namely, extranuclear existence. Recall the premise and conclusion of this objection: (7) The existent golden mountain is existent, golden, and a mountain, and (8) Some golden mountain exists. This conclusion is incompatible with the following fact: (9) No golden mountains exist. Parsons' response, therefore, is that the word "existence" as it appears in (8) doesn't signify what it signifies in (9). Consider the following description, where '$e!$' denotes nuclear existence, 'g' denotes nuclear goldenness, and 'm' denotes nuclear mountainhood:

(c) $(\imath x)(\forall f)(fx \equiv f = e! \lor f = g \lor f = m)$

Parsons uses description (c), which we abbreviate as '$(\imath x)\chi_3$,' to produce the following, true reading of (7):

(7') $e!(\imath x)\chi_3$ & $g(\imath x)\chi_3$ & $m(\imath x)\chi_3$

Moreover, Parsons' reading of (9) is (9'):

(9') $\sim(\exists x)(E!x$ & gx & $mx)$

That is, nothing exemplifies *extranuclear* existence, nuclear goldenness, and nuclear mountainhood. Clearly, (7') and (9') are consistent, since all that follows from (7') is:

(8') $(\exists x)(e!x$ & gx & $mx)$

So Parsons' defense against Russell's third objection does show that Meinongian principles do not conflict with contingent facts.

Parsons' defense against the third objection employs a hypothesis that seems rather different from the hypotheses employed to defend against the first two. Against the third objection, he utilizes a hypothesis about the meaning of 'exists,' whereas against the first two objections, he requires hypotheses about the range of certain quantifiers in both logical and non-logical contexts. By way of contrast, our defense against all three objections depends on the same two hypotheses, namely, that 'is' can also be read as 'encodes,' and that descriptions of the form 'the $G_1,\ldots,G_n$,' when used in Meinong's way, have readings on which they denote A-objects that encode the properties $G_1,\ldots,G_n$. Whether this explanatory elegance has any overriding merit must be left for the reader to decide.

8.2   A Strict Understanding of Meinong[3]

There is a strict understanding of Meinong's views that has been emphasized in the recent literature, and in the final sections of this chapter, we shall dissect this understanding piece by piece. The story we told in Chapter 6 about Brentano's puzzle, Meinong's solution, and the refined Meinongian solution based on Mally's ideas was cast in rather simple terms. But the literature on Meinong has grown to be very sophisticated, and recently, many philosophers have agreed that Meinong had a somewhat different solution to Brentano's puzzle. These scholars believe that Meinong's leading idea was not simply that there are nonexistent objects, but that there are objects which have no being whatsoever.

Recall the discussion of Meinong's solution to Brentano's puzzle in Chapter 6. A naive analysis of "Russell thought about the round square" seemed to require an object that really exemplifies roundness and squareness. It is not good enough simply to deny that such an object exists, i.e., deny that it fails to have a location in space (and time). For any object that exemplifies roundness and squareness, even a nonexistent one, is incompatible with the non-logical axiom that if a thing exemplifies being square then it fails to exemplify being round. Meinong seemed to be aware of this problem, and remarks he made in response have led recent scholars to attribute to him the view that the round square not only fails to exist, but has no being whatsoever. Indeed, Meinong seems to posit a domain of objects that "stand outside" of being.[4] On this understanding, then, the first principle of Meinongian metaphysics is the following:

(G) There are objects that have no being whatsoever.

The following authors understand Meinong in this way: Chisholm [1973], van Inwagen [1977], Routley [1980], Lambert [1983], and Smith [1985].

This understanding of Meinong is quite severe. The problem with it is that (G) is logically false. The standard logical analysis of Principle (G) is the following:

(G′) $(\exists x) \sim (\exists y)(y = x)$

There is no interpretation under which (G′) is true. If this is Meinong's view, then it would seem that he has made an egregious mistake. In Meinong's defense, it must be noted that Meinong prefaced his assertion of (G) with the disclaimer "one who was fond of paradoxical expression could ... say" ([1904a], p. 83). However, there are philosophers who,

---

[3]Some of the points made in this section were sketched in [1986].

[4]This is his realm of *Aussersein*; see his [1904a], §IV.

though clearly aware of this disclaimer, not only seem to attribute Principle (G) to Meinong, but view it as an insight and try to defend it. For example, Chisholm takes Principle (G) to be more clearly expressed by the claim "an object may have a set of characteristics whether or not it exists and whether or not it has any other kind of being" ([1973], p. 245). Actually, Chisholm's restatement of (G) is a paraphrase of another principle, Mally's Principle of Independence, upon which we shall focus later.[5] But Chisholm believes that his restatement captures the truth that lies behind (G), and he suggests that it is one of Meinong's most basic insights (p. 245).

Unfortunately, however, Chisholm never offers an analysis of his informal understanding of (G). It seems to be nothing more than the claim that there are objects that exemplify properties even though they have no being whatsoever. In logical notation, this is cashed out as: $(\exists x)((\exists F)Fx \ \& \sim(\exists y)(y=x))$. However, this is logically false as well (it implies Principle (G)). It is hard to regard it as an insight when there is no interpretation under which it is true. So Chisholm never explains how objects such as unicorns, golden mountains, and round squares can "have" properties and still fail to be something.

A philosopher who directly attributes Principle (G) to Meinong with no hedging is K. Lambert. Consider this passage from his [1983]:

> Meinong held that *existent* objects are objects having a location in space-time; objects not spatio-temporally locatable but nevertheless having being he called *subsistent* objects .... But what really sets Meinong apart from the majority of philosophers, however, is not the distinction between two kinds of being an object might possess [footnote] ...; rather it is his belief in *nonsubsistent objects*, objects that have neither existence nor subsistence (nor any other kind of being). ... most Meinong scholars agree that Meinong's most widely promulgated (and most interesting) insight is that there are objects having no being in some appropriate sense of 'there are.' (pp. 13–14)

So we find the view that Meinong's central doctrine ("what really sets him apart") is Principle (G).

Unfortunately, Lambert never tells us what sense of 'there are' makes Principle (G) true. He offers no direct analysis of (G). In fact, Lambert says some rather confusing things in this regard, which suggest that he doesn't really think that Principle (G) is Meinong's central doctrine. His

---

[5]Mally's Principle of Independence is: An object's having properties (*Sosein*), that is, its being such and such, is independent of its having being (*Sein*) (Mally [1904], p. 126; my paraphrase).

most damaging testimony comes when he claims that Terence Parsons, in his book of [1980], "champions something very much like Meinong's theory" ([1983], p.38). And he says later:

> Terence Parsons' *Nonexistent Objects* has provided a clear characterization of something analogous to the Meinongian conception of an object, and it is easily verifiable in that semantic account that not all objects have being. (p. 127)

The second conjunct of this statement is clearly false. To see why, note that Lambert's notion of 'being' squares pretty much with our own. He defines 'x has being' as: $[\lambda y\ (\exists z)(z=y)]x$ (p. 55). So the claim that there are objects that fail to have being, that is, $(\exists x)\sim[\lambda y\ (\exists z)(z=y)]x$, is a logical falsehood. But no such falsehood is derivable on Parsons' theory. On his theory, it is derivable that: $\sim(\exists x)\sim(\exists z)(z=x)$. By λ-abstraction, it follows that $\sim(\exists x)\sim[\lambda y\ (\exists z)(z=y)]x$. These consequences of Parsons theory directly contradict Principle (G). Parsons' theory implies that there are nonexistent objects, but it denies that there are "beingless objects."

So not only is Lambert wrong when he says that, on Parsons' theory, not all objects have being, but his claim that Parsons' theory is "very much like" Meinong's theory seems to be incompatible with his claim that Meinong's central doctrine is Principle (G). Actually, a careful reading of Lambert reveals that although he attributes (G) to Meinong, he never offers (G') as its analysis. Instead, given his definition of 'being,' it looks like he would offer the following analysis of (G):

(G'') $(\exists x)\sim([\lambda y\ (\exists z)z=y]x)$

Clearly, (G'') is equivalent to (G'), by λ-abstraction. In standard exemplification logic with identity, both are logical falsehoods from which contradictions may be derived in a few simple steps. But unlike (G'), one cannot derive a contradiction from (G'') without using the principle of λ-abstraction. And, indeed, Lambert believes that the best interpretation of Meinong requires the rejection of the principle of λ-abstraction. So by attributing Principle (G) to Meinong, analyzing (G) as (G''), and rejecting λ-abstraction, Lambert is able to defend Meinong against the charge of inconsistency. Unfortunately, that is not the same as providing an interpretation under which (G) or (G'') is true.[6] And what's more, Lambert's reasons for rejecting λ-abstraction are not good ones. This is a topic reserved for the last section, however.

---

[6] The inner domain/outer domain semantics for free logic that Lambert discusses (p. 15, footnote 8) is not a semantics in which (G'') is true. Nor are Quinean "virtual classes" or the other "virtual objects" he discusses (pp. 8, 98) genuine examples of "beingless objects."

Consequently, the strict understanding of Meinong, as embodied by Chisholm, Lambert, and others, does not attribute a clear insight to Meinong. The notion of a "beingless object" is completely mysterious, and none of these authors offers us any real understanding of what such things might be. Analyses of intentionality that invoke such a notion simply inherit its obscurity. Our theory, like Parsons', rejects this notion. Given our definitions for the identity symbol, it is easy to derive the negation of (G′). From our point of view, it seems clear that Meinong need not have committed himself to (G′) in order to explain the data of intentionality. However, it is interesting that the above-mentioned authors seem to think that there are some deep reasons compelling Meinong to assert such a claim, and it is instructive to try to understand what these reasons are.

8.3   Did Meinong Have to Commit Himself to Principle (G)?

Let us put aside the question, did Meinong in fact commit himself to Principle (G)? This is a scholarly question that we shall not try to answer here. Though the passages in which Meinong discusses the realm of *Aussersein* suggest that he did, there is some disagreement on this score. Instead, we shall be interested in the question of whether there are good reasons for trying to develop a coherent notion of a "beingless object." Are there data that would be better analyzed by appealing to "beingless objects" instead of A-objects? Why would anyone be tempted to develop such a notion?

To answer these questions, let us reconsider why Chisholm and Lambert believe that Meinong has to commit himself to Principle (G). When we try to isolate the reasons Chisholm cites for appealing to "beingless objects," we find only that *nonexistent* objects are required for the analysis of intentional states ([1973]):

> Meinong's best case, then, would seem to lie with those true *intentional* statements that seem to pertain to objects that do not exist. (p. 252)

The essential Meinongian doctrine required for the analysis of intentionality is not that there are "beingless objects," but rather that there are nonexistent objects of a certain kind. Such nonexistents must have (in some sense) the properties attributed to them in an intentional context (for example, the ghost John fears has to be a ghost in some sense, the set of all non-self-membered sets that Russell thought about has to be a set of all non-self-membered sets, in some sense).

When we try to track down the essential ideas that Lambert says forced Meinong to commit himself to "beingless objects," we're also left puzzled. At the end of an inconclusive passage ([1983], pp. 17–18) in which Lambert discusses Meinong's positive reasons for thinking there are "beingless objects," he directs us to the last section of Chapter 2, where we find:

> The deeper motive [for postulating nonsubsistent or "being-less" objects], one which Meinong does allude to now and then... can be expressed simply as the concern to explain how what he took to be clearly true statements, for example 'The *perpetuum mobile* is nonexistent' (in the broad and uni-vocal sense Quine attaches to the word 'nonexistent'), 'The round square is round,' and 'Goldberg thinks of the *perpetuum mobile*,' can be true. ... Similarly, he took the statements 'The round square is round' and 'The *perpetuum mobile* is nonexistent' to express attributions. It was quite natural, then, for Meinong to conclude that 'the round square' and 'the *perpetuum mobile*' stand for objects.... . The important question had to do with the character of these objects. (pp. 36–37)

In this passage, Lambert suggests that Meinong postulated "beingless objects" to account for the truth of certain sentences. We can agree with Lambert that Meinong was correct in positing objects to account for the data, but one of the alleged pieces of data Lambert produces must be challenged. "The *perpetuum mobile* is nonexistent" is *not* a datum when "existence" is given Quine's broad, and technical, sense. To claim that it is prejudges its analysis, by presupposing that the English sentence comes with a technical meaning already attached to its words. With such a presupposition, it is no wonder Lambert would think that Meinong is forced into adopting something like Principle (G).

The datum, of course, is just the English sentence "The *perpetuum mobile* doesn't exist," where 'exist' is a non-technical word. Given our pre-theoretical understanding of this word, we judge that the sentence is true. Though we may disagree on the best theoretical understanding of the word and sentence, we are not forced to postulate "beingless objects" for it to be true. By appealing to the story that grounds the description 'the *perpetuum mobile*,' we can represent 'the *perpetuum mobile*' as a description of an A-object, in the way described in the previous chapter.[7]

No piece of data directly entails Principle (G), not even the sentence "I am thinking about a beingless object." That's because data are

---

[7]The story might be: The *perpetuum mobile* is a machine that, once set into a cyclical motion, never ceases to move, even though it is totally disconnected from all external forces or power supplies.

expressed in non-technical language, whereas Principle (G) is a philosophical hypothesis, in which 'beingless object' is a technical term. The
deeper reasons why some philosophers seem tempted to make sense of
Principle (G) stem from the other data Lambert describes in this passage. Exemplification logic offers only one way to understand the nature
of the objects involved. Given the intuitions that underly this logic, it is
easy to discover reasons that may have led Meinong, Findlay, Chisholm,
Routley, Smith, and maybe even Lambert to the view that certain objects have to be "beingless."[8] Let us collate five such reasons.

The first reason is by now familiar. If we are to assign denotations
to 'the non-square square' or 'the round square' in exemplification logic,
then, as Parsons' work shows, we have to restrict logical and non-logical
laws. If we don't want to tinker with these laws, then something else
has to be done to prevent inconsistency. Exemplification logic offers
few alternatives, however. One possibility to consider is the notion of a
"beingless object." If clarified, this notion might evade the inconsistency.
It should be clear, however, that the theory of A-objects and the logic of
encoding offer an alternative that doesn't force us to try to make sense of
this notion. Objects that encode incompatible properties are consistent
with the logical and non-logical laws in question.

The second reason these philosophers may have had for seriously
considering this notion is the desire to avoid commitment to nonexistent objects that exemplify existence-entailing properties. A property
F is existence-entailing iff necessarily-always, anything that exemplifies F exemplifies existence. For example, being golden and being a
mountain seem to be existence-entailing properties. If so, then it is
rather puzzling to reconstruct "the golden mountain" as an object that
exemplifies goldenness and mountainhood but which fails to exemplify
existence. Unfortunately, however, exemplification logic offers no other
choice. To avoid this dilemma, one might be tempted to think that "the
golden mountain" has no being whatsoever, instead of saying that it
fails to exemplify existence. On our theory, however, there is no conflict, since the theory doesn't imply that nonexistent objects exemplify
existence-entailing properties.[9] It doesn't imply, for example, that anything exemplifies both goldenness and mountainhood. The notion of
"existence-entailing property" need not be abandoned or restricted.

The third reason why philosophers might have been attracted to the

---

[8]Lambert mentions frequently that free logicians don't quantify over "beingless
objects" (pp. 68, 97) and we take it, given his publications on free logic, that he
would not do so either. But we include him in this list because it is clear to readers
of his book that he believes that if 'the round square' were to denote an object, it
would denote a "beingless" one.

[9]This tension is present in Parson's reconstruction of Meinong, though he may have
some subtle way to undermine it.

notion of "beingless object" also stems from our traditional understanding of exemplification. Suppose, for example, that we know that some object x exemplifies being a mountain. It is part of our implicit knowledge of what it is to exemplify being a mountain that x exemplifies having some shape or other, that x has some location or other, that x is more than a meter in height, that x exemplifies not being a duck, that x is not made of styrofoam, etc. Here is another example. It is part of our implicit knowledge, when we know that y exemplifies being a detective, that we can hire y, shake y's hand, offer y money, etc. But we have to bracket such implicit knowledge if we are to accept that there is an object z that exemplifies just being golden and being mountain and no other properties, or if we are to accept that there is an object w that exemplifies just the properties attributed to Holmes in the novels.[10] In light of this, a philosopher might be attracted to the idea that though z and w exemplify the properties in question, respectively, they have no being. It might be thought that the implicit knowledge we have doesn't apply to "beingless objects."

We need not bracket any implicit knowledge for A-objects, however. Since our implicit knowledge that mountains aren't ducks, and that detectives aren't inanimate is exemplification knowledge, no bracketing is required to conceive of objects that encode just the properties of being a mountain and being golden, or just the properties attributed to Holmes in the novels. There is no tension with exemplification knowledge on this conception.

The fourth reason concerns logical completeness and modal closure. An object x is *complete* iff for every property F, either Fx or $\bar{F}x$. An object x is *closed* iff x exemplifies every property G necessarily implied by any property F that x exemplifies. Clearly, it follows on logical grounds alone that all objects are complete and closed. The supposition that there is an object that exemplifies just goldenness and mountainhood and no other properties is inconsistent with these logical theorems. On Parsons' theory, objects need not be complete nor closed with respect to nuclear properties, though every object is complete and closed with respect to the extranuclear properties.[11] But without the nuclear/extranuclear distinction, some other move is warranted. And that may be why "beingless objects" have seemed attractive.

---

[10]Again, this tension seems to be present in Parsons' reconstruction of Meinong.

[11]Since nuclear properties do not have true negations, one cannot derive the principle of completeness for nuclear properties. Nor can one derive the principle of closure for nuclear properties. On Parsons' theory, some objects do exemplify all of the properties "necessarily implied" by the properties they exemplify. But that's only because the notion of necessary implication for nuclear properties is defined as follows: f necessarily implies g iff $\Box(\forall x)(E!x \rightarrow (fx \rightarrow gx))$ (see Parsons [1980], pp. 106–107).

On our theory, all objects, including A-objects, are complete and closed with respect to the properties they exemplify. The following are both derivable as logical theorems: (a) $(\forall F)(\forall G)[Fx \ \& (F \Rightarrow G) \rightarrow Gx]$, and (b) $(\forall F)(\forall x)(Fx \ \lor \ \bar{F}x)$. No restrictions on any of the quantifiers are necessary, and our intuitive understanding of exemplification is preserved. There are, however, corresponding notions of completeness and closure that apply to encoded properties. Let us say: (a) x is *complete*[*] iff $(\forall F)(xF \ \lor \ x\bar{F})$, and (b) x is *closed*[*] iff $(\forall F)(\forall G)[xF \ \& \ (F \Rightarrow G) \rightarrow xG]$. It is easy to prove that there are A-objects that are neither complete[*] nor closed[*].

The final reason one might have for thinking there are "beingless objects" might be that the intentionality inherent in the very discussion of this notion requires them. Maybe the sentence, "I am thinking about a beingless object" requires that there be "beingless objects." But this reason is still undermined by the exemplification/encoding distinction. To see why, just stand back a bit and apply the theory at a deeper level to the language of this discussion. We need not believe that anything exemplifies being a beingless object (assuming that there is such a property). To analyze the alleged intentionality in this discussion, we can employ A-objects that encode this property. We can regard "beingless objects" as creatures of a philosophical fiction.

Mally's distinctions, therefore, undermine all of the reasons for trying to make sense out of Principle (G). They show that Meinong didn't have to accept Principle (G) to explain the data. Of course, scholars interested in the letter of Meinong's statements and not their spirit will continue to labor to produce a clear interpretation of Principle (G). To our knowledge, no one has yet succeeded in doing this. Such a task seems incompatible with the simple and natural laws of classical logic, and hence, incompatible with the idea that the proper axioms of metaphysics should not require revisions of the basic laws of logic. While it is of some interest to discover just which of these laws are incompatible with a strict reading of Meinong's words, it may be much more charitable to try to find an interpretation of Meinong's words that offer a classically consistent explanation of the data.

If this is right, then Meinong's most important contribution is not Principle (G), but the idea that there must be some unusual objects that account for intentionality. So, without trying to be revisionist historians of philosophy, we suggest that the following doctrines are what really set Meinong apart from his contemporaries:

- There are objects that, in some sense, are golden mountains, round squares, unicorns, ghosts, monsters, fictional characters, etc., and they play a role in (the analysis of) intentional acts and attitudes.

- Such objects are individuals, not properties or sets of properties.

- Such objects can be correlated with the formally possible combinations of properties.

- Such objects are not spatio-temporally located.

- There be many such objects that are, in some sense, incomplete.

- Sentences such as "the round square is round" are predications, in some sense, about these objects.

It seems that the real opposition between Meinong and Russell should be located among these doctrines.

8.4   The Principle of Independence[12]

Once Principle (G) goes, so does the infamous Principle of Independence. In his work of [1904], Mally asserted the following principle:

(H) An object can have properties (that is, be so and so), even though it lacks being.

Principle (H) has come to be known as the Principle of Independence. In his later work, Mally abandoned Principle (H), and with good reason. It is logically false if represented as the claim:

(H′) $(\exists x)((\exists F)Fx \ \& \ \sim(\exists y)y=x)$.

Mally did not need Principle (H) to explain the facts of intentionality in his later work. The notion of encoding a property gave him a means of "constituting" objects with the right sorts of properties required by the intentional phenomena. The objects so constituted are not beingless, and so there is no need to break the connection between being and being so and so (i.e., between *Sein* and *Sosein*).

Recently, K. Lambert has defended the Principle of Independence and concluded that Mally made a mistake in abandoning it. In his book [1983], Lambert offers an interpretation of this principle and argues that it is true. He doesn't analyze the principle in the material mode as a claim governing objects and properties. He doesn't describe a language and semantics in which (H′) is true. Instead, he analyzes (H) in the formal mode, and reads it as a metalinguistic assertion about the invalidity of a certain inference. Lambert analyzes Mally's Principle as the following claim: the inference from "$(\exists F)x$ exemplifies F" to "x has being" is invalid (p. 29). In formal terms, Lambert's interpretation of (H) is this:

---

[12]Some of the points made in this section were sketched in [1986].

the inference from '$(\exists F)Fx$' to '$(\exists y)y = x$' is invalid.[13]   His argument
for thinking that this reading of (H) is true has the following structure.
First, he establishes that, subject to a proviso, his interpretation of (H)
is equivalent to the failure of a traditional constraint on the principle of
exemplification predication (p. 52). Then, he argues that the traditional
constraint does indeed fail, because there are true predications that do
not conform to the constraint (pp. 152–156).

Lambert formulates the predication principle in question as follows: a
closed atomic exemplification formula is true iff the relation term applies
to the objects denoted by the object terms.[14] The traditional constraint
on this principle is that the object terms must all denote objects which
have being (p. 50). Note that this constraint would be violated if either
of the following two conditions were to obtain: (a) there are true atomic
predications having an object term that denotes a "beingless object,"
or (b) there are true atomic predications having an object term that
denotes nothing at all. So Lambert establishes the following link between
Meinong and the free logicians: Meinong thinks (a) is the reason the
constraint fails, whereas the free logicians think (b) is the reason. If
either is right, then the inference from "x exemplifies P" to "x has
being" is invalid. But then so is the inference from "$(\exists F)x$ exemplifies
F" to "x has being." Or so Lambert argues (p. 50).

An important proviso to Lambert's conclusion is that the princi-
ple of λ-abstraction (i.e., λ-*Equivalence*) has to be regarded as false.
Apparently, the truth of this principle undermines the equivalence of the
Principle of Independence and the failure of the traditional constraint.
The reasons for this are rather involved and somewhat obscure, and
interested readers may pursue the details in his book (pp. 52–53).[15]
However, Lambert is willing to accept that λ-abstraction is false. In
fact, he outlines independent reasons for thinking that λ-abstraction is
a seriously flawed principle which ought to be abandoned.

To restate then, the main conclusion of Lambert's book is that the
inference from "$(\exists F)x$ exemplifies F" to "x has being" is invalid. The
reasoning, from his point of view as a free logician, ultimately traces

---

[13]We should note that Lambert would read "x has being" with a more complex
   formula, namely, $[\lambda y (\exists z)z = y]x$ (p. 55). In a standard exemplification logic with
   identity and λ-abstraction, these two formulas are equivalent. But Lambert rejects
   λ-abstraction, for various reasons (some were discussed in Section 2; others will be
   discussed below). Nevertheless, we shall use the simpler reading for "x has being,"
   since this doesn't really affect the reasoning in what follows.

[14]Lambert states the principle so as to be neutral on the question of whether the
   relation term denotes a relation, but nothing hangs on this.

[15]Lambert's reasoning centers around a variant of the example we discussed in
   Chapter 7 in connection with Russell's second objection , namely, 'the non-square
   square.' We believe that Lambert's reasoning about this example is undermined
   by the analysis presented in Chapter 7, Section 2.

back to the alleged fact that there are true atomic predications that
have terms that do not denote anything. Lambert's last comment in the
proper part of his book is that Mally was in error when he abandoned
the Principle of Independence (p. 158), for analysis shows that it is a
truth.

In our view, Lambert's conclusions should be rejected. The traditional constraint on predication is a valid one, and Mally's eventual
rejection of the principle he developed was well-advised. The inference
from 'Fx' to '$(\exists y)y = x)$' is valid, and so is the inference from "$(\exists F)x$ exemplifies F" to "x has being." Moreover, the proviso to Lambert's conclusion is unjustified. λ-abstraction is a true logical principle, and the
independent reasons he offers for rejecting it are not good ones.

In defense of our point of view, note that the traditional constraint
governs both of our principles of predication. The clauses in the definition of satisfaction for atomic exemplification formulas and atomic encoding formulas (Chapter 3, Section 2) embody these constraints. And
when descriptions are added to the system, the traditional constraints
are built explicitly into these clauses (Chapter 5, Section 2). No atomic
formula is true unless all of its terms denote objects over which we can
quantify. So if we can successfully translate Lambert's crucial data into
our system, we can show that the constraint doesn't fail.

Lambert's main argument rests on the claim that there are true predications that contain terms that fail to denote. He offers the following
three statements as clear examples of true predications (p. 151):

(10) The winged horse of Bellerophon is the winged horse of Bellerophon.

(11) The winged horse of Bellerophon is mythological.

(12) Vulcan is the planet causing the perturbations in Mercury's orbit.

As a free logician, Lambert believes that 'the winged horse of Bellerophon,' 'Vulcan,' and 'the planet causing the perturbations in Mercury's
orbit' all fail to denote objects. However, as a *positive* free logician, he
believes that (10) – (12) are true predications. His arguments for this
view are mostly directed at *negative* free logicians, who agree that these
terms fail to denote but claim that (10) – (12) are false (pp. 152–156).
These arguments, therefore, simply presuppose that the terms involved
fail to denote. As such, they really do not show that "the weight of the
evidence supports the view that there are true predications containing
singular terms that specify no subsistent" (p. 156).[16] This conclusion of
Lambert's is not justified.

---

[16] By "subsistent," Lambert means "object that has being".

In our system, (10) – (12) have true readings, and the truth of the readings depends directly on the fact that the formal terms representing the English names and descriptions have denotations. The description in (10) denotes a character originating in Greek myth, namely, Pegasus. According to the myth, Pegasus is the winged horse captured by Bellerophon. Where 's_4' denotes the myth, 'Cxy' translates "x is captured by y," and the other abbreviations are obvious, we get the following representation for (10):

(13) $(\imath x)\Sigma_{s_4}(Wx \ \& \ Hx \ \& \ Cxb) = (\imath x)\Sigma_{s_4}(Wx \ \& \ Hx \ \& \ Cxb)$

This identity statement is true, since the A-objects denoted by the descriptions are identical (as this notion is defined). Note that the following is a consequence of (13):

(14) $(\exists y)y = (\imath x)\Sigma_{s_4}(Wx \ \& \ Hx \ \& \ Cxb)$

In other words, it follows that the winged horse of Bellerophon has being.[17]

By way of contrast, Lambert argues that (10) is a true predication even though 'the winged horse of Bellerophon' doesn't denote. He says that identity statements have the following, traditional analysis: '$a = b$' is true iff '$(\forall F)(Fa \equiv Fb)$' is true (pp. 152–153). He claims that the right side of the biconditional is (logically) true when 'the winged horse of Bellerophon' is substituted for both 'a' and 'b'; presumably, in interpretations where the description fails, the right side of the conditional is true by antecedent failures in both directions. But if this is his argument as to why (10) is true, then he cannot simultaneously maintain, as he does, that (10) is a predication (in which the identity sign is a two-place predicate). For he has analyzed this alleged predication as if it were a quantified statement. Clearly, lots of molecular and quantified statements with non-denoting terms may be true—their logical form alone may guarantee their truth. But to establish his version of the Principle of Independence, Lambert needs to produce a true atomic predication in which one of the terms fails to denote.

---

[17]There is a passage in Lambert's book which suggests that there is some disagreement about what the data are. Lambert says that the sentence "Holmes is a detective" seems undeniably true (p. 144). But, strictly speaking, this is not true. Rather, "In the Conan Doyle novels, Holmes is a detective" is true. Truth is not preserved when the story operator is dropped. We certainly agree with Lambert that the story operator cannot be plausibly prefixed to "Pegasus is fictitious," "Holmes is fictional," and "The winged horse captured by Bellerophon is mythological" (pp. 146, 154). But our theory does not require us to prefix the story operator to every statement about fictional characters. Only those that are part of the story should have the story operator prefixed to them. Failure to see that dropping the story operator from these sentences doesn't preserve truth but only hinders the philosophical investigation of fictional and mythical characters.

Lambert's example (11) is not conclusive either. In our framework, the description in (11) denotes an object that satisfies the definition of 'mythological.' This notion was defined in the previous chapter (Section 4). So the following representation of (11) in our system should be reasonably clear:

(15) $Mythological((\imath x)\Sigma_{s_4}(Wx\ \&\ Hx\ \&\ Cxb))$

The reason (15) is true is that the description picks out a character that originated in a myth. Note that (15) implies (14).

Constrast this with Lambert's account of why (11) is true. He suggests that 'mythological' is a nonsubsistence-entailing predicate. He says (p. 154), "The statements in which it occurs entail the *nonsubsistence* of the purported referents of the constituent singular terms of those statements." But what could this mean? What does a nonsubsistence-entailing predicate entail the nonsubsistence of? What does Lambert mean by "purported referent"? Can we append 'is mythological' to any denotationless name or description to produce a truth? Does Lambert's analysis require us to think of 'mythological' as a semantic predicate of terms?[18] Using what principle of predication does Lambert support his conclusion, and how is it to be applied?[19] The problem here is that *positive* free logicians offer us very little understanding of how there can be true atomic predications in which one of the terms fails to denote. There are lots of questions that surround such a view, but few answers.

We turn next to (12). On our view, Vulcan is a character originating in Leverrier's piece of science fiction. Where 's_5' denotes the story in question, 'Pxy' translates 'x causes the perturbations in the orbit of y,' and the other abbreviations are obvious, we may analyze the description in (12) as: $(\imath x)\Sigma_{s_5}(Px\ \&Pxm)$. This description denotes the same A-object that 'Vulcan' denotes, namely, the one encoding just the properties attributed to Vulcan in Leverrier's science fiction. Clearly, then, the following identity statement is true: $v=(\imath x)\Sigma_{s_5}(Px\ \&\ Pxm)$.

By way of contrast, Lambert argues that (12) is true by definition. The fact that Leverrier used 'Vulcan' as shorthand for 'the planet that

---

[18]Maybe the reason Lambert thinks (11) is true is that he understands it as the claim that 'the winged horse of Bellerophon' is a description grounded in fiction, and as such, fails to denote. But even this metalinguistic analysis of (11) is a predication involving terms that denote, since the term $\ulcorner$ 'the winged horse of Bellerophon' $\urcorner$ denotes the term 'the winged horse of Bellerophon.' So this claim is still a predication in which the subject term denotes something, namely, the description in (11).

[19]Are we, for example, supposed to apply the principle C$\bar{\mathrm{T}}$ (p. 82): predication joins an n-place general term to n singular terms to form a statement which would be true or false according as the n-place general term is true (false) of the n-tuple of objects referred to be the n singular terms were they to refer? If so, how does this principle show that (11) is a true predication?

causes the perturbations in Mercury's orbit' is the reason (12) is true. But how, then, can he argue that (12) is a predication? How does the stipulation that a symbol is to be used in a certain way evolve into a genuine predication? This seems rather mysterious.

We conclude, therefore, that Lambert has not conclusively established that there are true atomic predications containing non-denoting terms. The data Lambert cites have readings which show that they do not contain non-denoting terms. Moreover, our readings suggest that the sentences in question are not necessarily atomic predications either.[20] Consequently, the traditional constraint upon predication is not violated—no atomic predication is true unless all of the terms denote and the denotations stand in the right relation. Since the traditional constraint seems to be a good one, the Principle of Independence, as Lambert conceives of it, should be rejected. The inference from '$(\exists F)Fx$' to '$(\exists y)y = x$' is valid.

The traditional constraint on predication serves an important function. It places bounds on our philosophical conceptions. When operating under this constraint, we need not try to make sense of the notion of a "beingless object." Nor do we have to accept the claim that there are true atomic predications involving denotationless terms. It is difficult to reconcile this claim with the idea that the world makes atomic predications true. If one of the terms in an atomic predication fails to denote how could the world make the predication true?[21] How could the predication even signify anything? Furthermore, note that the free logicians' view leaves them with no means of explaining the successes of Existential Generalization. Until the underlying conception is made clear, until coherent analyses of sentences involving names and descriptions of fictional characters are developed, and until the validity and invalidity of inferences involving the existential quantifier are explained, free logic, in and of itself, offers no solution to the puzzles of intensionality.

Finally, let us defend λ-abstraction against Lambert's attack. This principle, formulated in our logic as λ-*Equivalence*, is basic to the logic of complex relation terms. Lambert argues that for his reading of Principle (H) to be equivalent to the failure of the traditional constraint, λ-abstraction must be false (p. 53). But to lessen the shock of rejecting such an important principle, Lambert offers independent grounds for thinking that it is false (p. 54). He points first to the [1969] study by Scales, in which the following instance of λ-abstraction is considered:

(16) $[\lambda x \sim (x \text{ has being})]$Vulcan $\equiv \sim$(Vulcan has being)

---

[20] Our representations of the data use defined notation that involves atomic formulas, but the representations themselves may not be simple predications.

[21] If the atomic predication is a metalinguistic claim about a term, then the subject term still has a denotation!

It is alleged that (16) is false, on the grounds that the left side of the biconditional is false ('Vulcan' fails to denote) while the right side is true (it is the negation of a false atomic predication).

This is not a good argument against λ-abstraction, however. It just presupposes that the name 'Vulcan' fails to denote. On our view, this presupposition is unjustified, since 'Vulcan' denotes a character of a myth. If there is such a property as $[\lambda x \sim (x \text{ has being})]$, then both sides of (16) are false, making the whole true.[22] The left side is false because 'Vulcan' denotes an object over which we can quantify (so it has being). The right side is false because it denies the truth that Vulcan has being. So from our point of view, no doubt is yet cast on λ-abstraction.

But Lambert also cites the [1968] study by Stalnaker and Thomason. The following instance of λ-abstraction is offered as a counterexample:

(17) $[\lambda x \ \Box(x \text{ is a citizen})]$the U.S. president $\equiv \Box$(the U.S. president is a citizen)

It is alleged that (17) is false, on the grounds that the right side of the biconditional is true while the left side is false. The right side is true, it is argued, because in every possible world, the U.S. president at that world is a citizen of the U.S. at that world. The left side is suppose to be false because the object denoted by the description, namely Reagan, is not a citizen of the U.S. in every possible world.

This isn't a good argument against λ-abstraction either. The argument depends crucially on treating the description in (17) as non-rigid, and so at best, it shows that instances involving non-rigid definite descriptions in modal contexts should be banished. If we treat 'the U. S. president' in (17) as a rigid description, then (17) is true, since both sides of the biconditional are false. Both the left and right sides are false for the same reason—the person denoted by the description at the actual world is not necessarily a citizen of the U. S. Our work in Chapter 5, Section 4 shows that a simple restriction on λ-abstraction is necessary when rigid definite descriptions are allowed into the system. Instances like (17) are permissible only when the definite description has a denotation. But such a restriction does not limit the principle as a completely general, material mode statement to the effect that objects that exemplify a complex relation stand in just the simple relations required by the complex one. Furthermore, our work in Chapter 5, Section 5 shows that it is no surprise that non-rigid descriptions in modal contexts cause

---

[22]In our system, the representation of 'x has being' is '$(\exists y)y = x$,' which is defined notation that includes encoding subformulas. Thus, there is no guarantee that '$[\lambda x \sim (x \text{ has being})]$' denotes a property, though an axiom could be added that requires it.

problems for λ-abstraction. But this doesn't justify completely abandoning the principle. There is no reason to accept Lambert's claim that
λ-abstraction does not hold. If this claim is necessary for the defense of
the Principle of Independence, then we ought to question Independence,
not λ-abstraction.

Part IV

Substitutivity and Existential Generalization

9

Direct Reference, Fregean Senses, and The Propositional Attitudes

To account for the informativeness of true identity statements of the form '$a = b$,' Frege proposed in [1892] that terms expressed a "sense" in addition to having a denotation. The true statement '$a = b$' is informative, according to Frege, because 'a' and 'b' have distinct senses. These distinct senses are different modes of presentation of one and the same object, and it is informative to learn that an object which has been presented in one way is the same object as one which has been presented in another way. Frege's theory gains some plausibility from the fact that, with the addition of the hypothesis that terms denote their senses in propositional attitude contexts, there is a simple explanation of the substitutivity failures that afflict such contexts. On Frege's view, the principle of substitution is a good one, and the reason we cannot interchange terms having the same ordinary denotation is that in such contexts, these terms denote their senses. Distinct terms having the same ordinary denotation typically have distinct senses, and so we cannot expect substitutions into such contexts to preserve truth, since truth is preserved only when a term is replaced by one having the same denotation.

Recently, doubt has been cast on this Fregean explanation of attitude report substitutivity failure, though in an indirect way. Convincing arguments by Kripke, Donnellan, Putnam, and Kaplan suggest that terms directly denote, that is, no intermediate entity plays a role in securing or determining the denotation of a term. Since many philosophers think that Fregean senses are the entities that determine or secure the denotation of the term with which they are associated, Fregean senses are rejected altogether. But once senses are rejected, we lose an elegant explanation of the failures of substitutivity. In this chapter, we hope to show that by modifying Frege's conception of senses just a little, the arguments of the philosophers who reject them lose their force. One may simultaneously accept the thesis of the direct reference theorists as well as suppose that terms have a sense, by identifying senses in such a way that they do not, except in the case of definite descriptions, determine or secure the denotation of the term. Such a view of terms and their senses preserves Frege's explanation of the informativeness of identity statements, as well as his account of the apparent failure of substitutivity of identicals in propositional attitude contexts. Thus, we shall try to reconcile what appears to be an incompatibility between Frege's views and that of the direct reference theorists, and at the same time provide an explanation for puzzles that currently lack an explanation in direct reference theory.

One comment should be made before we begin. It will not be the purpose of this chapter to find a precise modeling of Frege's philosophy of language. Clearly, since we take the denotation of a sentence to be a structured proposition, rather than a truth value, we are not following Frege in this regard. Moreover, the formal language we shall use to preserve at least some of Frege's insights concerning senses does not utilize two semantic relations. We will get by with just the one semantic relation of denotation. The senses of the terms of English will be *denoted* by special terms of our language. In what follows, our policy is to build a picture of the propositional attitudes that explains the data and preserves many of the *key* ideas Frege had. It makes no attempt to preserve them all.

9.1   Roles Senses Play in the Philosophy of Language

Frege never developed a *theory* of senses. He offered no definitions, axioms, or identity conditions for them. How then are we supposed to identify senses, or know whether a theoretical entity we're considering is to be regarded as a sense? All we're really told by Frege and his interpreters is that senses are the kind of thing which play certain roles in an account of language. Frege himself didn't provide us with a definitive list of such roles, but some of his recent interpreters have suggested a variety of roles that senses are supposed to play in Frege's theory. In the next few paragraphs, we'll look at some of these suggestions.

In [1977], Tyler Burge lists three roles senses are supposed to play (p. 356):

> **Sense₁**: The mode of representation to the thinker which is associated with an expression. Sense₁ accounts for the information value associated with an expression.

Sense$_2$: That which determines the reference or denotation associated with an expression; for singular terms, senses serve as "routes" to singling out the unique object, if any, denoted by the term.

Sense$_3$: The entity denoted by the term in oblique contexts.

Burge draws a number of conclusions about the identity of entities that might play these roles. For example, he argues that the entities playing the role defined as sense$_1$ do not play the role defined as sense$_2$. In what follows, we shall abbreviate this conclusion, as well as others like it, as follows: sense$_1$ $\neq$ sense$_2$. Burge's reason for concluding this is:

> ... a complete account of the mode in which an object is presented to us—the effect it has on our cognitive representations or on our store of information—may be insufficient to determine that one object rather than another is the subject of our beliefs. (pp. 357–358)

Burge's conclusion seems to be just the kind of conclusion one might draw once the force of the arguments by Kripke [1972], Donnellan [1972], Putnam [1973], and Kaplan [1977] is recognized (these arguments show that names directly denote their denotations).

However, Burge draws a conclusion that seems a bit hasty. He argues that the entities playing the role of sense$_1$ do not also play the role of sense$_3$. To argue for this conclusion (i.e., that sense$_1$ $\neq$ sense$_3$), Burge draws our attention to the case in which different persons, say K and K', both have the *same* belief, for example, that Aristotle is a philosopher. He claims that it is possible for the cognitive significance of the name 'Aristotle' to differ for K and K', but that it is not possible for the entity denoted by 'Aristotle' in the oblique construction ascribing the belief to K and K' to differ (for otherwise, he argues, they couldn't have the *same* belief).

In the next chapter, we shall look at Burge's argument for this conclusion in more detail and, in light of the work in the present chapter, propose a way to undermine it. There are A-objects that can play both the roles of sense$_1$ and sense$_3$, and different people may have the *same* belief even when the cognitive significance of a term differs for each person. For now, however, let us continue with our catalog of the work Fregean senses are suppose to perform.

Nathan Salmon, has identified a set of roles for Fregean senses that look similar to (and indeed, were based upon) the roles Burge describes. In [1981], Salmon proposes the following categorization (p. 12):[1]

---

[1] We are renumbering Salmon's senses 1, 2, and 3 as senses 4, 5, and 6, respectively.

Sense₄: The purely conceptual representation of an object which a fully competent speaker associates in a particular way with his or her use of the term. Sense₄ is a psychological or conceptual notion. The sense₄ of a term is something that a subject "grasps." It includes only purely qualitative properties; external things cannot "occur as constituents." Instead, there are only conceptual representations thereof.

Sense₅: The mechanism by which the reference of the term (with respect to a possible world and a time) is secured and semantically determined. Sense₅ is a semantic notion.

Sense₆: The information value of the term; the contribution made by the term to the information content of sentences containing the term. Sense₆ is a cognitive or epistemic notion. The sense of a term forms part of any belief expressed by means of the term and is relevant to the epistemological status (*a priori*, *a posteriori*, trivial, informative) of sentences containing the term.

It is interesting to note here the overlap between Burge's and Salmon's conceptions. Salmon proposes that Burge's sense₃ can be distinguished from sense₆ as yet another role for senses to play (p. 12, note 7). Although Burge takes issue with Salmon's revised classification, we shall not be concerned here to resolve the differences between these two philosophers. The fact that they disagree about the proper classification of roles proves to be interesting in the present context.

One of Salmon's major conclusions about his classification of roles is that the theory of direct reference is incompatible only with the view that a single entity plays all the roles simultaneously. In [1981], he says:

> Insofar as the central theses [of the theory of direct reference] are opposed to admitting sense at all, they oppose the full-blown Fregean notion of *Sinn* as applied to proper names, the idea that that which fills one of these three functions for a proper name fills the other two as well. If that is the sort of thing the sense of a term is supposed to be, then perhaps some definite descriptions so indeed have sense. Proper names and indexical singular terms, on the other hand, do not. (p. 14)
>
> ... Kripke does not argue in *Naming and Necessity* that names do not evoke certain concepts in the minds of speakers who have learned the name. Nor does he argue there that names make no contribution, beyond their reference, to beliefs and assertions whose expression involves the name, and

> it is doubtful he would want to. He certainly does not want
> to argue that there is nothing by means of which the refer-
> ence of a name is secured or semantically determined. [But]
> He clearly does endorse the thesis that names lack sense if
> "sense" is something that is simultaneously the conceptual
> content, the semantical method of determining reference, and
> the cognitive content, all at once. (p. 23)

In what follows, we accept the conclusion that Kripke apparently en-
dorses, namely, that names lack sense when "sense" is something that
is simultaneously the conceptual content, the determiner of reference,
and the cognitive content. And we accept Salmon's claim, in an earlier
passage, that "there are singular terms, to be sure, for which an identification of $sense_5$ and $sense_6$ seems unquestionably correct; these are
definite descriptions in attributive use" (p. 13).

However, Salmon argues in [1979] that $sense_4 \neq sense_6$ (p. 450). Very
briefly, his argument is that whereas the information that a competent
speaker associates with a name ($sense_4$) may contain misinformation, the
$sense_6$ contains no misinformation. In the next chapter, this conclusion
will also be challenged. Senses can contain misinformation and still play
both of the roles in question.

There is one final role that senses can play. This role is intimately
connected to $sense_1$ and $sense_4$. Salmon briefly mentions it in a footnote
to [1981], where he says:[2]

> There is yet another kind of 'sense' for a term which is a close
> variant of our $sense_4$. This is the set or cluster of properties
> ... which a speaker associates in a certain way with his or
> her use of the term. Philosophers often speak of this as a
> 'mental file' attached to the term .... The major difference
> [between $sense_4$ and this notion of sense] is that the latter
> is not, in general, purely qualitative or conceptual, and may
> involve nonintensional entities as constituents. As such, it is
> a notion which Frege would reject as playing no part in his
> notion of *Sinn*. (p. 12, note 7)

Let us call this notion of sense, insofar as it is distinct from $sense_1$
and $sense_4$, "$sense_7$." Leave aside for the moment Salmon's claim that
Frege would reject this as a part of the conception of senses. Focus
instead on the label "mental file." This notion is rather vivid, and some
philosophers find it to be intuitive. For example, John Perry, in [1980a],
appeals to files of some sort in the following remarks:[3]

---

[2] In the following quotation, we have followed our numbering system and renumbered Salmon's notions of sense accordingly.

[3] See also Lockwood [1971].

Now it may be that in the mind the work of files are done
by something like proper names. (p. 331)

Each such file card offers me ... a profile, a set of predicates.
(p. 330)

The notion of a mental file can be linked to sense$_1$ and sense$_4$ and the
way to link them seems to be through the notion of *content*. This notion
is not the same notion as *aboutness*. Some philosophers use "content"
to indicate what a term denotes, or what a mental presentation or state
is about.[4] We might call this "objectual content." But sense$_1$, sense$_4$,
and sense$_7$ deal with the "cognitive" rather than the objectual content
of the presentation or state. It is important to emphasize that these
cognitive contents are, in an important sense, *objective*, public entities.
The cognitive content of a term for person K could, in principle, be
something that is grasped by any other person (though, typically, K
and K' rarely associate the same cognitive content with a given term).
Moreover, the cognitive content a term has for one person may be the
same as the cognitive content that a different term has for a different
person.

This notion of cognitive content seems to be connected with Husserl's
notion of "noematic *Sinn*." Recall here the doctrines that characterize
Husserl's noemata that were discussed in Chapter 6. In fact, noematic
Sinne are somewhat more general than Fregean senses, since the latter apply to directed cognitions signified by pieces of language, whereas
the former apply to the content of any kind of directed cognitive event.
Other philosophers have also objectified this notion of cognitive content.
In [1981], D. W. Smith suggests that the following three doctrines characterize the notion of an objectified, cognitive content that is common
to Bolzano, Frege, Twardowski, and Husserl:

A. A content is an abstract entity

B. With each mental act, there is associated exactly one content and
   different acts may share the same content

C. The content of a mental act individuates the psychological or phenomenological structure or type of the act. But it is in no way
   part of the act and is in that respect a non-mental entity.

These doctrines form part of the conception that is common to notions
of sense$_1$, sense$_4$, and sense$_7$.[5]

---

[4]For example, Searle's notion of content is such a notion. The content of a state, for
example, is its condition of satisfaction, and this is something that Searle seems
to identify with what the state is about.

[5]Traditionally, Fregean senses have played one other role in the philosophy of lan-

9.2   A-Objects as Senses: The General Picture

In principle, A-objects can play all of these roles. In fact, however, they play all of the roles with the exception of sense$_2$ and sense$_5$. Before we look at each role in turn, here is a rough sketch of the general picture. We shall assume that names directly denote, and that what they denote is determined by something like the mechanism described by the direct-reference theorists.[6] In any situation in which we encounter a token of a name for the first time, a certain group of properties present themselves as being characteristic of the name bearer. The context always supplies us with some information about the bearer of the name. The information may be copious, as in cases where the name is introduced by ostension, labels a photograph, or heads a biographic entry. Or the information may be scarce, as in cases where the name is simply part of some list. Furthermore, the information may be good or bad—the name bearer may or may not exemplify the properties featured. If the name token in question is a proper name, the properties that present themselves will be properties of individuals. If the token in question is a name of a relation or property, the properties that present themselves will be properties of relations or properties of properties.

It seems clear that the properties featured in the name-learning situation are linked directly to the sense the name has for a given individual in that situation. The natural way to objectify this link within the present framework is to regard the A-object that encodes the properties in question as the sense of the name. In the case of individual names, our comprehension principle for abstract individuals guarantees that there will be an A-object that encodes just the properties of individuals which are presented (in a given context, for a certain person) as characteristic of individual denoted. In the case of definite descriptions of individuals, there will be an A-object that encodes the properties involved in the description. In the case of names of properties and relations, however, we need abstract entities that encode properties of properties, or properties of relations, if we are to provide a general account of the sense of names.

---

guage, namely, to serve as the significance of "non-denoting" names like Pegasus, Zeus, Raskolnikov, etc. This role, however, shall not figure in the present discussion, for two reasons. One is that this role is not specifically linked in any special way with the attitudes. More importantly, however, such a role is unnecessary from our perspective, since such names are not considered to be non-denoting.

[6]We say "something like" the mechanism described by direct reference theorists because there is a *non-causal* step involved in the dubbing or baptism of certain entities. For example, names of fictional characters and names of properties and relations denote entities that are not part of the causal order, and so dubbing does not take place by simple ostension. So we deviate slightly from the strict doctrine of direct reference.

In fact, it is a simple matter to extend the theory described so far in order to generate both abstract properties and abstract relations in addition to abstract individuals. There is a simple typing of the theory that suffices. Let 'i' be the type of individuals, and '$\langle t_1, \ldots, t_n \rangle$' be the type of relations having as arguments objects of type $t_1, \ldots, t_n$, respectively (where $t_1, \ldots, t_n$ are any types). So, for example, the type of properties of individuals is: $\langle i \rangle$. The type of properties of properties of individuals is: $\langle \langle i \rangle \rangle$. The type of a 3-place relation between individuals is: $\langle i, i, i \rangle$, whereas properties of such relations are of type: $\langle \langle i, i, i \rangle \rangle$. It is a straightforward matter to type our entire formal language, theory, and logic with this characterization of types. For example, where $\tau_1, \ldots, \tau_n$ are any terms of types $t_1, \ldots, t_n$, respectively, and F is any term of type $\langle t_1, \ldots, t_n \rangle$, then '$Fx_1, \ldots, x_n$' will be a well-formed atomic exemplification formula. And where x is a term of type t, and F is a term of type $\langle t \rangle$, 'xF' will be a well-formed atomic encoding formula. The system that results is formally developed in the Appendix. But for now, these remarks should make this latest theoretical turn clear to our readers.

The most important consequence of the typing is this: the comprehension principle for abstract individuals becomes a typed comprehension schema that generates abstract entities at every type. At every level of the type theory, there will be ordinary things of that type as well as abstract things of that type. But the comprehension principle circumscribes only the latter. Where ϕ is any condition on properties having type $\langle t \rangle$, the principle asserts that there is an abstract entity of type t that encodes just the properties satisfying the condition. This means, for example, that in addition to the ordinary properties with type $\langle i \rangle$, there will be abstract properties with type $\langle i \rangle$ that encode properties having type $\langle \langle i \rangle \rangle$. And in addition to ordinary relations with type $\langle i, i \rangle$, there will be abstract relations with type $\langle i, i \rangle$ that encode properties with type $\langle \langle i, i \rangle \rangle$. So the abstract entities of a given type encode properties that are typically exemplified by things of that type.

In what follows, we shall use "A-individual," "A-property," and "A-relation" to talk about abstract individuals, abstract properties, and abstract relations, respectively. All such entities shall fall under the general category "A-object."

Clearly, we now have a straightforward way to unify our analysis of the senses of names. In the final case to consider, that of names of relations, our typed comprehension principle guarantees that there will be an A-relation that encodes just the properties of relations which are presented as being characteristic of the relation named. This, then, is the general picture behind the idea that A-objects serve as the senses of names and descriptions.

9.3   Sense$_1$, Sense$_4$, and Sense$_7$

Sense$_1$:   Clearly, A-objects can play the role sense$_1$. By encoding the same kinds of properties that are exemplified by the denotation of the term with which they are associated, these abstract objects seem to be objectified modes of presentation. Consider a fifth grader, Mary, who comes upon a book in her parents' library entitled: *Life on the Mississippi*, by Mark Twain. At that moment, Mary becomes part of an historical chain of events connecting her with the name 'Mark Twain.' This chain traces back to certain actions by Samuel Clemens in which he used a pseudonym to refer to himself. As Mary reads the book, various properties may present themselves as being characteristic of the author. Just which properties depends on how much attention she is paying, her cognitive abilities, how much literature she has already assimilated, etc. The following properties could certainly be relevant to the experience: being a man, being an author, having authored a book in such and such year with such and such press (information she gleans from the back of the title page), being humorous, being knowledgeable about piloting a steamboat on the Mississippi, etc. And furthermore, should there happen to be a picture of the author on the frontispiece, extremely vivid properties (like having a walrus moustache) will be available.

For simplicity, let us consider a point in time soon after all of this information about Twain has been presented. Let 'Twain$_m$' denote the A-individual that encodes the properties that still significantly affect Mary's cognitive apparatus with respect to the name 'Twain.' Clearly, Twain$_m$ objectifies a certain way or mode of presenting Samuel Clemens.

Suppose Mary has an identical twin, Anna, and that they have flipped through the pages of the book together. Twain$_m$ need not be the same A-individual as Twain$_a$. Anna may have been paying closer attention to the information than her sister. And having read and assimilated a greater variety of literature, she may have been able to associate with 'Twain' more sophisticated properties, such as those linking him to literary traditions. Strictly speaking, the sense of a name is relativized to a person and a context, though in what follows, we will frequently ignore the contextual relativization in order to simplify matters. Note that nothing we've said rules out there being a sense$_1$ that encodes properties the entity denoted by the name fails to exemplify. Had Mary encountered a book by George Eliot, Eliot$_m$ might have been an A-individual that encodes the property of being a man.

A-properties and A-relations can be the modes of presentation associated with property and relation denoting terms. For example, 'being a woodchuck' and 'being a groundhog' denote the same property. A perfectly competent speaker of English, say K, may learn these terms in different circumstances yet not know that they denote the same property; one term may have been looked up in the dictionary, whereas the other may have been learned out in the field. Different properties of type $\langle\langle i \rangle\rangle$ would have been featured as being characteristic of the property denoted by the name. Let $\underline{W}_k$ denote the sense of the name 'being a woodchuck' for K. It is the A-property (type $\langle i \rangle$) that encodes the group of properties (having type $\langle\langle i \rangle\rangle$) presented in the dictionary. Also, let $\underline{G}_k$ denote the sense of the name 'being a groundhog' for K. The A-property denoted encodes the group of properties presented out in the field. Consequently, $\underline{W}_k$ is distinct from $\underline{G}_k$. The identity statement "Being a woodchuck just is being a groundhog" would be informative for K, since the senses of the names differ.

As modes of presentation, A-objects become especially important in cases where we learn new terms of a language without being directly acquainted (in the epistemological sense) with the entities denoted. Certainly one way of introducing an individual (or relation) is by referring to the properties that individual (or relation) exemplifies. This is an important role played by sense$_1$.

Sense$_4$: Salmon conceives of sense$_4$ as the *purely conceptual* representation that a speaker associates with a term. There is nothing in principle that prevents us from identifying such representations as A-objects, though his further characterization of this notion is somewhat puzzling. Senses$_4$ are things that a subject may "grasp." But what is it to grasp a conceptual representation? Salmon seems to suggest that to be graspable, senses$_4$ must have no "external" things as constituents. But aren't ordinary properties and relations "external" things, in the sense that their existence is independent of the mind? Does that mean that only representations of properties and relations, and not the properties and relations themselves, may be constituents of senses$_4$? Or can we grasp these external properties and relations directly?

The notion of "grasping" being used here seems to presuppose that whatever is grasped somehow becomes "part" of the mind. This would explain why Salmon banishes external constituents from conceptual representations. But is "the thing that is grasped" a part of the mind or part of the content of the mental state? Do we have to accept the idea that to grasp something, it must become part of the mind? The notion of grasping is notoriously obscure. Instead of talking about "grasping," maybe we should be talking about individuating mental states. Sometimes, the natural way to individuate a mental state is to appeal to an object that exists outside the mind. In particular, it seems best to individuate *de re* thoughts and attitudes by ignoring the cognitive content of such thoughts and attitudes and by appealing to the external objects which they are about. The fact that these external objects are essential to individuating the mental state does not imply that the external objects are part of anyone's mind!

Consequently, it may be that we can individuate the cognitive content of these states (that is, individuate conceptual representations) by appealing to external objects without implying that such objects are part of the mind. We might want to say that a subject has "grasped" a conceptual representation, even though the properties used to individuate that representation contain physical constituents. In other words, the A-objects that serve as senses$_4$ may encode relational properties involving physical objects. Such A-objects may still be "graspable," for this does not imply that they are taken into the mind in some way.

However, even if Salmon is right in thinking that no external constituents are "involved" in conceptual representations, then we simply need to consider the A-objects that encode a certain restricted class of purely qualitative properties that fail to contain physical constituents. Actually, this class of properties is not as restricted as one might think. For in our system, not only does this class contain the usual kinds of qualitative properties, but it also contains properties with abstract constituents. These properties are like properties involving ordinary physical constituents except that their physical constituents have been replaced by the A-individuals that represent them! For example, our fifth grader, Mary, may have been struck by the fact that Mark Twain was born in Missouri (having read this somewhere). The property *native of Missouri* may become part of the sense 'Twain' has for her. If Salmon is right, then $\underline{\text{Twain}}_m$ doesn't encode this property, but rather the property: native of $\underline{\text{Missouri}}_m$ (this property is the result of plugging $\underline{\text{Missouri}}_m$ into the second place of the relation *native of*). The abstraction principle ensures that there is such a property. Note that the representation of an object is an A-object of the very same logical type. Both the sense and the denotation of an English term of type t are entities of the same type.

Actually, there is another possibility that arises in the context of our theory. That is, the A-objects that serve as sense$_4$, instead of encoding ordinary properties and relations, may encode instead the A-properties and A-relations that represent the ordinary ones. Recall that even ordinary properties and relations are "external" in the sense that they exist independently of the mind. Maybe the conceptual representations Salmon has in mind consist of those A-objects that encode A-properties having abstract constituents. For example, instead of encoding native of $\underline{\text{Missouri}}_m$, $\underline{\text{Twain}}_m$ might encode the property: $\underline{\text{native of}}_m$ $\underline{\text{Missouri}}_m$. In this property, $\underline{\text{native of}}_m$ is the A-relation that represents the ordinary relation *native of* for Mary. It is an A-relation of type $\langle i, i \rangle$.

Consequently, we may plug any individual into its second argument place, even Missouri$_m$. We're talking *very* abstract now—in this situation, we have an A-individual (Missouri$_m$) plugged into an argument place of an A-relation (native of$_m$), and the property that results is encoded into the A-individual Twain$_m$.

We shall discover shortly that in order to describe correctly the logic of certain mixed *de re/de dicto* contexts, the full range of combinations just described are required. An appeal must be made to ordinary and abstract properties having both ordinary and abstract constituents to do justice to the logic of certain attitude reports. But more about this in the final section.

Sense$_7$: A vivid way to understand the notion of grasping a conceptual representation is through the notion of accessing a "mental file." The mental file imagery of sense$_7$ is compatible with the above picture as long as it is not supposed that these files are literally part of anyone's mind. Instead, they are public—anyone can access any given file. By associating a particular A-object with a given name, a person associates a file of properties that appear to characterize the name bearer. This seems to be what Perry has in mind when he talks about "file cards" and "predicates." However, A-objects have more structure than just a list of predicates. They are essentially characterized by the properties they encode, in roughly the same way that our mental image of Mark Twain is characterized by the properties involved in that image. Indeed, Twain$_m$, as described above, constitutes one of Mary's rather vivid files on Samuel Clemens (though, unless she knows that Twain and Clemens are the same person, she may not know that the conception she brings to mind with the label 'Twain' is a conception of Samuel Clemens). A-objects, therefore, seem well-suited to this imagery of "mental files."

9.4   Sense$_2$, Sense$_5$, and Direct Reference

There is a special group of A-objects that could determine unique denotations for the names and terms with which they are associated. They could serve as the "semantic mechanism" for determining reference. These are the A-objects that encode properties exemplified by at most one object. Let us call such A-objects "individuating concepts," where this is defined as follows:

x^t *is an individuating concept* $=_{df}$

$$(\forall y^t)(\forall z^t)[(O!^{\langle t\rangle}y \ \& \ O!z \ \& \ (\forall F^{\langle t\rangle})(xF \to Fy \ \& \ Fz)) \Rightarrow y=z]$$

In other words, x is an individuating concept iff necessarily-always, at most one ordinary object exemplifies every property x encodes. This definition operates at every level of type theory. So, for example, an A-property F of type $\langle i \rangle$, which encodes properties of properties (i.e., encodes type $\langle\langle i \rangle\rangle$ properties), will be an individuating concept just in case there could never be more than one type $\langle i \rangle$ property that exemplifies all of the properties F encodes. Now by stipulating that only an individuating concept of type t may serve as the sense of an English name κ of type t, then the semantic route to the denotation of κ is simply this: it is the object of type t, should there be one, that in fact uniquely exemplifies every property encoded by the individuating concept.

Frege seems to have endorsed the idea that something like individuating concepts served as the senses of proper names. However, the arguments by the direct reference theorists show that proper names do not work this way. The cases of mistaken identity described by Kripke, Donnellan, and Putnam suggest that senses do not determine the denotations of names. The conclusion we draw from these cases is that the A-objects serving as modes of presentation need not be individuating concepts. In fact, they may encode properties that the denotation of the term fails to exemplify. Alternatively, they may encode properties that individuate some object other than the denotation of the term.

The one group of terms that may indeed have something like sense₂ or sense₅ are the definite descriptions. The theory generates a plausible candidate for the sense of an English description 'the so and so,' namely, the A-object that encodes just the property of being the so and so. Take, for example, the description 'the teacher of Aristotle,' represented as: $(\imath x)Txa$. Consider the A-individual that encodes just the property of being the teacher of Aristotle, namely, $(\imath x)(\forall F)(xF \equiv F = [\lambda y \ (\forall z)(Tza \equiv z =_E y)])$. This A-individual is a natural candidate for serving as the sense of 'the teacher of Aristotle' because it is an individuating concept. As the sense of 'the teacher of Aristotle,' it determines the denotation of the description: the denotation is that object, should there be one, that in fact exemplifies being the teacher of Aristotle (i.e., that exemplifies $[\lambda y \ (\forall z)(Tza \equiv z =_E y)]$).

In general, where ϕ is any propositional formula, we write '$(\imath x)\phi$' to denote the A-object that encodes just the property of being the x such that ϕ. That is:

$$(\imath x)\phi =_{df} (\imath x)(\forall F)(xF \equiv F = [\lambda y \ (\forall z)(\phi_x^z \equiv z =_E y)])$$

So when '$(\imath x)\phi$' is the ordinary representation of an English description in standard exemplification logic, $(\imath x)\phi$ is the sense$_2$, or sense$_5$, of the description.[7]

9.5   Sense$_3$, Sense$_6$, and the Propositional Attitudes

Let us stipulate that a *de re* attitude report is one for which truth is preserved when any embedded term is replaced by another having the same denotation. Otherwise, it is a *de dicto* report. Informally, we shall sometimes refer to the attitude described by the report as being *de re* or *de dicto*, though strictly speaking, this is a feature of the report, and not of the attitude reported. Finally, let us modify our type theory in a trivial way. Let '$\langle\ \rangle$' be a well-formed type. It shall be the type of *propositions*. Since propositions are zero-place relations, they have a relational type with no arguments. For simplicity, we abbreviate '$\langle\ \rangle$' with the single letter 'p'. Propositional attitude verbs are of the type $\langle i, p\rangle$. They denote 2-place relations between individuals and propositions.

To show that A-objects can play the roles sense$_3$ and sense$_6$, we consider an example that involves not only the substitutivity failure of descriptions but also the substitutivity failure of relation names. Consider (1):

(1) John believes that the animal in the cage is a woodchuck.

To formulate the standard logical representation of (1), let 'B' denote a relation of type $\langle i, p\rangle$. This relation will represent the belief relation. Furthermore, let '$(\imath x)\phi_1$' abbreviate the standard logical translation of 'the animal in the cage.' Then, where the other abbreviations are obvious, the natural way to read (1) is as follows:

(1a) $B(j, W(\imath x)\phi_1)$

The formal representation (1a) is true just in case John stands in a certain relation to the proposition that has the ordinary individual denoted by '$(\imath x)\phi_1$' plugged into the ordinary property denoted by 'W.' On this analysis, the truth conditions of (1) are determined by the objectual content of its terms. In particular, the description 'the animal in the

---

[7]It should be mentioned here that a hierarchy of Fregean senses will *not* be necessary. The reason is that only the names and descriptions of natural language have a sense. The formal expressions used to designate the senses of English names and descriptions are not part of natural language. No data is expressed by sentences containing 'Twain$_m$' and '$(\imath x)\phi$.'

However, there are interesting cases of attitude reports where the sense of a description such as 'the wife of Cicero,' for example, cannot be represented as the wife of Cicero. Instead, we have to use the wife of Cicero$_s$. See [1983], pp. 137–138. A hierarchy of senses is not required for such representations, however.

cage' and the predicate 'is a woodchuck' contribute their denotations to the truth conditions. Thus, (1a) is a pure *de re* reading of (1), since on this reading, any replacement of an expression in (1) by an expression having the same denotation preserves truth.

In some contexts, (1a) would be a good representation of the conditions under which (1) is true. In such contexts, the function of the report is to identify in some way or other the individuals and properties towards which John's belief state is directed. The particular way in which John is cognizing the individual and the property in question is not important to the truth of the report. Were one to characterize John's belief by using a different description of the same individual, or a different name of the property, the truth of the report would be unaffected. For example, if 'experimental animal #107' is another description for the same animal, and the property of being a groundhog is the same property as the property of being a woodchuck, then in the contexts in question, (2) would be a perfectly good recharacterization of John's state:

(2) John believes that experimental animal #107 is a groundhog.

This is just what we would expect when the *de re* reading of (1) is the most appropriate for the given context.

There are contexts, however, in which the truth of the attitude report depends specifically on the way in which John is cognizing the individual and property denoted by the embedded terms. In such contexts, the sentences (1), (3), (4), (5), (6), and (7) are all true:

(3) John doesn't believe that experimental animal #107 is a woodchuck.

(4) The animal in the cage is experimental animal #107.

(5) John doesn't believe that the animal in the cage is a groundhog.

(6) John doesn't believe that experimental animal #107 is a groundhog.

(7) Being a woodchuck just is being a groundhog.

The fact that these sentences are consistent suggests that the very meaning of the attitude reports is more closely linked to the cognitive, rather than objectual, content of the embedded terms. Thus, (1a) does not represent the proper truth conditions of (1) in such contexts. Were we to substitute co-denotational terms for 'the animal in the cage' or 'is a woodchuck,' the truth of (1) would not be preserved. To see this, let '$(\imath x)\psi_1$' represent 'experimental animal #107', and 'G' denote the property of being a groundhog. Then the following *de re* representations of (3) – (7) generate numerous inconsistencies in the presence of (1a):

(3a) $\sim B(j, W(\imath x)\psi_1)$

(4a) $(\imath x)\phi_1 =_E (\imath x)\psi_1$

(5a) $\sim B(j, G(\imath x)\phi_1)$

(6a) $\sim B(j, G(\imath x)\psi_1)$

(7a) $W =_E G$

How, then, do we explain the fact that in the contexts in question the English sentences appear to be true?

The answer brings us to sense$_3$ and sense$_6$: in the contexts in question, the embedded sentences signify a proposition constructed out of the cognitive contents of the terms of the embedded sentence. The cognitive content of an individual term is an A-individual. The cognitive content of property term is an A-property. When an A-individual is plugged into an A-property, the result is a proposition that has abstract constituents. This proposition can serve as the second argument of the relation that represents belief. This means that sentences embedded in attitude reports are ambiguous—in some contexts they signify the propositions they usually denote, while in others they signify propositions that have abstract constituents.

An Essential Distinction: If these ideas are to bear fruit, an important distinction must be observed. This is the distinction between the truth of the *belief report* and the truth of the *belief* that is being reported. In other words, the conditions under which the report is true must be distinguished from the conditions that must obtain for the belief to be correct or felicitous. In *de re* reports and beliefs, this distinction collapses. But in *de dicto* reports and beliefs, it is essential. The condition that makes such reports true may simply be that the person stands in the right relationship to a certain intermediate representation. But the condition that makes the belief true may be that the proposition represented is true. In other words, that someone has a belief may simply be a matter of that person being in a mental state that is directed in a certain way. But the correctness of the mental state depends on the proposition towards which the state is ultimately directed.

In *de dicto* attitude reports in general, then, the propositional representations that make the report true are to be distinguished from the propositions that make the attitude a felicitous one. The propositional representations are the entities in virtue of which the mind of a cognizing being is directed towards the world. Whether or not a person is related in the appropriate way to such representations determines whether a given attitude report is true. But, in the standard cases, it will be the propositions with ordinary constituents that determine whether or not the attitude so reported is a felicitous one.

A special feature of this analysis is that the propositional representations may be identified as objects of the same logical type as the propositions they represent. This is what allows us to develop the idea that embedded sentences are ambiguous. The embedded sentences denote propositions, but whether they denote a proposition constructed out of the denotations of its terms or one constructed out of the cognitive contents of its terms depends on whether the report in question is *de re* or *de dicto*.

The Formal Representation: To make these ideas formally precise, let us return to our example. The suggestion is that the embedded sentences in (1), (3), (5), and (6) have a secondary significance. What they signify is a proposition constructed out of the cognitive contents of their terms. This analysis is formalized by the following logical representations, which are offered as the second readings of the sentences in question:

(1b) $B(j, \underline{W}_j(\imath x)\phi_1)$

(3b) $\sim B(j, \underline{W}_j(\imath x)\psi_1)$

(5b) $\sim B(j, \underline{G}_j(\imath x)\phi_1)$

(6b) $\sim B(j, \underline{G}_j(\imath x)\psi_1)$

Clearly, (1b) relates John to a proposition that has the A-individual $(\imath x)\phi_1$ plugged into the A-property $\underline{W}_j$.[8] (3b) tells us that John is not so related to the proposition that has the A-individual $(\imath x)\psi_1$ plugged into the A-property $\underline{W}_j$. (1b) and (3b) are consistent. The negation of (1b) may not be derived from (3b) and (4a) by the principle of substitutivity.

Though (1b) provides the truth conditions of the English report (1), it doesn't tell us the correctness conditions of the belief reported. But those are easily stated: the belief reported by (1) is felicitous just in case the proposition denoted by '$W(\imath x)\phi_1$' is true. In formal terms, where ϕ^* is the result of deleting all of the underlines and subscripts from ϕ, we may define:

$$Felicitous(B(x, \phi)) =_{df} B(x, \phi) \ \& \ \phi^*$$

---

[8]It is best to think of (1b) as presenting the following conditions under which (1) is true: K stands in the relation B to the proposition: $\mathbf{PLUG}_1(\mathbf{d}(\underline{W}_j), \mathbf{d}((\imath x)\phi_1))$. The proposition to which John is related does have a truth value, but its truth value should simply be ignored. After all, it doesn't have to *be* a truth for our purposes, rather, it has to *represent* a truth. Its truth value doesn't play a part in its representational role.

Note that this definition works no matter how much incorrect information is encoded by the constituents of the intermediate proposition. Even if $(\imath x)\phi_1$ encodes properties that the animal in the cage doesn't exemplify, or $\underline{W}_j$ encodes properties that the property of being a woodchuck doesn't exemplify, the belief reported by (1) is felicitous iff the animal in the cage is a woodchuck.

The foregoing remarks about the consistency of the triad (1)-(3)-(4) apply not only to the triads (1)-(5)-(7) and (1)-(6)-(7), but also to the entire group of sentences (1), (3), (4), (5), (6) and (7). In some contexts, all of the sentences in this latter group appear to be true. The appearances are explained by the fact that the representations (1b), (3b), (4a), (5b), (6b), and (7a) are jointly consistent. No contradictions may be derived from the identities (4a) and (7a), since the principle of substitutivity simply fails to apply. The English reports in these contexts are ultrasensitive to the cognitive content that the embedded terms of the report have for John. Truth is preserved only when terms having the same cognitive content are substituted for one another. Note that the apparent substitutivity failure of co-denotational relation terms receives the same explanation as that of individual terms. No special treatment is required. Moreover, the definition of felicity works properly for these representations as well. If the proposition denoted by '$W(\imath x)\phi_1$' is true, then (3b), (5b), and (6b) each imply that John fails to have certain felicitous beliefs.

These analyses demonstrate that A-objects can serve as the sense$_3$ of embedded terms in *de dicto* reports. They are signified by such terms in certain contexts. Moreover, A-objects are the "parts" to the content of the belief, something that is required by the description of sense$_6$.[9]

Some Added Flexibility: The method of forming sense-terms in our formal language (by using underlines and subscripts) maximizes flexibility for representing propositional attitude reports. On the strict Fregean analysis of these reports, it is typically assumed that *every* term inside the attitude report denotes its sense. The problem with this assumption, however, is that this forces every attitude report to be interpreted as a

---

[9] When Salmon talks about "information content" with respect to sense$_6$ in [1981], he seems to be using, in an intuitive way, the technical notion that he develops in [1986]. When he says that sense$_6$ forms part of the belief expressed, he probably means that it is a constituent of the Russellian proposition that embodies the "information content" of the embedded sentence. But if this is what information content is, then sense$_6$ doesn't seem to be a notion of sense but rather of denotation, since the Russellian proposition is constructed with the denotations of the terms in the embedded sentence. In our system, the notion of "information content" is simply ambiguous between the objectual content and the cognitive content of a term or sentence.

pure *de dicto* report. However, in some contexts, it is best to interpret reports as having a mixed *de re/de dicto* character.

To see why, consider the report "John hopes that the strongest man in the world beats up the man who just insulted him." Clearly, there are contexts in which the truth of the report depends just on the denotations of the two descriptions. And there are contexts in which it depends just on the cognitive content of the two descriptions. But there are also contexts in which the truth of the report depends on the cognitive content of the first description and the denotation of the second description (and *vice versa*). In such contexts, John's mental state is more accurately characterized by appealing to the cognitive content of 'the strongest man in the world' and to the objectual content of 'the man who just insulted him.' The former term signifies John's conception of the strongest man, whoever he might be. However, the latter term does not signify a conception, but rather the man himself. In such a situation, the intersubstitution of other names or descriptions of the person denoted by 'the man who just insulted him' does not affect the truth of the report![10]

Let us say that any term under the scope of the main verb in an attitude report is in *de re position* iff substitutions for that term are truth preserving; otherwise it is in *de dicto position*. In the case just described, the term 'the strongest man in the world' is in *de dicto* position while the term 'the man who just insulted him' is in *de re* position. This suggests that embedded terms in attitude reports should not automatically be interpreted as being in *de dicto* position. Consequently, we shall suppose that each term under the scope of a propositional attitude verb may be ambiguous. A term signifies its denotation when it is in *de re* position; it signifies its cognitive content when in *de dicto* position. When all of the embedded terms of a report are in *de re* position, we shall say that the report is *pure de re*. When some of the terms are in *de re* position and others are in *de dicto* position, the report is *mixed de re/de dicto*. When all of the embedded terms are in *de dicto* position, the report is *pure de dicto*.

Flexibility is maximized if, within any given attitude report, embedded terms in *de re* position can be given one reading while those in *de dicto* position can be given another. That is why the underline and subscript notation is designed to operate on embedded terms rather than on the entire embedded sentence. Consider that the following four readings of "John hopes that the strongest man in the world beats up the man who just insulted him" are available in our logic:

(a) $H(j, B'((\imath x)\chi, (\imath x)\theta))$ (pure *de re*)

---

[10]This case is examined in some detail in [1988c].

(b) $H(j, B'((\imath x)\chi, (\imath x)\theta))$ (mixed *de dicto/de re*)

(c) $H(j, B'((\imath x)\chi, (\imath x)\theta))$ (mixed *de re/de dicto*)

(d) $H(j, B'((\imath x)\chi, (\imath x)\theta))$ (pure *de dicto*)

Flexibility such as this is missing in some recent analyses of attitude contexts. In Richard [1983], we find two distinct belief relations, one for *de re* belief, and one for *de dicto* belief. Also, Forbes [1987] offers a Fregean-style analysis that automatically forces *de dicto* belief reports to be given pure *de dicto* readings. In such systems, it is impossible to represent mixed *de re/de dicto* reports like the above.

This flexibility extends even to relation-denoting expressions. In some situations, a relation-denoting term inside the scope of a propositional attitude verb signifies its ordinary denotation, whereas in others, such a term signifies its cognitive content. For example, (1) contains two terms under the scope of the attitude verb. Depending on the context, the most relevant characterization of John's belief state may be any one of the following four readings:

(1a) $B(j, W(\imath x)\phi_1)$ (pure *de re*)

(1b) $B(j, \underline{W}_j(\imath x)\phi_1)$ (pure *de dicto*)

(1c) $B(j, W(\imath x)\phi_1)$ (mixed *de re/de dicto*)

(1d) $B(j, \underline{W}_j(\imath x)\phi_1)$ (mixed *de dicto/de re*)

Representation (1a) is a purely *de re* reading of the English sentence (1). Representation (1b) is a pure *de dicto* reading of (1)—it is constructed out of the cognitive content that the embedded terms have for John. However, (1c) and (1d) are mixed readings—the former treats the English predicate as *de re* and the English description as *de dicto*, whereas the latter treats the predicate as *de dicto* and the description as *de re*. For each reading, it is a straightforward matter to describe a context in which that reading is a more appropriate representation of the English than the others. In general, then, if there are n terms under the scope of the main attitude verb, there will be 2^n different readings of the report.

9.6   Summary

It should be clear that Frege's general insight concerning attitude contexts has been preserved. Although Frege seems to have required that the terms of natural language inside such contexts always denote their senses, we have relaxed this constraint somewhat. Our view is that English terms inside such contexts are ambiguous—sometimes they signify their ordinary denotations, sometimes they signify the cognitive content that they have relative to the subject of the attitude. The attitude verb itself, however, is not ambiguous. We do not need one belief relation to represent *de re* belief reports and another belief relation to represent *de dicto* reports. Only a single belief relation between individuals and propositions is necessary.

This view preserves intact the principle of Substitutivity. No restrictions need be placed on this principle. Once the ambiguities of natural language are eliminated through analysis, it becomes clear that the ambiguities are the source of the apparent failures.

Finally, it seems clear that A-objects can perform the tasks for which Fregean senses were designed. Unfortunately, Frege believed that senses determine the reference of the terms with which they are associated. This is incompatible with the theory of direct reference. Since direct reference theory offers a better understanding of how denotations are acquired, this part of Frege's theory must be abandoned. On our analysis, the A-objects that serve as senses do not have to determine denotations. They may encode incorrect information—even information that would cause them to determine the wrong denotation. Nevertheless, these A-objects play an important role in mediating our propositional attitudes to the world. Fortunately, the incorrect information they might encode is not used to determine the conditions under which the propositional attitudes in which they are involved are felicitous.

10

Further Issues Concerning the Attitudes

10.1 Possible Objections to the Theory

In this first section, we consider various objections that might be raised against the present view. For the most part, we examine recent work that suggests it would be a mistake to employ A-objects to perform the kinds of tasks that our theory requires them to perform. We shall consider, in turn, some related ideas of Burge and Salmon, and then the ideas of Kripke. These authors arrive at conclusions that appear to run counter to the theory presented so far.

Burge's Objection: In his paper of [1977], Tyler Burge argues that the entities serving as modes of presentation (sense$_1$) cannot also be the objects denoted inside attitude constructions (sense$_3$). To support the conclusion that sense$_1$ $\neq$ sense$_3$, he says (pp. 359ff):

> A touchstone for dealing with the relation between sense$_1$ and sense$_3$ is the consideration of when people are said to share a belief. For example, we often want to say that A, B, and C all believe that Sam Rhodes is a fine fellow, where 'Sam Rhodes' does not have purely transparent position. If the sense$_1$ of a name in a context of potential use is taken to be the descriptions, images and so forth that the user would associate with it, then sense$_1$ and sense$_3$ must be distinguished. For A, B, and C's descriptions and so forth may not coincide .... But none of the aspects of an account of sense$_1$, at least the sense$_1$ of proper names or other demonstrative constructions, is promising as an account of sense$_3$.

Burge's conclusion is warranted only if we accept his view of what it is to have the *same* belief. Once a more detailed understanding of the notion of "having the same belief" is developed, it does not follow from the fact that different individuals have different senses for a given name that they do not share the same belief expressed by means of the name. In the cases of pure *de re* reports, one may say that A, B, and C all have the same belief just in case there is a single proposition to which they bear the relevant attitude. But in the *de dicto* cases, like the example in Burge's argument, what it is to share a belief is different. In this particular case, even though each person has a different sense of 'Sam Rhodes' and is thereby related to distinct intermediate propositions, they share the same belief if there is a single proposition in virtue of which A, B, and C each *truly believe* that Sam Rhodes is a fine fellow. And this is just what happens on our account of true belief.

The definition of felicity from the previous chapter makes the notion of "truly believes" more precise. Here is the definition again, with a different definiendum:[1]

$$x \text{ truly believes that } \phi =_{df} B(x, \phi) \ \& \ \phi^*$$

In pure *de re* contexts, ϕ^* is identical with ϕ (since no underlined terms are used in the pure *de re* readings). But now consider an analysis of Burge's example in which 'Sam Rhodes' is in *de dicto* position. Let us use 'r' to abbreviate 'Sam Rhodes,' 'F' to abbreviate 'being a fine fellow,' and '$\underline{r}_k$' to denote the sense of the name 'Sam Rhodes' for person K. Then, we may represent "K believes that Sam Rhodes is a fine fellow," where 'Sam Rhodes' is the only term that fails to be purely referential, as: $B(k, F\underline{r}_k)$. Now look at the consequences of the definition of true belief ('TB') with respect to persons A, B, and C:

$$TB(a, F\underline{r}_a) \equiv B(a, F\underline{r}_a) \ \& \ Fr$$

$$TB(b, F\underline{r}_b) \equiv B(b, F\underline{r}_b) \ \& \ Fr$$

$$TB(c, F\underline{r}_c) \equiv B(c, F\underline{r}_c) \ \& \ Fr$$

A single proposition, namely the one denoted by 'Fr,' determines whether A, B, and C each truly believes that Samuel Rhodes is a fine fellow. It is in virtue of this fact that they may be said to *share* this belief. Each is directed towards the *same* objective piece of information, namely the proposition denoted by "Samuel Rhodes is a fine fellow." For each person x, the directed state is objectified by an intermediate proposition that has as a constituent x's own particular cognitive association with the name 'Sam Rhodes.' The language is holding everything together for us,

---

[1] Recall that ϕ^* is the result of deleting all of the underlines and subscripts in ϕ.

because no matter what sense each attaches to 'Sam Rhodes,' this name is causally/contextually tied to Sam Rhodes. This is what allows the definition of believing truly to work properly. And this is why abstract objects can simultaneously play the roles $sense_1$ and $sense_3$.

Salmon's Objection: Salmon argues in [1979] that $sense_4 \neq sense_6$. His reasoning is that the $sense_4$ of a name may contain misinformation, whereas the $sense_6$ may not ([1979], p. 450).[2] He considers the following sentence:

(1) K believes that Aristotle wrote *The Metaphysics*.

Salmon assumes that (1) is both true and informative, and that when someone believes that Aristotle wrote *The Metaphysics*, there is nothing incorrect in what is believed. He then argues that the name 'Aristotle' seems to make some contribution to this correct and *a posteriori* information. Its contribution can't be its $sense_4$, however, since that may be replete with misinformation. So, he concludes that $sense_6$, which forms "part" of the belief expressed by means of the term, must be distinct from $sense_4$.

Salmon is correct in thinking that the $sense_4$ may contain misinformation. But the problem with the argument is the assumption that were there such misinformation in the $sense_6$ of a term, it would cause the belief to be incorrect. In our theory of belief, this assumption is false. The notion of "correct belief" operative here is just the notion of "true belief." In the problematic *de dicto* cases, which, presumably, are the ones Salmon has in mind, the truth conditions of the belief report involve propositions having abstract constituents that may encode misinformation (the properties encoded need not be exemplified by the denotations of the terms used to express the belief). But the conditions under which the belief is true (or correct) are not affected by this misinformation, for these conditions are linked to the propositional object of the belief.

Reconsider (1). If K's associations with the name 'Aristotle' includes misinformation, then $\underline{Aristotle}_k$ encodes properties Aristotle fails to exemlify. For simplicity, let us investigate the *de dicto* reading of (1) on which 'Aristotle' is the only term inside the attitude context for which substitutions aren't permitted. That is, consider (1a):

(1a) $B(k, W\underline{a}_k m)$

The definition of "truly believes" yields the following theoretical consequence, relative to (1a):

---

[2] If you look up the reference, remember that we've renumbered his '$senses_i$' to square with our own numbering system.

(2) $TB(k, W\underline{a}_k m) \equiv B(k, W\underline{a}_k m) \,\&\, Wam$

In other words, the truth of K's belief depends on the standard proposition denoted by 'Wam.' Despite the fact that the sense 'Aristotle' has for K forms part of the proposition to which K is related by the relation B, the correctness of his belief is tied to the proposition that Aristotle wrote *The Metaphysics*. So there is a clear sense in which K's belief is correct.

It should be clear that the definition of "truly believes" has the following consequence. *Whenever it is appropriate to embed English sentence S, and S alone (i.e., substitutions aren't permissible), in a belief report to ascribe a belief, the definition ties the truth of the belief to the truth of S.* So there is no incompatibility between the roles sense$_4$ and sense$_6$ as long as one distinguishes the truth conditions of the belief report from the felicity conditions of the belief reported.

Kripke's Objection: Finally, we turn to some arguments of Kripke that imply that a picture such as ours is flawed and does not account for the phenomena it was designed to explain. He offers two arguments. The first concludes that sentences like "Some people are unaware that Cicero is Tully" cannot be properly represented if the sense of a name is allowed to vary from person to person; the second concludes that the apparent failure of substitutivity of codesignative names is not to be explained by differences in the senses of names, since people often associate exactly the same sense with different names.

Before looking at these objections in detail, we need to remember that Kripke sometimes takes it as an axiom about senses that they determine reference ([1979], pp. 243–244). Moreover, he seems to hold the view that Fregean senses typically involve properties that uniquely individuate things, and that this is how they determine reference. But our view is that senses need not determine the reference nor encode properties that, either singly or jointly, are uniquely exemplified. Our view even differs from Kripke's understanding of "the extreme Frege-Russellian view" on which the senses of a proper name varies from speaker to speaker. Kripke links this view with the idea that senses involve identifying descriptions. He says in [1979]:

> All this appears at first blush to be powerful support for the view of Frege and Russell that in general names are peculiar to idiolects, with 'senses' depending on the associated 'identifying descriptions'. (p. 245)

In our theory, though the sense of a name does vary from speaker to speaker, it does not necessarily encode identifying descriptions.

This fact plays an important role in undermining Kripke's first objection, which runs as follows:

> Note that, according to the view we are now entertaining [i.e., that senses might vary from person to person], one cannot say, 'Some people are unaware that Cicero is Tully.' For according to this view, there is no single proposition by the 'that' clause, that the community of normal English speakers expresses by 'Cicero is Tully.' ... There is no single fact, 'that Cicero is Tully,' known by some but not all members of the community. ([1979], p. 245)

From our perspective, this objection is not a good one. Clearly, the sentence "Some people are unaware that Cicero is Tully" is true. The reason is that some people fail to take the appropriate attitude to a certain representation of the fact that Cicero is self-identical. For every person x, there is a representational proposition P_x that has the A-objects $\underline{c}_x$ and $\underline{t}_x$ plugged into the gaps of the $identity_E$ relation. There are some individuals x that adopt a certain attitude, namely awareness, to P_x. There are other individuals y that fail to adopt this attitude to P_y. The latter individuals make the sentence in question true. The former individuals have a felicitous attitude, for no matter how widely the individual senses of 'Cicero' and 'Tully' vary relative to the members of this group, the felicity of their awareness depends on the fact that Cicero is $identical_E$ to Tully.

Consequently, if we represent the attitude of awareness by the relation A, the truth conditions of the report "Some people are unaware that Cicero is Tully" are:

$$(\exists x)(Px \ \& \ \sim A(x, \underline{c}_x =_E \underline{t}_x))$$

Note that on this reading, it would be illegitimate to replace 'Tully' by 'Cicero' in the English, since the denotations of these names do not play a role. And, indeed, this is the reading of the English in which we are interested. Suppose Ralph ('r') is a person who makes this quantified English claim true. Then: $\sim A(r, \underline{c}_r =_E \underline{t}_r)$. Ralph, therefore, fails to bear the A relation to P_r. Had Ralph been so related to this proposition, then his attitude would have been a felicitous one, since '$c =_E t$' is true.

Kripke states the second objection as follows:

> But the clearest objection, which shows that the others should be given their proper weight, is this: the view under consideration does not in fact account for the phenomena it seeks to explain. ...Common men who clearly use 'Cicero' as a name for Cicero may be able to give no better answer

to 'Who was Cicero?' than 'a famous Roman orator,' and
they probably would say the same (if anything!) for 'Tully.'
... Similarly, many people who have heard of both Feynman
and Gell Mann, would identify each as 'a leading contemporary theoretical physicist.' ... But to the extent that the
indefinite [his emphasis] descriptions attached or associated
can be called 'senses,' the 'senses' assigned to 'Feynman' and
'Gell Mann,' are *identical* [footnote]. ... The premise of the
argument we are considering for the classic position of Frege
and Russell—that whenever two codesignative names fail to
be interchangeable in the expresson of a speaker's beliefs, failure of interchangeability arises from a difference in the 'defining' descriptions the speaker associates with these names—is,
therefore, false. The case illustrated by 'Cicero' and 'Tully'
is, in fact, quite usual and ordinary. So the apparent failure
of codesignative names to be everywhere interchangeable in
belief contexts, is not to be explained by the differences in
the 'senses' of these names. (pp. 246–247)

Clearly, Kripke has a valid argument here. However, one of the premises
is false. And that is the assumption that two different names may have
the same sense. This is something we emphatically deny, and there are
several good ways to show that the senses of distinct proper names are
always going to be distinct. It seems to us undeniable that every proper
name a person encounters is encountered in a distinct situation. It is not
possible to grasp two proper names simultaneously, in exactly the same
circumstances.[3] This means that in cases like the ones Kripke describes,
distinct senses can be associated with distinct names. This will happen
even if, for example, the only encounter one has with 'Feynman' and
'Gell Mann' is that one has heard the names read off a list of "leading
contemporary theoretical physicists."

  There are, in general, two minimal pieces of information always
available to distinguish the files of information associated with distinct
names. For one thing, we can always use the properties of being called
'Cicero' and being called 'Tully.' These are non-trivial pieces of information that can be encoded by the A-object a person associates
with 'Cicero' and 'Tully,' respectively. The footnote in the above passage from Kripke contains his objection to this move. It is an objection that he discussed in [1972] (pp. 283–286). In [1972], Kripke
agrees that such properties as being called so-and-so are not trivial but

---

[3]If the two names are read successively off a list, then the circumstances in which
the names are learned are different. The second name is learned in a circumstance
in which the first name was just uttered. This difference might be exploited.

argues that the use of such properties violates the "circularity condition." The circularity condition is simply that the properties used to
determine the denotation of the name are not themselves allowed to
involve the notion of denotation. *But note that Kripke's argument is
directed against a Fregean theory on which senses determine the denotation of names.* Ours is not such a theory. We do not appeal to
properties such as being called 'Cicero' to determine that Cicero is the
denotation of 'Cicero,' and in fact, as the reader should be aware, we
rely on Kripke's ideas about direct reference to explain what it is that
does determine the denotation of a name. So this argument of his has
no force against the claims that distinct names always carry with them
the information that their bearers are so-called and that this information is always distinct for distinct names. No dire consequences result
as long the information is not used for determining the denotation of a
name.[4]

We turn next to a second kind of minimal information that distinct proper names may encode. Note that when we encounter distinct
names and there is no evidence for thinking that they denote the same
thing, we usually assume that the names denote different things. Sometimes, part of the information that we attach to different names learned
one right after the other is that they denote different things. So if K
hears 'Feynman' and 'Gell Mann' read off a list of leading contemporary theoretical physicists, K would naturally assume that Feynman is
not Gell Mann. This assumption may get encoded into the the senses
of both names. But in such a situation, K has no epistemological acquaintance with either man. It is important to characterize K's mental
state without employing properties that have Feynman or Gell Mann as
constituents.

Once K has heard both 'Feynman' ('a') and 'Gell Mann' ('b') read
off the list, the sense of 'Feynman' for K might encode $[\lambda y \ y \neq_E \underline{b}_k]$ and

---

[4] Another passage in [1972] is also of interest. Kripke says:

> Suppose we amend the thesis so that it reads: it's trifling to be told
> that Socrates is called 'Socrates' by us, or at least by me, the speaker.
> Then in some sense this is fairly trifling. I don't think it is necessary
> or analytic .... As a theory of the reference of the name 'Socrates' it
> will lead immediately to a vicious circle. ... Actually, sentences like
> 'Socrates is called "Socrates" ' are very interesting ... " (pp. 286–287)

Kripke here lends support to the idea that such properties are genuinely informative by admitting that sentences such as "Socrates is called 'Socrates' (by speaker
K in context c)" are neither necessary nor analytic. Thus, we can suppose that the
sense of 'Cicero' for K can be distinguished from the sense of 'Tully' for K by the
fact that the former encodes the informative property of being called 'Cicero' (in
learning context c) whereas the latter encodes the property of being called 'Tully'
(in learning context c').

the sense of 'Gell Mann' for K might encode $[\lambda y \; y \neq_E \underline{a}_k]$. We could not have used the properties $[\lambda y \; y \neq_E b]$ and $[\lambda y \; y \neq_E a]$, in which the physicists themselves are constituents. Such properties would not do the job in the Cicero-Tully case, since $[\lambda y \; y \neq_E c]$ is the same property as $[\lambda y \; y \neq_E t]$. But for an individual K who heard the names read from a list of famous Roman men of letters, the following properties would work: $[\lambda y \; y \neq_E \underline{c}_k]$ and $[\lambda y \; y \neq_E \underline{t}_k]$.

To complicate the example somewhat, suppose that K is told that Cicero might in fact be the same person as Tully. We could still distinguish the sense of 'Cicero' for K from that of 'Tully' with the properties $[\lambda y \; \Diamond y \neq_E \underline{t}_k]$ and $[\lambda y \; \Diamond y \neq_E \underline{c}_k]$. Properties like these are available, and this seems to be a good way to put them to work.[5] Properties having abstract constituent can therefore help to distinguish the information content of names in the kinds of cases that Kripke describes.

So there are two reasons for thinking that the senses of distinct proper names can always be distinguished. If at least one is right, then Kripke's claim, that the appeal to senses doesn't explain the apparent substitutivity failure, is false. A refined theory of senses is immune to Kripke's charge.

10.2   The Triadic Theory of Belief

Recently, a certain theory of belief has captured the attention of many philosophers. It is known as "the triadic theory of belief." The theory is, roughly, that the two-place relation of belief is definable in terms of a certain three-place relation that relates persons, propositions, and "ways" of believing propositions. David Kaplan formulated this theory in [1977] (Section XVII), by applying his distinction between content and character at the sentential level. He suggests that a given content (proposition) may be presented under various characters, which are something like manners of presentation. We may hold a propositional attitude toward a given content under one character without holding that attitude toward that content under some other character. John Perry developed a somewhat different version of the triadic view in [1979] and [1980b]. For Perry, propositions are believed relative to a belief state, the latter

---

[5]Recall that the axioms of the theory require that for at least some distinct A-objects a and b, $[\lambda y \; y =_E a] = [\lambda y \; y =_E b]$. Cardinality considerations do not permit us to generate a distinct property $[\lambda y \; y =_E x]$ for each A-object x (since the A-objects are correlated one-to-one with the power set of the set of properties, it would be a violation of Cantor's theorem to suppose that $[\lambda y \; y =_E x]$ is distinct for each distinct A-object x). However, we may consistently suppose that there are many pairs of distinct A-objects a and b such that $[\lambda y \; y =_E a] \neq [\lambda y \; y =_E b]$. These may be used in the analysis of minimal information just proposed.

being individuated in terms of the sentence meanings that a person in
such a state accepts.[6]

Other philosophers have adopted a version of the triadic theory. In
Salmon [1986], the relation of belief is analyzed in terms of a ternary
relation BEL as follows: K believes p iff $(\exists x)(K$ grasps p by means of x
and $BEL(K, p, x))$ (p. 111). And in Soames [1988], there is a somewhat
more general version for any propositional attitude V: a person K V's
that p iff there is a sentence (or mode of presentation) S' such that K
bears a certain attitude (related to V) toward S' and S' expresses the
proposition p. For these authors, then, the three-place attitude relations
are basic, and the two-place relations are derived. Consequently, the
notation '$B(k, p)$' used to translate English belief reports is not primitive
notation, but rather defined.

The triadic view of belief developed by Salmon and Soames identifies the semantic information content of a sentence with structured
Russellian propositions (see Soames [1987], and Salmon [1986]).[7] On
their triadic view, this objective content of a sentence is semantically
signified even when the sentence appears under the scope of an attitude
verb. On their view, terms embedded in such contexts are not ambiguous. Salmon and Soames agree that the principle of substitution is valid,
and that substitutions of co-denotational terms are truth preserving, despite appearances and intuitions to the contrary. They locate the source
of the apparent failures in the *pragmatics* of reporting attitudes.

The triadic theory raises some rather puzzling questions, however.
One concerns the philosophical analysis of the third term of the triadic
relation. In the closing passages of his book, Salmon acknowledges:

> The major problem remaining for the sort of theory I have
> advocated here is to provide a more complete account of the
> things corresponding to proposition recognition failure, the
> things that serve as the third relatum for the BEL relation.
> ([1986], p. 126)

Outside of set-theoretic reconstructions of the notions of character and
sentence meaning, very little is said about these mysterious entities that

---

[6]In another paper, [1977], Perry breaks the connection between thoughts (or propositions) and senses, and suggests that we use senses (these are later referred to as
sentence meanings) to individuate psychological states.

[7]There is an important difference between their conception of propositions and
ours, however. On our conception, the truth of a proposition is basic—it is not
evaluated with respect to anything else. Facts are just true propositions. Compare
Soames' approach in [1987]. He assigns Russellian propositions to sentences, and
then evaluates the propositions in terms of "truth supporting circumstances." But
what are "truth supporting circumstances? Are they something like facts? Do they
have a logical structure? Can they be complex? The answers to these questions
may reveal important differences between our respective points of view.

present propositions to us. Although sets may be useful for describing certain structural relationships, they are not the kind of thing that would help us to understand the nature of presentation. There is nothing about a set in virtue of which it may be said to present something to us. So what are these entities and how do they mediate attitudes towards propositions? How do they function as manners or ways of presenting propositions?

A second problem with the triadic view has do do with apparent substitutivity failure. To explain these failures, triadic theorists draw some important distinctions. Both Soames and Salmon, for example, distinguish between the information semantically encoded by the embedded sentence from pragmatically imparted information. The apparent failure of substitutivity does not arise from any semantic invalidity, they argue, but rather from the pragmatics of reporting attitudes. Unfortunately, however, many of us share the intuition that there are at least some readings of these reports on which substitutions appear to be semantically invalid. Even Soames, who has probably gone the farthest in arguing that substitution is always legitimate, acknowledges:

> Still, a residual uneasiness remains. We do, I think, ordinarily suppose that it is possible to believe and assert that Cicero bears R to Tully without believing or asserting that Cicero bears R to Cicero. This intuition may well remain even after the facts about reflexives and pragmatics have been accommodated. ([1988], Section VI)

The present theory offers some help with respect to both of these concerns about the triadic view. Our metaphysics provides a kind of entity that seems well suited for occupying the third term of the triadic attitude relations. The mysterious, intermediate x's by which we are directed towards propositions are just the special propositions with abstract constituents. These special propositions can represent other propositions with which we have no perceptual or epistemological acquaintance. The constituents of the former represent, and direct us toward, the constituents of the latter, and the structure of the former represents the structure of the latter.

On our theory, however, the two-place attitude relations are basic. *De re* reports link the subject of the attitude directly with the propositional object. *De dicto* reports link the subject of the attitude directly with a way of conceiving the propositional object. In either case, the attitude involved holds between persons and propositions. This seems to be the way attitude verbs work in natural language. They seem to involve a subtle ambiguity. Moreover, our analysis of attitude felicity suggests that the three-place attitude relations can be derived. That's because the abstraction principle for relations guarantees that, for a given two-place attitude relation V, there is a three-place relation of type $\langle i, p, p \rangle$ that holds among an individual x and propositions F and G just in case both VxF and the felicity of V depends on the truth of G. In other words, when considering the felicity conditions of the attitude that is reported rather than the truth conditions of the *de dicto* report, three different entities are related in a special way: the individual, the proposition that does the representing, and the proposition that is represented.

Secondly, the present analysis also explains the intuition that the apparent failures of substitutivity signal a *semantic* invalidity of some kind. Substitutions based on identity statements of the form '$a = b$' are invalid when either 'a' or 'b' is in *de dicto* position. Since natural language attitude reports involve terms in *de dicto* position, substitutivity will appear to fail. For example, the report "Ralph believes that Cicero is a Roman", on our view, does have a reading for which the substitution of 'Tully' for 'Cicero' is illegitimate. But this is no fault of the Principle of Substitutivity, but rather of the fact that, for the reading in question, 'Cicero' does not denote Cicero.

It is for these reasons, then, that we prefer the present analysis to that of the triadic view. It gives us a somewhat sharper picture of how propositions can be believed, desired, expected, etc., in one way but not in another. "Ways" of holding an attitude towards a proposition are not so metaphysically mysterious, once they are individuated with propositions having abstract constituents. No appeal is made to sets, structured meanings, or any other theoretical entity that's not a part of the explicitly stated background ontology. Moreover, intuitions about the semantic invalidity of certain inferences are not ignored.[8]

10.3   Existential Generalization

The last issue that we consider in this chapter concerns Existential Generalization. The theory yields a simple explanation of the apparent

---

[8]There is one other interesting feature of our view. And that is that the analysis of belief involves a direct reference theory that can cover the cases of names of nonexistent objects. This leaves us with a more complete defense of the modified "naive" theory of information content. Compare, for example, Salmon [1986], in which we find: "...the other major sources of objection to the modified naive theory have traditionally been the apparent existence of true negative existentials involving nonreferring names and the more general problem of the truth value and information content of sentences involving nonreferring names. ...a complete defense of the modified naive theory would require a complete defense of the latter source" (p. 127).

failure of this principle. Recall the example of Quine's that was described in Chapter 1:

(3) Ralph believes that the tallest spy is a spy.

Clearly, there is a reading of (3) that does not imply "Ralph believes that someone is a spy," where this means "There is a particular person who Ralph believes to be a spy." This reading of (3) is not captured by the pure *de re* analysis, namely (4), in which '$(\imath x)\phi_1$' represents 'the tallest spy':

(4) $B(r, S(\imath x)\phi_1)$

Let us assume that there is a tallest spy. Then (5) is a consequence of (4):

(5) $[\lambda y \ B(r, Sy)](\imath x)\phi_1$

Sentence (5) tells us that the tallest spy has the property of being believed by Ralph to be a spy. If we assume that spies are persons, then we can derive (6):

(6) $(\exists y)(Py \ \& \ B(r, Sy))$

Clearly, then, since (4) implies (6), it is not the reading that explains why Existential Generalization appears to fail.

A reading of (3) that does not imply (6) is captured by the following:

(7) $B(r, S\underline{(\imath x)\phi_1})$

On this reading, the English 'the tallest spy' is in *de dicto* position.[9] Since '$\underline{(\imath x)\phi_1}$' denotes a particular A-object, (7) has some interesting consequences. One is:

(8) $(\exists x)B(r, Sx)$

So from the *de dicto* reading of (3), it follows that there is something that Ralph believes to be a spy. But then why does Existential Generalization appear to fail? The answer is found in the fact that (8) doesn't imply (6). So even if (3) describes a case in which Ralph is doing nothing more than contemplating consequences of the fact that there is a tallest spy (having no particular spy in mind), our analysis allows quantification over the A-individual that serves to represent the tallest spy to Ralph. Even in such a case, it must be true to say that there is something that Ralph believes to be a spy, even though we cannot suppose that there

---

[9]Of course, there are other readings of (3) that take 'is a spy' to be in *de dicto* position, but these will not play a role in the explanation of the puzzle.

is some person (or some particular thing that exemplifies being a spy) who Ralph believes to be a spy.

Note that by representing descriptions in *de dicto* position in this way, there are two ways to distinguish "the information content" of two arbitrary sentences S and S' which differ only by the fact that a name in S is replaced by a co-referential description in S'. To see this, note that in ordinary contexts, descriptions contribute their denotation to the proposition denoted by the sentence as a whole. Consequently, when a name such as 'b' and a description such as '$(\imath x)\phi$' have the same denotation, the sentences 'Rab' and '$Ra(\imath x)\phi$' denote the same proposition. They have *different* truth conditions, however, as can be seen by considering the definition of truth$_I$. Moreover, 'Rab' and '$Ra(\imath x)\phi$' typically have distinct *cognitive* information content, since relative to a given individual, the cognitive content of 'b' and '$(\imath x)\phi$' will typically be distinct. In attitude contexts in which the description is in *de dicto* position, '$Ra(\imath x)\phi$' signifies an intermediate proposition that has a constituent encoding the information embodied in the description. Consequently, there are two ways in which "the information content" of 'Rab' can differ from the information content of '$Ra(\imath x)\phi$', even when 'b' and '$(\imath x)\phi$' have the same denotation—they have different truth conditions, and their cognitive significance is different. The latter suffices for analyzing the crucial cases where someone believes the one and not the other.

Other Substitutivity Puzzles

11.1   Russell's Puzzle About George IV

The brief discussion of descriptions at the end of the last chapter puts us in a position to reexamine Russell's puzzle about the propositional attitudes. This is the only puzzle in his [1905a] that we have not yet discussed, and a successful solution would show that the present framework constitutes an alternative to the theory of descriptions. There is no reason to think that every name is a disguised definite description, and there is no need to eliminate descriptions by contextual definition.

Russell notes that using the law of substitutivity, we may deduce (3), which is clearly false, from (1) and (2), which seem clearly true:

(1) George IV wished to know whether Scott was the author of Waverley

(2) Scott was the author of Waverley

(3) George IV wished to know whether Scott was Scott

Russell's solution to this puzzle must have certainly seemed like positive evidence in favor of his theory, for it allowed him to preserve the principle of substitutivity. Using his notion of scope, Russell gives the following two readings of (1), in which '$W(x, \phi)$' abbreviates 'x wishes to know whether ϕ,' 'Axy' abbreviates 'x authored y,' 'g' denotes George IV, 's' denotes Scott, and 'w' denotes the novel in question:[1]

---

[1] Strictly speaking, Russell would eliminate every occurrence of a proper name in the formal representations that follow. They would be replaced by the definite description for which they are but shorthand. However, the symbolizations that follow represent the case in just enough detail for stating Russell's principal solution to the puzzle.

(4) $W(g, (\exists x)(Axw \ \& \ (\forall y)(Ayw \rightarrow y=x) \ \& \ s=x))$

(5) $(\exists x)(Axw \ \& \ (\forall y)(Ayw \rightarrow y=x) \ \& \ W(g, s=x))$

In addition, Russell asserts that (2) is not really a simple identity statement of the form '$x=y$.' Instead, its form is given by (6):

(6) $(\exists x)(Axw \ \& \ (\forall y)(Ayw \rightarrow y=x) \ \& \ s=x)$

Finally, the reading of (3) that Russell wants to avoid seems to be (7):

(7) $W(g, s=s)$

Russell's argument in ¶30 and ¶31 of [1905a] continues as follows: (4) is the reading of (1) that best represents George IV's concerns. In (4), however, there is no syntactic constituent corresponding to the English description. And in a similar manner, (6) is the proper analysis of (2). Not only does (6) fail to have a syntactic constituent corresponding to the description, but it also fails to be a simple identity statement (though it does have an identity statement as a part). Consequently, one cannot legitimately apply the principle of substitutivity to (4) and (6) to produce (7), since the formulas don't have the appropriate form. Since (7) does not follow from (4) and (6), Russell argues, analysis shows that (3) is not a conclusion of (1) and (2).

Russell also has an explanation for why it was thought that (3) followed in the first place: when the description in (1) is construed as having primary occurrence, (1) has the alternative reading (5). So (7), the reading of (3), follows from (5) and (6), using the principle of substitutivity in conjunction with other laws of logic.

Recent theorists tend to accept Russell's view that (1) is ambiguous. Though Montague doesn't contextually eliminate descriptions before evaluating sentences in which they occur, he does follow Russell in utilizing scope distinctions to give at least two readings for (1) (see his [1974]). Montague's analysis yields a *de dicto* reading similar to (4), for which the inference does not go through, and a *de re* reading similar to (5) for which it does.[2]

Though we agree with Russell that (1) is ambiguous, we prefer not to tamper with the logical form of the embedded sentence. The English terms in propositional attitude reports are ambiguous, and once their

---

[2]In the *de dicto* reading, Montague builds up the logical form by developing a tree in which the noun phrase 'George IV' is concatenated with the verb phrase 'wished to know whether Scott was the author of Waverley.' In the *de re* reading, he builds up the logical form with a tree in which 'the author of Waverley' is substituted into the open sentence "George IV wished to know whether Scott was him$_0$." The semantic representations associated with the two distinct syntactic trees are also distinct, and the *de dicto* representation accounts for the failure of substitutivity.

senses are identified as entities of the same logical type as their denotations, the ambiguity may be resolved without destroying the apparent logical form of the report. The sense of the 'the author of Waverley' is the A-object that encodes the property of being the author of Waverley. The sense of 'Scott' for George IV is a distinct A-object. If we let '$\underline{s}_g$' denote George IV's sense of 'Scott,' and '$(\imath x)Axw$' denote the sense of 'the author of Waverley,' the following representations help to explain Russell's puzzle:

(1a) $W(g, s =_E (\imath x)Axw)$

(1b) $W(g, \underline{s}_g =_E (\imath x)Axw)$

(2a) $s =_E (\imath x)Axw$

(3a) $W(g, s =_E s)$

Clearly, (1b) is a *de dicto* reading of (1), and since it, together with (2a), does not imply (3a), there is a reading of (1) and (2) which neither forces us to accept (3) nor forces us to revise the rule of substitution. However, (1a) and (2a) do imply (3a), and this reading reveals why we are tempted to think that the English inference is valid. Note that (3a) is false. Though it relates George IV to the proposition which, if true, would positively satisfy his desire for knowledge, (3a) says that George IV is directly related to this proposition. This doesn't seem to be the case. Note also that the distinction between the primary and secondary occurrence of the description does not play a role. The English description in (1) and (2) is always treated as a genuine syntactic constituent.

11.2   Kripke's Puzzles

In his paper of [1979], Kripke produces an interesting puzzle about the attitudes. An analysis of this puzzle provides a good showcase for our theory. It provides us with a clearer picture not only of the phenomena being considered but also of how the puzzle arises. In this section, we state Kripke's puzzle, state the solution, and then show that the solution is sophisticated enough to disarm the challenges Kripke raises to the standard Fregean position.

The Principal Puzzle: The puzzle concerns one Pierre, a normal French speaker who lives in France, speaks no English, and on the basis of what he has read and heard of the famous foreign city, assents to the sentence "Londres est jolie." Later, after moving to an unattractive part of London (which he fails to realize is the same city as Londres), and after acquiring some English and some beliefs about the unattractiveness of the city in which he finds himself, assents to the sentence "London is not pretty" (without withdrawing his assent from "Londres est jolie"). Kripke notes that (10) is a consequence of Pierre's sincere assent to (8) and the French version of the disquotation principle (9):

(8) Londres est jolie

(9) If normal speaker, on reflection, sincerely assents to 'p', then he believes that p

(10) Pierre croit que Londres est jolie

He also notes that we get (12) from (10) coupled with an ordinary principle of translation (11):

(11) If a sentence of one language expresses a truth in that language, then any translation of it into any other language also expresses a truth

(12) Pierre believes that London is pretty.

The puzzle is that we may simultaneously deduce (14) (which conflicts with (12)) from the disquotation principle and Pierre's assent to (13):

(13) London is not pretty

(14) Pierre believes that London is not pretty

The puzzle, at this stage, is simply to try to explain how both (12) and (14) can be true together. There is not yet any contradiction in our judgments about Pierre's beliefs, but rather a contradiction in Pierre's judgments. But we can in fact get a contradiction in our judgments about Pierre's beliefs by appealing to a strengthened disquotation principle, namely, (5′):

(5′) A normal speaker, on reflection, sincerely assents to 'p' iff he believes that p.

We could build the case of Pierre in such a way that it is reasonable to assume that he does not assent to (15):

(15) London is pretty

Then, by the strengthened disquotation principle (5′), we get (16):

(16) Pierre doesn't believe that London is pretty

This, Kripke argues, is a real paradox, for we have deduced a contradiction, namely, the conjunction of (12) and (16), from apparently acceptable principles and some uncontroversial facts. So which principle needs to be given up?

From the point of view of the theory and intensional logic of abstract objects, both the disquotation principle and the translation principle are simply too crude. For consider the following description of Pierre's situation using the concepts available in our framework.[3] In the story we tell concerning Pierre's situation, we can say that while still in France, Pierre encountered the name 'Londres' and utilized an abstract object, $Londres_p$, as the sense of that name. This object represents London (under the label 'Londres') to him. It may encode the property of being pretty. When he uses the term 'Londres,' the intermediate propositions that he grasps contain $\underline{Londres}_p$ as a constituent. Such propositions are essential for individuating Pierre's states of mind. For explaining most of Pierre's behavior, the appeal to standard propositions would suffice. But we are now concerned with his reponses to questions about his beliefs, and this may require us to appeal to the senses of the words involved in the questions.

From the fact that Pierre reflectively and sincerely assents to (8) we may conclude (10), but only if we recognize that the French belief report is ambiguous. Our intensional logic now becomes essential to the disambiguation process because "Londres est jolie" does not distinguish $\mathbf{PLUG_1}(\mathbf{Being\ pretty}, \mathbf{London})$ from $\mathbf{PLUG_1}(\mathbf{Being\ pretty},$ $\mathbf{\underline{Londres}_p})$. The disquotation principle, while moving us to (10) from Pierre's assent to (8), doesn't distinguish the two important readings of the latter. And since there is no sentence of French which unambiguously expresses the *de dicto* reading of the report, the translation principle to which Kripke appeals is not attuned to the fact that Pierre's sense of the word 'Londres' is an important component of this reading. A translation principle that fails to take into account the senses of names will not be discriminating enough.

To see this, let 'ls' be an abbreviation in our logic for 'Londres,' 'ln' be an abbreviation for 'London,' '$\underline{ls}_p$' denote $\underline{Londres}_p$, and '$\underline{ln}_p$' denote $\underline{London}_p$. Then, given that Pierre has assented to (8) ("Londres est jolie"), the belief report "Pierre croit que Londres est jolie" has the following truth conditions:

(17) $B(p, P\underline{ls}_p)$

---

[3] In the description that follows, we shall simplify matters by ignoring Pierre's sense of the French property denoting term 'jolie,' since Kripke's puzzle concerns only the individual denoting terms 'Londres' and 'London.' We shall return later to the question of whether a Kripkean puzzle concerning relation-denoting expressions can be constructed.

That is, were we using 'C' for 'croit' instead of 'B' for 'believes,' and
'J' for 'jolie' instead of 'P' for 'pretty,' these same conditions would be
described in our logic as:

(18) $C(p, J\underline{ls}_p)$

(17) and (18) are both true just in case Pierre stands in that special re-
lationship to the proposition $\mathbf{PLUG}_1(\mathbf{Being\ pretty},\underline{\mathbf{Londres}}_p)$.[4] A
properly sensitive disquotation principle would yield only (18) from
Pierre's assent to (8). (18) is a disambiguated reading of (10).

Now any translation principle that fails to take into account the fact
that Pierre's sense of 'Londres' is essentially involved in the truth conditions of the belief report will not be sensitive enough to the conditions
that make (18) true. In our intensional logic, (17) is a translation of (18),
and it will not do to just decode (17) back into (12) ("Pierre believes
that London is pretty"). The reason is that the word 'London' has a
sense for Pierre which is different from the sense of 'Londres.' This seems
to be the most natural explanation of the fact that Pierre both assents
to (13) ("London is not pretty") and fails to assent to (15) ("London
is pretty"). From the fact that Pierre assents to the former, the weak
version of the disquotation principle yields (14). But, of course, this report is ambiguous, and a refinement of this weak disquotation principle
would do no more than yield (19) from Pierre's assent to (13):

(19) $B(p, \sim P\underline{ln}_p)$

This saves Pierre from the charge that he has inconsistent judgments
and explains the first version of the puzzle. Thus, the proper readings of
(10) and (14) yield only (17) and (19). The actual propositional objects
of Pierre's state of mind are not inconsistent, though our definition of
true belief tells us that Pierre cannot truly believe both of the propositions in question. This is important evidence in favor of our theory,
for the definition of true belief explains why we feel that despite Pierre's
ignorance of the identity of Londres and London, his beliefs, as they are
described in setting up the puzzle, appear to be inconsistent.

Furthermore, from the fact that Pierre withholds his assent from
(15) ("London is pretty"), the strengthened version of the disquotation
principle yields (16) ("Pierre does not believe that London is pretty").
But, of course, (16) is also ambiguous, and the proper reading for it is
(20):

(20) $\sim B(p, P\underline{ln}_p)$

---

[4]It seems reasonable to think that the intermediate proposition also has Pierre's
sense of 'jolie' as a constituent. But recall that we have simplified matters by
focusing only on the sense of 'Londres.'

And now we have a solution to the second version of the puzzle, for (17) and (20) can both be true together. There is no contradiction as long as we are sensitive to the Pierre's senses of 'Londres' and 'London.' This gives us a good reason to reject Kripke's demand that we answer a certain question concerning Pierre. He says:

> But none of this answers the original question. Does Pierre, or does he not, believe that London is pretty? I know of no answer to this question that seems satisfactory. It is no answer to protest that, in some other terminology, one can state 'all the relevant facts.' To reiterate, this is the puzzle: Does Pierre, or does he not, believe that London is pretty? ([1979], p. 259)

It should be clear to our readers that the question involves an ambiguous belief report. If the query is about the state of affairs represented in our logic as '$B(p, P\underline{ls}_p)$,' then the answer is yes. If the query is about the state of affairs represented in our logic as '$B(p, P\underline{ln}_p)$,' the answer is no.

Kripke's Challenge to Fregeans: Kripke anticipates a Fregean's response to his puzzle. Though he admits that there is something to the Fregean solution (pp. 244–245), he produces arguments to show that such a solution is ultimately not successful. However, his arguments are persuasive only against a strict Fregean view. They have no force against our modified Fregean view.

We dealt with Kripke's first objection to the strict Fregean position in the previous chapter. He asserts that the puzzle remains even if Pierre associates exactly the same identifying properties with both names (pp. 260–261). The case is developed so that Pierre, while in France, associates certain identifying properties with 'Londres,' such being the capital of England, being the location of Buckingham Palace, being the residence of the Queen of England (such properties, of course, being expressed in French with such words as 'Angleterre', 'le Palais de Buckingham,' and 'la Reina'). Then, after he comes to England, Kripke asserts, the same identifying properties (this time expressed in English), could be associated with 'London.' But, Kripke suggests, Pierre need not conclude that 'Londres' and 'London' name the same city. He need only conclude that 'England' and 'Angleterre' name different countries, that 'Buckingham Palace' and 'le Palais de Buckingham' name different palaces, and so on (p. 261).

On our view, however, 'Londres' and 'London' would not be associated with the same properties (identifying or otherwise). Even if the situation is exactly like the one Kripke describes, Londres$_p$ might encode the property of being called 'Londres' whereas London$_p$ might encode the property of being called 'London.' Moreover, when Pierre is in France, the relational properties he associates with 'Londres' are expressed in terms of other names like 'le Palais de Buckingham.' But since Pierre has no direct acquaintaince with Buckingham Palace, Londres$_p$ might not encode the property of being the location of Buckingham Palace (this property has Buckingham Palace as a constituent). Rather Londres$_p$ would encode the structurally similar property that has the sense of 'le Palais de Buckingham' as a constituent, in the place of Buckingham Palace. The other relational properties encoded by Londres$_p$ would also have abstract representations as constituents, rather than the objects represented. And when Pierre learns English, the structurally similar properties encoded by London$_p$ will have distinct abstract representations as constituents, since Pierre's associations with these English names will differ, in the manner suggested, from the associations he has with their French equivalents.

Consequently, there are several reasons why Londres$_p$ and London$_p$ will be distinct. The learning contexts for 'Londres' and 'London' are radically different in this case (there is even a language switch), and these two names thereby carry different information for Pierre. It is not puzzling why Pierre denies that Londres is identical with London, or why he can assent to "Londres est jolie" while denying "London is pretty," even in this last version of the case. There are different senses and different belief states involved, even though the states are directed at the same propositional objects.

In most ordinary contexts and for most ordinary purposes, translating "Pierre croits que Londres est jolie" as "Pierre believes that London is pretty" preserves truth. For these contexts and purposes, the precise way in which Pierre represents this city is unimportant. But in contexts in which we are interested in the special way in which a person represents the world, greater sensitivity to the particular words used in the *de dicto* readings of attitude reports is required (that's why we call them "*de dicto*"). In these special contexts, it is unacceptable to translate 'Londres' as 'London,' for example. So translating the *de dicto* readings of attitude reports from one language to another becomes a real problem. We may indeed have to restrict ourselves to phonetically identical names to translate these readings. But none of this means that we have to give up our the normal translation procedure for ordinary contexts and purposes.

This, then, is the way to reply to Kripke when he says that it is too "desperate" and "drastic" a move to suggest that we not translate 'Londres' as 'London' (p. 263). He argues that it is contrary to our normal practice, as well as implausible, to use "word salads" (in which names from one language are imported into another) to translate these reports.

However, for ordinary purposes, we need not translate "Pierre croit que Londres est jolie" as "Pierre believes that *Londres* is pretty." For special philosophical purposes, though, this may be necessary. Kripke acknowledges that the practice of importing foreign names into a language for certain purposes of translation is acceptable (p. 264).

Nevertheless, Kripke is still concerned that such a procedure is too drastic. He argues that this procedure would have to be extended to natural kind terms as well, so that, for example, we would have to import 'lapin' into English, rather than translate it as 'rabbit.' Otherwise, we get the same puzzle. He says:

> We were considering a 'strict and philosophical' reform of translation procedures which proposed that foreign proper names should always be appropriated rather than translated. Now it seems that we will be forced to do the same with all words for natural kinds. (For example, on price of paradox, one must not translate 'lapin' as 'rabbit'!) No longer can the extended proposal be defended, even weakly, as 'merely' universalizing what we already do sometimes. It is surely too drastic a change to retain any credibility. (p. 265)

But Kripke's conclusion is far too strong. All that follows is that 'lapin' should not be translated as 'rabbit' when the context and occasion is sensitive to the senses that words have for the subject of a belief report. Such occasions are rare, and usually arise only in the context of philosophical discussions about predicting (verbal) behavior.

Actually, our intensional logic is designed to handle the puzzles concerning natural kind terms as well. The 'woodchuck'/'groundhog' example described in Chapter 9 shows that we cannot substitute these expressions in certain *de dicto* readings of attitude reports and preserve truth. In such contexts, the truth of the report depends on propositions having the senses of these words as constituents. The senses of 'woodchuck' and 'groundhog,' as we construe them, play an important role in explaining why K can believe that something is a woodchuck without believing that it is a groundhog. The same applies to the case of 'lapin' and 'rabbit.' In the special context of a *de dicto* report of Pierre's attitudes, we may not be able to translate 'lapin' as 'rabbit' and preserve truth, since the sense that 'lapin' has for Pierre is distinct from the sense that 'rabbit' has for him. The abstract properties in question encode distinct properties of properties, since the circumstances in which 'lapin' and 'rabbit' are learned will be distinct.

Finally, Kripke suggests that the restriction requiring the use of phonetically identical names for translation is still ineffectual against another version of the puzzle. His 'Paderewski' case involves an agent who

misconstrues two tokens of the same name as tokens of different, but
phonetically identical, names of two different individuals. The example concerns one Peter, who on the basis of learning 'Paderewski' as
the name of a famous pianist, believes that Paderewski had musical talent. Later, in different circumstances, Peter learns of someone called
'Paderewski' who was a politician, and on the basis of skepticism regarding the musical abilities of politicians, concludes that Paderewski
(the politician) had no musical talent. Since one is still faced with the
puzzling question of whether Peter believes Paderewski had musical talent, Kripke concludes that the restriction requiring that phonetically
identical names be used in translation is ineffectual (pp. 265–266).

Though this may be an objection to the "word salad" approach
that Kripke considers, it is no objection to our theory. Throughout
our discussion, we've simplified matters by ignoring the fact that senses
of names may vary from time to time. In the present case, however,
this fact is relevant. The sense of 'Paderewski' for Peter when he first
learned the name is different from the sense it has for him when he
later hears the name in the political circles. We may designate these as
$\underline{\text{Paderewski}}_{p,t_1}$ and $\underline{\text{Paderewski}}_{p,t_2}$. The logical representation of "Peter
believes that Paderewski had musical talent" involves $\underline{\text{Paderewski}}_{p,t_1}$,
whereas the logical representation of "Peter believes that Paderewski
had no musical talent" involves $\underline{\text{Paderewski}}_{p,t_1}$. This is simply a case
where the cognitive significance of the name changes with the change of
context, and the truth conditions of the *de dicto* reading of the belief
report will therefore depend on the context. The *de re* reading will not
change, however, since the denotation of the 'Paderewski' is the same in
both contexts.

11.3   Indexical Belief

Since the notion of context has now become significant, it is appropriate to conclude this chapter with a brief discussion of belief reports
that contain context-sensitive terms. The denotations of indexicals vary
from context to context. They are to be contrasted with unambigu-
ous proper names and property-denoting expressions, the denotations
of which remain fixed through context change. From the discussion in
the previous section, it is clear that the sense of a name may vary from
context to context. Consequently, since indexicals are essentially just
context-dependent names, they constitute a special class of terms which
are such that their senses *and* denotations vary from context to context.

The sense of an indexical is not its linguistic meaning. Its linguistic meaning is typically embodied by a rule that any competent language user has to know to use the indexical properly. For example, the

linguistic meaning of 'I' might be the rule: 'I' is a nominative case, singular pronoun that is used by the speaker to refer to himself or herself other than by name. In [1977], Kaplan calls this kind of meaning the 'character' of the indexical, and he represents the character of an expression semantically with a function that maps each context of use to the content (denotation) of the expression in that context.

In contrast, our view is that the sense of an indexical is the cognitive significance that the indexical has in a given context for a given individual. Unlike the cognitive significance of non-context dependent names, the cognitive significance of an indexical is not closely tied to an individual's historical encounters with the expression. Instead, it reflects the fact that an individual cognizes the object denoted by an indexical (in a given context) in a certain way. In any given context, a person who utters or hears such words as 'I,' 'you,' 'he,' 'that,' etc., typically cognizes the object in a certain way. Their mental state (which may be a perceptual state, if there is a demonstration along with the indexical) has a certain content. This content can be objectified by abstract entities. We may call the abstract entity that objectifies such content "the cognitive character" of the indexical for a given individual in a given context. Semantically, there is a function that maps each indexical, relative to a context c and an individual i in c, to an A-object that serves as the cognitive character of the indexical for i in c. We can name the values of this function by underlining the indexical, and subscripting the name of the individual in question. Thus, relative to context c, '$\underline{I}_k$' denotes the cognitive character of 'I' for person K in c. To relativize the denotation of term τ to context c, we shall sometimes write '$[\tau]_c$.' So the cognitive character of 'I' for person K in c is written '$[\underline{I}_k]_c$.'

The cognitive character of an indexical is the key to the substitutivity puzzles about attitude reports containing such expressions. There is an extensive literature on these puzzles, in which it is made patently clear that codesignative terms cannot be substituted for indexicals in certain readings of attitude reports.[5] By analyzing two representative cases, we should give the reader a good idea of how the theory applies to "indexical beliefs."[6]

Soames's Puzzle: In Soames [1987], we find the case of Professor K, who is looking through a class yearbook. He points to a picture of a student and says "I believe that he is a scholar." Then he points to a picture of a football player in full uniform and says, "I don't believe that he is a scholar." Unknown to the professor, he has pointed to two

---

[5]Some noteworthy papers are Castañeda [1966] and [1967], Perry [1979], Lewis [1979], Stalnaker [1981], Richard [1983], and Soames [1987].

[6]The two case studies that follow also appear in [1988c], forthcoming.

different pictures of the class valedictorian, Alex Jones. Consider the
following two reports:

(21) I believe he is a scholar (pointing to the first picture).

(22) I don't believe he is a scholar (pointing to the second picture).

Most of us share the intuition that by uttering (22), Professor K has
not directly contradicted himself. But the pure *de re* readings of these
two sentences reveal them to be directly contradictory. When the professor points to the second picture, there is a change of context. Let us
call the two contexts c and c', respectively. The indexical 'he' denotes
the same object in both contexts (in Kaplan's terms, the value of the
character function is the same for both c and c'). In other words, the
identity statement, "He is Alex Jones" is true in both c and c', because
$[he]_c = [he]_{c'}$. Now consider the pure *de re* readings of (21) and (22),
respectively:

(23) $[B(I, S(he))]_c$

(24) $[\sim B(I, S(he))]_{c'}$

Clearly, since 'Alex Jones' has the same denotation as 'he' in both contexts, substitution is permissible. This, unfortunately, reveals that Professor K has contradicted himself when he utters (22). Obviously, the
de re reading does not capture our intuitions about the case.

Though the indexical 'he' has the same denotation in c and c', its
cognitive character changes with the change of context. Professor K is
cognizing Alex Jones in two different ways. The content of these two
cognitions is represented by distinct A-objects. Consequently, $[\underline{he}_k]_c \neq$
$[\underline{he}_k]_{c'}$. These objects figure into the *de dicto* readings of (21) and (22).
For these readings, the propositions signified by the embedded sentence
"He is a scholar" are different. The proposition signified by "He is a
scholar" in c has $[\underline{he}_k]_c$ as a constituent, whereas the one signified in c'
has $[\underline{he}_k]_{c'}$ as a constituent. Consequently, the *de dicto* readings of (21)
and (22) may be consistent.

Formally speaking, (25) and (26) are such *de dicto* readings:

(25) $[B(I, S(\underline{he}_I))]_c$

(26) $[\sim B(I, S(\underline{he}_I))]_{c'}$

In both (25) and (26), '$\underline{he}_I$' denotes the sense of 'he' for Professor K
in the context in question.[7] There is no inconsistency between (25) and

---

[7]Given the way these special sense terms are constructed, $[\underline{he}_k]_c = [\underline{he}_I]_c$. The
subscripts 'k' and 'I' both denote Professor K in c. So both expressions denote

(26), since (25) relates K in a special way to the proposition denoted by '$S(\underline{he}_I)$' in **c**, while (26) relates K to the proposition denoted by '$S(\underline{he}_I)$' in **c'**. So (25) indicates that K is in a certain belief state, while (26) indicates that K fails to be in a certain other belief state. Both belief states are directed towards the same proposition, however.

Note that if Professor K strengthens his belief report from "I don't believe that he is a scholar" to "I believe that he is not a scholar" (when pointing to the second picture), then one of K's beliefs is not felicitous. Consider (27) and its *de dicto* representation (28):

(27) I believe that he is not a scholar (pointing at the second picture) .

(28) $[B(I, \sim S(\underline{he}_I))]_{\mathbf{c'}}$

The definition of true belief, when relativized to contexts, requires in the case of (26), that K has a true belief iff Alex Jones is a scholar. But in the case of (28), the definition requires that K believes truly iff it is not the case that Alex Jones is a scholar. In formal terms, the definition has the following consequence for (26):

$$[TB(I, S(\underline{he}_I))]_{\mathbf{c}} \text{ iff } [B(I, S(\underline{he}_I)) \ \& \ S(he)]_{\mathbf{c}}.$$

However, for (28), the definition yields:

$$[TB(I, \sim S(\underline{he}_I))]_{\mathbf{c'}} \text{ iff } [B(I, \sim S(\underline{he}_I)) \ \& \ \sim S(he)]_{\mathbf{c'}}$$

Since $[\sim S(he)]_{\mathbf{c'}}$ is the negation of the true proposition $[S(he)]_{\mathbf{c}}$, it follows that the belief reported by (26) is felicitous and that the belief reported by (28) is not. These results square with our intuitions about the case.

Perry's Puzzles: We conclude the discussion of substitutivity failure by looking at John Perry's puzzles about indexical belief. In [1979], Perry describes the case of a person in a store who notices that a messy trail of sugar is being made by a shopper with a torn sack. However, the person, let us call him 'Bill,' doesn't realize that the trail leads back to his own sack of sugar and that he is the shopper making the mess. We may assume that Bill would accept (29) and (30) because he is ignorant of (31):

(29) I believe that the shopper with a torn sack is making a mess

---

the sense of 'he' relative to K in **c**. Note that the sense terms constructed out of names and indexicals are not entirely compositional. That is, the denotation of '$\underline{he}_k$' relative to any context **c** is not constructed out of the denotations of 'he' and 'k' relative to **c**. The denotation of 'he' in **c** is not relevant to the truth of the report, but rather to the truth of the belief reported. The underline forces us to consider the cognitive character of the term, rather than its character.

(30) I don't believe that I am making a mess

(31) I am the shopper with the torn sack

In this case, there is a single context **c**, and in that context, 'I' denotes Bill. But though (31) is true relative to **c**, and 'I' and 'the shopper with the torn sack' both denote Bill, we cannot substitute the former for the latter in (29), even if the verb was modified to agree with the new subject. The pure *de re* readings of (29) and (30) suggest that we can, however, and this is the source of the puzzle. Here are the pure *de re* readings of (29) – (31):

(32) $[B(I, M((\imath x)\phi))]_{\mathbf{c}}$

(33) $[\sim B(I, M(I))]_{\mathbf{c}}$

(34) $[I =_E (\imath x)\phi]_{\mathbf{c}}$

Since $[I]_{\mathbf{c}} = [(\imath x)\phi]_{\mathbf{c}}$, (34) is true. But then 'I' may be substituted for '$(\imath x)\phi$' in (32), contradicting (33). This doesn't explain why (29) and (30) appear to be consistent.

A consistent reading of (29) and (30) may be found by supposing that the description and the indexical are in *de dicto* position. This reading is sensitive to the cognitive characters of the English terms. The cognitive character that the English description has for Bill in **c** is distinct from the cognitive character that the indexical has for Bill in **c**, even though both terms have the same denotation in **c**. The relevant *de dicto* readings of (29) and (30) are:

(35) $[B(I, M(\underline{(\imath x)\phi}))]_{\mathbf{c}}$

(36) $[\sim B(I, M(\underline{I}_I))]_{\mathbf{c}}$

These readings explain why we cannot substitute the indexical for the description in (29): the two English terms signify different things in **c**. According to (35), the English description signifies $[\underline{(\imath x)\phi}]_{\mathbf{c}}$, whereas according to (36), 'I' signifies $[\underline{I}_I]_{\mathbf{c}}$. The latter is the sense that Bill attaches to 'I' in **c**, whereas the former is the sense that the description has in **c**. These are distinct A-objects, since we may reasonably assume that $[\underline{I}_I]_{\mathbf{c}}$ doesn't encode being the shopper with a torn sack. And Bill has no reason to think he is in fact the object being conceived through the sense of the description.

As it stands, Bill's state of mind as described by (35) is a felicitous one, whereas (36) tells us that he fails be in a certain other felicitous state of mind. The state that he fails to be in is rather informative and would make it possible for him to avoid embarassment. So from (35) and (36), we can make certain predictions about Bill's behavior. On the other hand, were Bill's state accurately characterized by the representation '$[B(I, M(\underline{L_I}))]_c$,' we could predict that if he were an honest character, he would be disposed to clean up the mess or report it to the store management.

These basic ideas concerning the analysis of indexical belief make it possible to understand other problematic cases that Perry discusses. These cases suggest that the cognitive character of indexicals that signify the self are special. For example, in [1977], Perry describes the case of the amnesiac Rudolf Lingens, who, being lost in the Stanford Library, finds and reads a biography of Rudolf Lingens without realizing that this is none other than himself. He ends up learning quite a bit about Lingens, even the fact that Lingens is lost in the Stanford Library. But none of this information allows him to conclude "I am Rudolf Lingens" or "I am lost in the Stanford Library." The explanation for this is that the cognitive character that 'Rudolf Lingens' has for Lingens does not encode the same information that the cognitive character of 'I' encodes for Lingens. As long as the information encoded is distinct, the identity statement "I am Rudolf Lingens" will be informative to Lingens. Indeed, this may be what happens to amnesiacs—the cognitive significance of their names becomes disassociated from the cognitive significance that they normally attach to the word 'I.'

This case suggests that indexicals signifying the self have a special cognitive character. It is tempting to say that no matter how much information Lingens associates with 'Lingens' as a result of reading the biography, he would not acquire the kind of information that would allow him to conclude "I am Rudolf Lingens." If this is right, then it may be that the senses of indexicals that signify the self encode special kinds of properties, properties that are not typically associated with proper names. Do we need to appeal here to Frege's strong hypothesis that there is a primitive and unique way by which each person is presented to himself? Or would it suffice to think that there is a single, generic concept of self that is encoded, possibly along with other properties, by the A-object that serves as the cognitive significance 'I'?[8] Actually, we plan to leave it an open question as to exactly how the cognitive character of indexicals that signify the self are to be distinguished from the cognitive character of names. No matter how the question is decided, the answer seems to be consistent with the theory.[9]

---

[8] This self-concept might also be encoded by the significance of 'he', for example, in the sentence "Lingens believes that he is lost" or "Bill believes that he is making a mess," where the occurrences of 'he' denote the believer and are ineliminable.

[9] In G. Forbes' recent article of [1987], there is a defense of Frege's treatment of indexical belief. Forbes appeals to Frege's hypothesis that every person is pre-

The analysis of Perry's [1977] Heimson and Hume case suggests that the answer to this question should be flexible enough to permit distinct persons to be in exactly the same belief state. Recall that mad Heimson believes that he is Hume, something which Hume believes as well. Both Heimson and Hume assert "I am Hume." Intuitively, Heimson and Hume seem to be in exactly the same belief state—they both use the same special sense of 'I,' and both associate the same sense with 'Hume'. Heimson's disturbed conception of his own identity is so completely bound up in the details of Hume's life that his cognitive associations with 'I' and 'Hume' exactly match Hume's. So "I am Hume" has the same cognitive significance for both Heimson and Hume—the intermediate proposition that both Heimson and Hume grasp when they utter "I am Hume" is the same. But this intermediate proposition represents one proposition for Heimson, and a distinct one for Hume. For Heimson, the intermediate proposition represents the proposition that Heimson is Hume. Since this is false, Heimson fails to have a true belief. However, for Hume, the intermediate proposition represents the proposition that Hume is Hume. This proposition is true, and so Hume has a true belief. So though Heimson and Hume are in exactly the same belief state, only the latter can truly utter "I am Hume."

---

sented to himself in a unique way. His neo-Fregean analysis of indexical belief has some similarity to our own. However, Forbes relies on Peacocke's [1983] views about the individuation of thoughts and modes of presentation. Peacocke's theory of senses, though, seem rather obscure when compared to the present theory, in which propositions and A-objects are precisely characterized. The real problem with Forbes' analysis, therefore, is that it is given in terms of *uninterpreted notation*! No semantics is offered for his sense-denoting terms or the concatenation symbol that indicates that senses are coupled together to produce thoughts. Compare our technically precise way of plugging together property senses and individual senses to produce propositions with abstract constituents. Our technique is rather straightforward, once the sense of a term is identified as an entity of the same logical type as the denotation of the term.

Part V

Conclusion

12

A Comparison with Montague's Intensional Logic[1]

Although many systems have been developed for treating intensional contexts, few have the capacity to analyze the full variety of such contexts. Some are designed principally to treat relations as non-strongly extensional objects (see the cited works of Bealer, Cocchiarella, Menzel, and Chierchia and Turner). Others offer useful analyses of nonexistent objects and the principle of *Existential* Generalization (Parsons [1980]). And still others are designed solely to handle the propositional attitudes and the failures of Substitutivity and Existential Generalization (Thomason [1980]). But none of these systems, to our knowledge, offers a single framework that can resolve the basic puzzles associated with all four kinds of intensionality.

The system that still comes the closest to doing so is Montague's intensional logic in [1974]. His system contains a semantical treatment of propositional attitudes, modality and tense, and nonexistence. Montague identifies relations, properties, and propositions as strongly extensional, set-theoretic objects and then concentrates on the problems associated with the other kinds of intensionality. Since our system is designed to analyze the full range of intensional contexts, it would be useful to see what new features the logic exhibits when compared with Montague's. One of the principal differences that emerges concerns the very definition of intensionality. In Montague's system, modal and temporal contexts are inherently intensional contexts. In our system, such contexts are not intensional by nature.

In Section 1, we try to develop a broad perspective both on the general features of the two logics and on the overall approach to language

---

[1]An earlier version of this chapter appeared as [1988b].

they embody. In Section 2, there is a detailed look at the way each logic represents the puzzles of nonexistence, while in Section 3, the analyses of the propositional attitudes are compared. In Section 4, the focus is on modality and definite descriptions. This topic is a key to one of the important differences between the conceptions of intensionality embodied by the two systems.

12.1 General Comparison

For certain heuristic purposes, it will prove useful to compare our system as it is defined in the Appendix with Montague's as it is explained in the recent text, *An Introduction to Montague Semantics*, by Dowty, Wall, and Peters [1981] (hereafter referred to as: [DWP]). These authors outline very clear motivations for certain features of Montague's logic and some of these motivations will be examined in light of the features of our intensional logic.[2]

The comparison is hampered somewhat by the fact that Montague uses the method of extension and intension in his semantics, whereas we use the method of denotation and satisfaction in ours. Montague's method is to place both terms and formulas into the more general category of "meaningful expression," and to assign every meaningful expression both an extension and an intension. Once an interpretation $\mathbf{M}$ and an assignment to the variables $\mathbf{g}$ is fixed, he assigns to every meaningful expression an extension at each world-time pair. Where η is a meaningful expression, "$[\eta]^{\mathbf{M},\mathbf{w},\mathbf{t},\mathbf{g}}$" indicates the extension of η at $\mathbf{w}$ and $\mathbf{t}$ with respect to model $\mathbf{M}$ and assignment $\mathbf{g}$ (this notation follows [DWP]). Montague then recovers from this assignment an intension for each expression, namely, that function which takes each world-time pair to the extension of the expression at that world-time pair. What distinguishes formulas from other meaningful expressions is the fact that they are of a specific type, namely, the type of expression that is assigned a truth value as its extension at each world-time pair.

Our method of denotation and satisfaction doesn't quite correspond in a nice way to Montague's method. The terms of our language receive only denotations; they are not assigned intensions. Moreover, the denotations of terms are not relativized to world-time pairs. They are relativized only to interpretations of the language and assignments to the variables. This automatically makes every term a rigid designator. In addition, there is a whole class of formulas that fail to be terms. These are the formulas that contain encoding subformulas. Though they

---

[2]See also Partee [1975] for a good discussion of the motivations that underlie various features of Montague's system.

don't denote propositions, such formulas are, nevertheless, meaningful. That's because they have well-defined satisfaction and truth conditions. Despite these differences, it makes some sense to compare the denotation of a term (in our sense) with the extension of a meaningful expression (in Montague's sense).

The following list of features crystallize the general differences between the two systems and will form the basis of discussion in what follows. We use "MIL" to refer to Montague's intensional logic, and "ILAO" to refer to the intensional logic of abstract objects:

i. In MIL, relations, properties, and propositions are represented as sets of a certain sort. This representation requires them to be strongly extensional. In ILAO, these entities are neither represented as sets nor are they strongly extensional.

ii. In MIL, the extension of a formula is a truth value and the extension of an n-place predicate is a set of n-tuples. The intensions of formulas and n-place predicates are strongly extensional relations and propositions, respectively. In ILAO, formulas that are terms denote propositions, and n-place predicates denote relations. No term of any kind receives an intension.

iii. The theory of predication upon which MIL is based is the application of a function to an argument. In ILAO, it is based upon the exemplification of relations by objects and the encoding of properties by abstract objects.

iv. In MIL, the extensions of meaningful expressions are relativized to world-time pairs. In ILAO, the denotations of terms are independent of worlds and times; all terms rigidly designate what they denote at the base (actual) world. It is the extensions of *relations* that vary from world-time pair to world-time pair.

v. In MIL, the rules of identity elimination and λ-conversion are restricted in intensional, tense, and modal contexts. In ILAO, there are no such restrictions.

vi. In MIL, there are two simple types and two complex types. In ILAO, there is one simple type and one complex type.

vii. The intended interpretation of MIL is not finitely representable. The intended interpretation of ILAO is.

Consider, first, features (i) – (iii). They embody a certain understanding of how language relates to the world. Montague's system is based on an extensional, set-theoretic reconstruction of relations and propositions. Though this reconstruction clearly fails to capture the fact that these entities fail Strong Extensionality, it also has another interesting consequence. And that is that the semantic value of the parts of the complex expression cannot be recovered from the semantic value of the entire expression. For example, one cannot recover the extension of the terms of a formula (or λ-expression) from the extension of the formula (or λ-expression) itself. Nor can one recover the intensions of the terms of a formula (λ-expression) from the intension of the entire formula (λ-expression).

To see this clearly, consider a simple atomic formula such as 'Pa' with respect to a model $\mathbf{M}$, where both 'P' and 'a' are constants of type $\langle e, t \rangle$ and e, respectively.[3] In MIL, $[P]^{\mathbf{M},\mathbf{w},\mathbf{t},\mathbf{g}}$ (the extension of 'P' relative to $\mathbf{M}$, $\mathbf{w}$, $\mathbf{t}$, and $\mathbf{g}$), is a function that maps each individual to a truth value (the truth values in MIL are 1 and 0). $[a]^{\mathbf{M},\mathbf{w},\mathbf{t},\mathbf{g}}$ is a particular individual. Consequently, the formula 'Pa' is true under $\mathbf{M}$ iff $[P]^{\mathbf{M},\mathbf{w},\mathbf{t},\mathbf{g}}([a]^{\mathbf{M},\mathbf{w},\mathbf{t},\mathbf{g}}) = 1$ (i.e., iff the result of applying the function denoted by 'P' to the individual denoted by 'a' is the truth value 1).

Once the extension of a sentence is defined to be the relevant truth value, the denotation of the parts of the sentence are not recoverable from the denotation of the sentence. All true sentences have the same denotation, and as Frege realized when he first suggested that the denotation of a sentence is a truth value, all that is specific to the denotation of the parts is lost in the denotation of the sentence as a whole. Strictly speaking, this approach to language does satisfy the demands of compositionality, for the denotation of the sentence is a function of the denotation of the parts. But the demands are not satisfied in quite the way one might expect, for the function in question is not something else in addition to the parts, but has instead been identified with one of the parts.

Recovery of the parts from the whole is not a feature of Montague's intensions either. That is, the intensions of complex expressions do not have as parts the intensions of the parts of the complex expression. The intension of an arbitrary complex functional expression such as $\eta(\gamma)$ does not have the intension of η and the intension of γ as parts. For example, the intension of 'Pa', designated "$[Pa]^{\mathbf{M},\mathbf{g}}_{\mathscr{A}}$" in [DWP], is a function from world-time pairs to truth values (type $\langle s, t \rangle$). The intensions of its parts are as follows: $[P]^{\mathbf{M},\mathbf{g}}_{\mathscr{A}}$ is a function (type $\langle s, \langle e, t \rangle \rangle$) from world-time pairs to functions from individuals to truth values, and $[a]^{\mathbf{M},\mathbf{g}}_{\mathscr{A}}$ is a function (type $\langle s, e \rangle$) from world-time pairs to individuals. The intension of the entire expression 'Pa' is *defined* in terms of the intensions of its parts. The definition is: $[Pa]^{\mathbf{M},\mathbf{g}}_{\mathscr{A}}$ is that function $\mathbf{h}$ with domain $\mathbf{W} \times \mathbf{T}$ such

---

[3]Type e in MIL corresponds to our type i. It is the type of ordinary individuals.

that $\mathbf{h}(\langle w, t \rangle) = 1$ iff $\{[P]_{\mathscr{A}}^{\mathbf{M},\mathbf{g}}(\langle w, t \rangle)\}([a]_{\mathscr{A}}^{\mathbf{M},\mathbf{g}}(\langle w, t \rangle)) = 1$. However, the function $\mathbf{h}$ is simply a set of ordered pairs, and one cannot recover the intensions of the parts of the sentence from this function.

Our system is based on an entirely different approach to language. An assignment $\mathbf{f}$ satisfies$_{\mathbf{I}}$ 'Pa' at $\langle w, t \rangle$ iff $\mathbf{d}_{\mathbf{I},\mathbf{f}}(a) \in \mathbf{ext}_{\mathbf{w},\mathbf{t}}(\mathbf{d}_{\mathbf{I},\mathbf{f}}(P))$ (ignoring contexts), where both 'P' and its denotation are of type $\langle i \rangle$, and both 'a' and its denotation are of type i. In addition, since 'Pa' is constructed entirely out of exemplification subformulas, it denotes a proposition. Dropping subscripts for simplicity, $\mathbf{d}(Pa) = \mathbf{PLUG}_1(\mathbf{d}(P), \mathbf{d}(a))$. So the denotations of the parts of the sentence are preserved as parts of the denotation of the whole sentence. Moreover, $\mathbf{ext}_{\mathbf{w},\mathbf{t}}$ is constrained so that the following condition holds (Appendix, §A.2.1):

$$\mathbf{ext}_{\mathbf{w},\mathbf{t}}(\mathbf{PLUG}_1(\mathbf{d}(P), \mathbf{d}(a))) = T \text{ iff } \mathbf{d}(a) \in \mathbf{ext}_{\mathbf{w},\mathbf{t}}(\mathbf{d}(P))$$

So the condition under which $\mathbf{ext}_{\mathbf{w},\mathbf{t}}$ assigns this proposition the truth value T at $\mathbf{w}$ and $\mathbf{t}$ is the same condition under which the formula 'Pa' is satisfied at $\mathbf{w}$ and $\mathbf{t}$.

This example reveals essential differences between the systems. The most important difference is: *Montague's intensions serve as the extensions of our relations and propositions!* In our system, necessarily equivalent expressions such as '$[\lambda x\, Px \to Px]$' and '$[\lambda x\, Rx \to Rx]$' may denote distinct properties, even though the properties denoted have the same extension at each world-time pair. Furthermore, not only is the denotation of the whole sentence a function of the denotation of the parts, the denotations of the parts are recoverable from the denotation of the whole. The denotations of necessarily equivalent sentences such as '$\Box\mathcal{H}(Pa \to Rq)$' and '$[\lambda xy\, \Box\mathcal{H}(Px \to Ry)]aq$' have a difference in structure that mirrors the difference in structure of the sentences.[4] The denotation function satisfies compositionality without obliterating the denotation of the parts when constructing the denotation of the whole. This Russellian conception of relations is central to the theory.

The divergence between the two approaches to language persists throughout the entire type hierarchy. In the above example, 'a' could be a term of any type t, in which case, 'P' is of type $\langle t \rangle$. The denotations of these expressions fall into the domains of type t and $\langle t \rangle$,

---

[4] The former denotes:

$$\mathbf{NEC}(\mathbf{WAS}(\mathbf{COND}(\mathbf{PLUG}_1(\mathbf{d}(P), \mathbf{d}(a)), \mathbf{PLUG}_1(\mathbf{d}(R), \mathbf{d}(q))))).$$

The latter denotes:

$$\mathbf{PLUG}_1(\mathbf{PLUG}_2(\mathbf{NEC}(\mathbf{WAS}(\mathbf{COND}(\mathbf{d}(P), \mathbf{d}(R))))), \mathbf{d}(q)), \mathbf{d}(a)).$$

respectively. The definitions of $\mathbf{ext_{w,t}}$ and satisfaction$_I$ relate the denotations of these expressions in the appropriate way (Appendix, §A.2.3).
The logical functions are typed as well. $\mathbf{PLUG}_i$ is defined so that the
result of plugging an individual of any type t into a property of type $\langle t \rangle$
is a proposition. The other logical functions, $\mathbf{NEG}$, $\mathbf{UNIV}_i$, $\mathbf{CONV}_{j,k}$,
$\mathbf{REFL}_{j,k}$, $\mathbf{VAC}_{j,t'}$, $\mathbf{COND}$, $\mathbf{NEC}$, $\mathbf{WAS}$, and $\mathbf{WILL}$ map the various propositions and relations into complex propositions and relations.
They work throughout and across the type hierarchy, in just the way
one would expect. $\mathbf{ext_{w,t}}$ ensures that the extensions of the complex
proposition or relation cohere in a natural way with the extensions of
its parts.

So much then for the basic differences between the two logical systems that arise out of the features (i) – (iii). Let us turn next to feature
(iv), namely the treatment of tense and modal contexts. Note that the
systems disagree on the question of whether these contexts are intensional! Montague's extension function, which assigns denotations to the
terms of his language is a binary function, the second argument of which
is a world-time pair. The denotations of his terms are essentially relativized to worlds and times, and this embodies a certain approach to
the way tense and modal contexts of language work. The idea is that
to determine the truth of a formula inside a tense or modal context, one
looks both at how the denotations of the terms of the formula vary from
world-time pair to world-time pair, and at how the denotations relate
to each other at each world-time pair. Look at the truth conditions of
a modal formula: $[\Box Pa]^{\mathbf{M},\mathbf{w}_0,\mathbf{t}_0,\mathbf{g}} = 1$ iff for all $\mathbf{w}'$ and $\mathbf{t}'$, $[Pa]^{\mathbf{M},\mathbf{w}',\mathbf{t}',\mathbf{g}}$
$= 1$. For the right side of this conditional to be satisfied, every $\mathbf{w}'$ and
$\mathbf{t}'$ must be such that: $[P]^{\mathbf{M},\mathbf{w}',\mathbf{t}',\mathbf{g}}([a]^{\mathbf{M},\mathbf{w}',\mathbf{t}',\mathbf{g}}) = 1$.[5] That is, for each
world-time pair $\langle \mathbf{w}', \mathbf{t}' \rangle$, the denotation of '$a$' at $\langle \mathbf{w}', \mathbf{t}' \rangle$ must be mapped
by the denotation of 'P' at $\langle \mathbf{w}', \mathbf{t}' \rangle$ to the truth value 1.

Again, a rather different approach to tense and modal contexts is
embodied in ILAO. The way we have set things up, once an interpretation is specified and an assignment to the variables is fixed, every term
of the language receives a denotation with respect to that interpretation
and assignment (some descriptions may fail to denote, however). The
denotation of a closed term will be a function only of the denotation
of its (elementary) parts (i.e., its primitive constants) and the way in
which they are arranged (Appendix, §A.2.3). This means that absolutely all of our simple and complex terms are "rigid designators." The
truth conditions of tense and modal formulas do not depend on what
the terms of the formula denote at other worlds and times. Instead, the
truth conditions of such formulas involve just the denotations *simpliciter*

---

[5]The '$\Box$' in MIL means: necessarily-always.

of the terms—the relationships among those denotations are evaluated from world-time pair to world-time pair.

For example, '$\Box Pa$' is true$_I$ just in case every assignment $\mathbf{f}$ satisfies it with respect to the actual world $\mathbf{w}_0$ and and present moment $\mathbf{t}_0$ (ignoring the contexts; Appendix, §A.2.3). An assignment $\mathbf{f}$ satisfies$_I$ $\Box Pa$ at $\langle \mathbf{w}, \mathbf{t} \rangle$ iff for every world $\mathbf{w}'$, $\mathbf{f}$ satisfies$_I$ 'Pa' at $\langle w', t_0 \rangle$, that is, iff for every world $\mathbf{w}'$, $\mathbf{d}_{I,f}(a) \in \mathbf{ext}_{\mathbf{w}',t_0}(\mathbf{d}_{I,f}(P))$. In other words, we begin with the denotations of 'a' and 'P' and look to see whether the former is an element of the exemplification extension of the latter at $\langle \mathbf{w}', \mathbf{t}_0 \rangle$, for each world $\mathbf{w}'$. Since the formula is also a term that denotes a proposition, there is an alternative, though equivalent, method of evaluation: '$\Box Pa$' is true iff $\mathbf{ext}_{\mathbf{w}_0,t_0}(\mathbf{d}_{I,f}(\Box Pa)) = T$. The denotation of the formula is the proposition $\mathbf{NEC}(\mathbf{PLUG}_1(\mathbf{d}_{I,f}(P), \mathbf{d}_{I,f}(a)))$. The exemplification extension of this proposition at $\langle \mathbf{w}_0, \mathbf{t}_0 \rangle$ is the truth value T just in case for every world $\mathbf{w}'$, the extension$_{\mathbf{w}',t}$ of the proposition $\mathbf{PLUG}_1(\mathbf{d}_{I,f}(P), \mathbf{d}_{I,f}(a))$ is T. This is guaranteed by the definition of the function $\mathbf{ext}_{\mathbf{w},t}$ (Appendix, §A.2.1).

Using this model of how tense and modal formulas work, we may reexamine the way Montague and other philosophers and linguists define the notion of intensionality.[6] Dowty *et al.* begin their introduction to intensionality by examining the simple tense operators (p. 141). They consider the following sentences:

ϕ: Iceland is covered with a glacier.
ψ: Africa is covered with a glacier.
$\mathcal{P}\phi$: Iceland was once covered with a glacier.
$\mathcal{P}\psi$: Africa was once covered with a glacier.

ϕ and ψ are now false, whereas $\mathcal{P}\phi$ is now true and $\mathcal{P}\psi$ is now false. Since formulas denote truth values in MIL, this example shows that the denotation of tensed formulas is not a function of the denotation of their simple parts. Formulas that have the same denotation may not be substituted for one another inside temporal contexts, and such a substitutivity failure marks these contexts as intensional. Dowty *et al.* conclude:

> But how can this fact about the interpretation of tenses be reconciled with our principle that the semantic value of a whole expression be a function of the semantic value of its parts? The answer would seem that we cannot consider the semantic value of $\mathcal{F}\phi$ to be merely a function of the *denotations* [their emphasis] of $\mathcal{F}$ and ϕ, but it must be a function

---

[6]See, for example, van Benthem [1985].

of something other than the denotation (as we have defined
it) in the case of ϕ. (p. 142)

Montague, therefore, evaluates tense and modal contexts in terms of the
intensions rather than extensions of the embedded formulas. Note that
this treatment of tense and modality essentially assimilates non-truth-
functionality to intensionality. The non-truth functionality of formulas
such as $\mathcal{F}\phi$ and $\Box\phi$ is the source of their intensionality.

The parenthetical remark "as we have defined it" in the above quote
is crucial. For if denotations are defined differently, it can be seen that
non-truth-functionality does not imply intensionality, as Dowty *et al.*,
and others, seem to suggest. In our logic, the denotation of formulas
such as $\Box\phi$ and $\mathcal{H}\phi$ are indeed functions of the denotation of ϕ. For
any interpretation $\mathbf{I}$ and assignment $\mathbf{f}$, $\mathbf{d_{I,f}}(\Box\phi) = \mathbf{NEC}(\mathbf{d_{I,f}}(\phi))$, and
$\mathbf{d_{I,f}}(\mathcal{H}\phi) = \mathbf{WAS}(\mathbf{d_{I,f}}(\phi))$ (Appendix, §A.2.3). Of course, the extension
of $\mathbf{WAS}(\mathbf{d}(\phi))$ at $\langle\mathbf{w_0},\mathbf{t_0}\rangle$ does not depend solely on the extension of
$\mathbf{d}(\phi)$ at $\langle\mathbf{w_0},\mathbf{t_0}\rangle$. This is the reason why these complex formulas are not
truth-functional. But co-designative formulas may be substituted for ϕ
in $\mathcal{H}\phi$ and $\Box\phi$ preserving truth. Modal and temporal contexts are not
essentially intensional contexts.

So part of the reason that modal and temporal contexts were thought
to be intensional has to do with the choice of truth values as denotations
for formulas. Another reason concerns the interaction of modality and
descriptions in natural language. This will be our focus in Section 4.

The next feature of general comparison is item (v), or the fact that
the rules of identity elimination and λ-conversion must be restricted in
Montague's intensional logic. This is partly a result of his treatment
of tense and modality. Consider the following pair of rules that govern
MIL, as described in [DWP] (p.165 and 167):[7]

> Identity Elimination: $\alpha = \beta \rightarrow [\phi \equiv \phi_\alpha^\beta]$, where α does not stand
> in the scope of $\hat{\,}$, $\Box$, $\mathcal{P}$, or $\mathcal{F}$ in ϕ

> λ-Conversion: $\lambda u[\phi](\alpha) \equiv \phi_u^\alpha$, provided that u does not stand
> within the scope of $\hat{\,}$, $\Box$, $\mathcal{P}$, or $\mathcal{F}$ in ϕ

Readers who are uncertain why it is Montague must restrict these rules
should consider the following examples. Take two formulas such as $\hat{\,}B(m)$
and $\hat{\,}B(n)$. Suppose that '$m = n$' is true, i.e., $[m]^{\mathbf{M},\mathbf{w}_0,\mathbf{t}_0,\mathbf{g}} = [n]^{\mathbf{M},\mathbf{w}_0,\mathbf{t}_0,\mathbf{g}}$.
It is a consequence of this identity that $[B(m)]^{\mathbf{M},\mathbf{w}_0,\mathbf{t}_0,\mathbf{g}}$ is identical with
$[B(n)]^{\mathbf{M},\mathbf{w}_0,\mathbf{t}_0,\mathbf{g}}$. So '$B(m) = B(n)$' is true. But since m and n may

---

[7]We've used our convention of abbreviating the result of substituting β for α in ϕ
as ϕ_α^β. Also, $\mathcal{P}$ and $\mathcal{F}$ are taken as primitive in Montague's logic, instead of $\mathcal{H}$
and $\mathcal{G}$.

not rigidly designate, there may be a world $\mathbf{w}_1$ where they denote different objects. Hence, it may be that $[B(m)]^{\mathbf{M},\mathbf{w}_1,\mathbf{t}_0,\mathbf{g}}$ is not identical with $[B(n)]^{\mathbf{M},\mathbf{w}_1,\mathbf{t}_0,\mathbf{g}}$. If so, then the intensions of '$B(m)$' and '$B(n)$' will differ, that is, $[B(m)]^{\mathbf{M},\mathbf{g}}_{\mathscr{A}}$ is not identical with $[B(n)]^{\mathbf{M},\mathbf{g}}_{\mathscr{A}}$. Hence, $\hat{}B(m) \neq \hat{}B(n)$. But without restrictions on identity elimination, one would be able to deduce $\hat{}B(m) = \hat{}B(n)$ from the fact that $m = n$.

There is an analogous argument that reveals why the restriction on λ-conversion is required.[8] The deeper reason why Montague has to restrict these principles is that his entire logical set-up is based on the idea that the extension (or denotation) of a term varies from world-time pair to world-time pair. Identity statements and λ-equivalences given us information only about the extensions of terms at the base world and time. But intensional contexts are sensitive to the extensions of terms at all world-time pairs. Thus, substitutions and conversions based solely on contingent identities and equivalences will not be valid when performed in intensional contexts.

Compare this with the logical set-up of ILAO. The following are the counterparts of the above, and they do not have relevantly similar restrictions (Appendix, §A.3 and §A.4):[9]

Substitutivity: $\alpha = \beta \rightarrow (\phi(\alpha,\alpha) \equiv \phi(\alpha,\beta))$, where $\phi(\alpha,\beta)$ is the result of replacing some, but not necesarily all, free occurrences of α by β in $\phi(\alpha,\alpha)$, provided β is substitutable for α in the occurrences of α it replaces.

λ-Equivalence: Where ϕ is any propositional formula with no ordinary descriptions, and $x^{t_1}, \ldots, x^{t_n}$ are substitutable for $\alpha^{t_1}, \ldots, \alpha^{t_n}$, the following is an axiom:

$$(\forall x^{t_1}) \ldots (\forall x^{t_n})([\lambda \alpha^{t_1} \ldots \alpha^{t_n} \, \phi] x^{t_1} \ldots x^{t_n} \equiv \phi^{x^{t_1}, \ldots, x^{t_n}}_{\alpha^{t_1}, \ldots, \alpha^{t_n}})$$

If one just looks at the two logics as formalisms, then there seems to be no reason to prefer a logic free of restrictions on identity elimination and λ-conversion. Viewed as pure symbols, '$=$' and 'λ' may be defined to operate any way one pleases. However, not all formalisms define '$=$' and 'λ' in ways that capture certain intuitions we may share about the notion of identity and about the nature of complex relations. Our axiom of Substitutivity captures the intuition that if two, apparently distinct,

---

[8]For a good discussion of why λ-conversion must be restricted, see [DWP], p. 166. The example used to outline the reason for the restrictions on Identity Elimination was taken from [DWP], p. 164.

[9]The axiom for identity substitution is a proper axiom, since identity is defined. It constitutes part of our *theory* of identity. The axiom for λ-conversion is a logical axiom.

objects really are identical, then anything true about one is true about the other. And λ-*Equivalence* captures the intuition that objects which are related by a complex relation (even tense or modal relations) stand in just those simple relations to one another that one would expect given the structure of the complex relation. In λ-*Equivalence*, the restriction on ϕ banishing definite descriptions preserves the spirit of this intuition, since the appearance of non-denoting descriptions would otherwise yield instances in which the λ-expressions fail to denote relations. If a description denotes something, it may appear in the λ-principle.

The deeper reason why these principles do not need restrictions similar to Montague's has to do with the fact that the denotations of terms do not vary from world-time pair to world-time pair. The truth conditions of a formal sentence do not vary, even when the sentence is embedded in a modal, temporal, or attitude context. Identity statements and λ-equivalences express necessary and timeless truths, and substitutions and conversions based upon such truths is always valid. This is not really an advantage that our system has over MIL, but just a difference in approach. Had we included non-rigid descriptions in the language, substitutions and λ-conversions involving such terms would have to be restricted. The modifications required for this were discussed in Chapter 5.

The penultimate feature of comparison is (vi), which concerns the simplicity of the respective type theories. MIL is based on two simple types, e and t, and two complex types, $\langle a, b \rangle$, and $\langle s, a \rangle$ (where a and b are any types). In complex types of the form $\langle s, a \rangle$, the symbol 's' indicates semantically that the type in question is a function from world-time pairs to entities of type a. Worlds and times are primitive semantic entities—they do not receive analysis at any level of the theory.

By contrast, ILAO requires just one simple type, i, and one complex type, $\langle t_1, \ldots t_n \rangle$ (where $t_1, \ldots, t_n$ are any types, $n \geq 0$). The type for propositions is defined ($p =_{df} \langle \, \rangle$). Though worlds and times are taken as primitive entities in the semantics, they are defined in the theory by applying the ideas presented in Chapter 4. These definitions yield "world-states" in addition to worlds and times. Each world-state encodes all of the exemplification propositions true at some world-time pair. These definitions simplify the theory, and allow us to get rid of Montague's complex type $\langle s, a \rangle$.[10]

---

[10]Some might argue that the appeal to world-states in the semantics commits us to them. This would be a mistake however, for the theorems governing world-states demonstrate that they are individuals which have all of the features such entities are supposed to have. Though it is true that the semantics contains a set of worlds and times, the analysis in Chapter 4 shows that such domains may be thought of as subsets of the domain of individuals.

Finally, consider point of comparison (vii), which concerns the epistemological notion of finite representability. This is the property that a theory of language has just in case the way it represents the interaction between language and the world could be internalized by beings with finite minds. Montague's logic, unlike ours, doesn't seem to be finitely representable. Though this notion is difficult to make precise, it seems clear that a theory about the truth conditions and entailments of sentences of natural language must square with the fact that people understand those sentences. And it must square with the fact that in some sense, our minds do not seem to have an infinite capacity to store information. But it is reasonable to assume that there are an infinite number of world-states. So if the meaning of a predicate is its intension, and its intension is a function from world-states to sets of individuals, it seems that to genuinely understand the meaning of a predicate, one must somehow store an infinite mapping. Similarly, if propositions are functions from worlds-states to truth values, and propositions are the objects to which we are related by such attitudes as belief, it would seem that one must register these functions with infinite domains. It seems unlikely, however, that we can do this.

Such a puzzling situation does not arise in ILAO. The meaning of a predicate is the property it denotes. No attempt is made to define or reconstruct the property out of other things. They are not defined in terms of an infinite domain. Properties such as being red, being round, being soft, etc., are things with which we are all familiar. We are directly acquainted with such things and there is no point in trying to reconstrue them as something else that is supposedly more familiar. The best way to explain why just certain objects and not others are members of the set of round things at a given world and time is that they exemplify this property there and then.[11] Once we grasp the connection between the predicate 'is round' with the property of being round, we could visit any world at any time and identify just those objects that 'are round' there and then. Sentences are also the kind of thing we may understand without having to master some function defined on an infinite domain. Once we grasp the connection between the sentence "A is round" and the particular proposition it denotes, we could be placed in any world and time and determine, as a result of our epistemological acquaintance with the proposition, whether the sentence is truly assertable. This view of the semantic competence doesn't require our minds to be infinite in any way.

---

[11]In MIL, it remains a mystery why certain objects and not others are members of the set of round things; see [DWP], p. 151.

12.2   Montague and Nonexistence

To compare MIL and ILAO on the analysis of nonexistence, two kinds
of sentences are considered—those containing names of nonexistent objects and those involving indefinite phrases like 'a unicorn.' Presumably,
a name like 'Zeus' would be translated into MIL as '$[\lambda F\ \check{}F(z)]$,' where
F is a variable of type $\langle s, \langle e, t \rangle \rangle$, '$z$' abbreviates 'Zeus,' and '$\check{}F(z)$' says
that the entity denoted by 'z' is in the extension of the property F at
the actual world and time. The whole expression denotes the set of
properties Zeus exemplifies. Note that this set can't contain only the
properties attributed to Zeus in the myth, for then one could not explain the truth value of the sentence "Augustus worshipped Zeus." The
property of being worshipped by Augustus is not a property exemplified
by Zeus in the myth.

It may be that a view like van Inwagen's [1977] is the best way to
extend Montague's logic. Van Inwagen identifies Zeus as an abstract
object that exemplifies the following sorts of properties: being the most
powerful god in the myth, living on Mt. Olympus in the myth, being worshipped by Augustus Caesar, being the god most feared by the Greeks,
etc. But if this is the best way to incorporate a treatment of fictional
names into MIL, a great deal of work needs to be done, for an analysis of
the notion of a story and of the story operator is necessary. This is crucial for understanding properties such as being-F-in-story-s. Without
such an analysis, there would have to be, for example, a different primitive property of being a god in story s, for each story s. In addition,
something needs to be said about the kind of object denoted by 'z' in the
expression '$[\lambda F\ \check{}F(z)]$.' How are they to be distinguished from objects
like you and me? By way of contrast, one of the principal motivations
for developing the theory and logic of abstract objects was to produce
analyses that answered such questions. The stories and native characters are systematically identified as abstract, intentional objects, the
story operator is analyzed in terms of encoding, and sentences involving names of stories and characters are given relatively straightforward
translations into ILAO.

A more revealing comparison of the two theories involves the case
of the indefinite noun phrase 'a unicorn,' since the analysis in MIL has
received so much attention. Consider how the two readings of "John
seeks a unicorn" are produced in MIL ([DWP], pp. 216–220):

(1) John seeks a unicorn.

(2) $Seek'(j, \hat{}\lambda Q (\exists x)[unicorn'(x)\ \&\ Q\{x\}])$ (non-specific)

(3) $\exists x[unicorn'(x)\ \&\ [seek'(j, \hat{}\lambda P[P\{x\}])]]$ (specific)

Recall that '$Q\{x\}$' and '$P\{x\}$' are abbreviations of '$^\vee Q(x)$' and '$^\vee P(x)$.' Properties of individuals map worlds to sets of individuals, and so to predicate a property of an individual one has to first take its extension at the actual world and claim the individual is in the set.

Dowty, Wall, and Peters regard this analysis as a *tour de force* of Montague's intensional logic. Even so, it seems to leave an important feature of the logic of this English sentence unexplained. Before we look at this, let us briefly explain the analysis. Both readings identify the *seek* relation as a relation between individuals and properties of properties. In (2) and (3), the expressions beginning '$\lambda Q \ldots$' and '$\lambda P \ldots$' denote things of type $\langle s, \langle \langle s, \langle e, t \rangle \rangle, t \rangle \rangle$. The non-specific reading relates John to the property of being a property some (possible) unicorn has (such a property is a function that maps each world-time pair to the set of properties that some unicorn there has), whereas the specific reading says that there is some (existing) unicorn x such that John is seek-related to the property a property P has just in case it is a property actually exemplified by x.

This treatment clearly has many of the features required to explain the logic exhibited by the English. (2) may be true even if there are no unicorns, for the property John is related to would still exist. This explains why (1) can be true even when there are no unicorns. Moreover, this analysis can distinguish (1) from "John seeks a centaur." In order for it to have done so, it was important for Montague's treatment that the object of John's search be a property of properties, and not just a set of properties. For in MIL, the set of properties exemplified by some (actual) unicorn is the same as the set of properties exemplified by some (actual) centaur (since no unicorns or centaurs exist). But the property of being a property some (possible) unicorn has is distinct from the property of being a property some (possible) centaur has (since in other worlds, the extensions of 'unicorn' and 'centaur' are distinct, and so the properties in question will map those worlds to different sets of properties). And finally, the specific reading of (1) entails that some unicorn exists, just as the specific reading of "John seeks a friend" has a reading on which there exists some particular friend whom John seeks.

But there seems to be a problem with Montague's analysis in that it doesn't capture the apparent fact that no matter how one understands (1), it always entails (4):

(4) John seeks something.

Even if John is non-specifically seeking a unicorn, he is looking for something. The problem is that the translations in MIL of "John seeks something" are not consequences of (2). To see this, note that (4) could be produced syntactically either: (a) by combining 'seeks' with 'some thing' to produce a verb phrase, and then adding 'John' as subject (this will yield a non-specific reading), or (b) by combining 'seeks' with 'he$_0$,' adding 'John' to produce "John seeks him$_0$," and quantifying in 'some thing' into the position occupied by 'him$_0$' (this will yield a specific reading). This produces the following representations, respectively, for (4):

(5) $seeks'(j, {}^\wedge\lambda Q(\exists x)[thing'(x)\ \&\ Q\{x\}])$

(6) $(\exists x)[thing'(x)\ \&\ seeks'(j, {}^\wedge\lambda P[P\{x\}])]$

However, neither (5) nor (6) follow from (2), which means that there is a reading of (1) for which it doesn't follow that John seeks something. This is counterintuitive.

Montague could add a meaning postulate governing $seek'$ that would ensure that (5) followed from (2). The following would do the trick, where F and G range over properties of properties:

(7) $seek'(x, F)\ \&\ \Box(\forall P)(F\{P\} \to G\{P\}) \to seek'(x, G)$

This guarantees, for example, that since the properties some possible unicorn has will necessarily be in the set of properties some possible thing has, whenever someone seeks the property of being a property some possible unicorn has, they seek the property of being a property some possible thing has. To see that (5) now follows formally from (2) and (7), assume that there is also a meaning postulate governing $thing'$, namely, $\Box(\forall x)thing'(x)$. From this, one may deduce that $\Box(\forall x)(unicorn'(x) \to thing'(x))$. This yields: $\Box(\forall P)([\lambda Q(\exists x)(unicorn'(x)\ \&\ Q\{x\})](P) \to [\lambda Q(\exists x)(thing'(x)\ \&\ Q\{x\})](P))$. Now by inserting ''$^\wedge$'' in front of the λ-expressions (as we are allowed to do in MIL), one gets something of the form: $\Box(\forall P)[{}^\wedge F(P) \to {}^\wedge G(P)]$ ('F' can be substituted for expressions like '$[{}^\wedge\lambda Q\ldots Q\ldots]$'). Now the brace convention applies and yields: $\Box(\forall P)[F\{P\} \to G\{P\}]$, which is clearly of the form of the second conjunct in the antecedent of (7). Clearly then, (5) follows from (2) using the instantiated (7).

Contrast this situation with the representations available to us in ILAO. The point of this contrast will not be to criticize the MIL analysis of noun phrases (since we will not offer an alternative), but rather to observe simple advantages of having abstract individuals of type i that encode properties of type $\langle i\rangle$. With the extra expressive power this affords, $seek$ may be regarded as a two-place relation between individuals (type $\langle i, i\rangle$). There are two different conditions under which (1) is true, both of which are conditions under which (4) is true. Consider the following representations of (1), where 'U' denotes the property of being a unicorn, and 'S' represents the $seek$ relation:

(8) $(\exists x)(xU \ \& \ Sjx)$ (non-specific)

(9) $(\exists x)(Ux \ \& \ Sjx)$ (specific)

So the non-specific reading of (1) is true just in case John bears a certain relation to an object that encodes the property of being a unicorn. This "nonspecific" reading of (1) still entails that there is a specific abstract object which is the "intentional" object of John's search. In other words, (8) tells us that there is a certain objectified conception which John is seeking to instantiate. Of course, this objectified conception may encode other properties as well, since he may have some mental picture of what it is he is seeking. But the important point here is that (8) may be true even if there are no real unicorns (i.e., even if nothing exemplifies being a unicorn). And, in addition, this non-specific reading of (1) is distinct from the non-specific reading of "John seeks a centaur," for by assuming that the property of being a unicorn is distinct from the property of being a centaur, there will be objects encoding the former that do not also encode the latter (and vice versa). Finally, the specific reading of (1), namely (9), does imply that there is something which exemplifies being a unicorn that John is seeking.

Here is the representation of (4), where 'T' denotes the property of being a thing:[12]

(10) $(\exists x)(Tx \ \& \ Sjx)$

Now consider the relationships between (1), (4), (8), (9) and (10) in light of the axiom that $\Box \forall x Tx$. From this axiom, it follows that: $(\forall x)[(Ux \ \lor \ xU) \rightarrow Tx]$. This just says: any individual that either exemplifies or encodes the property of being a unicorn exemplifies being a thing. Consequently, both (8) and (9) imply (10), and so both readings of (1) imply (4). We get this result without requiring a special meaning postulate to govern the *seek* relation.

The contrast between the analyses of (1) and (4) in MIL and ILAO should reveal the importance of having individuals of type i that can serve as the intentional objects of the verb 'seek.' Even if a general treatment of noun phrases requires us to interpret English at the higher type levels utilized in PTQ, many of the ordinary features of intensional verbs will not be preserved unless such verbs are ultimately grounded in relations between individuals.

---

[12]The following is also a reading of (4): $(\exists x)(xT \ \& \ Sjx)$. But since it will play no role in the following explanation, we may ignore it.

12.3   Propositional Attitudes

Consider the case of belief Dowty *et al.* use to show that MIL can successfully explain the intensionality of propositional attitude contexts ([DWP], pp. 164–167). The case involves the following triad of sentences:

(11) John believes that Miss America is bald

(12) John doesn't believe that Norma is bald

(13) Norma is Miss America

Though this case can be handled in MIL, it requires terms that are not employed in the formal language of PTQ. Dowty *et al.* propose to treat 'Miss America' as a non-rigid name, and this is essential for giving a consistent reading of these sentences (in PTQ, there are no non-rigid names, since Montague uses a meaning potulate to require that names rigidly designate). These authors present (14) and (15) as readings for (11), (16) and (17) as readings for (12), and (18) as the reading of (13) (in what follows, '*Bel*' represents the belief relation of type $\langle\langle s, t\rangle, \langle e, t\rangle\rangle$, and '*B*' represents being bald):[13]

(14) $\lambda x[Bel(j, \hat{} B(x))](m)$ (*re*)

(15) $Bel(j, \hat{} B(m))$ (*dicto*)

(16) $\lambda x[\sim Bel(j, \hat{} B(x))](n)$ (*re*)

(17) $\sim Bel(j, \hat{} B(n))$ (*dicto*)

(18) $n = m$

The authors now point out that (15), (17), and (18) are consistent,[14] that the negation of (15) can not be derived from (18) and (17) using the restricted law of identity (substitution), and that (15) can not be derived from (14) using the restricted law of λ-conversion.[15]

The only problem with this analysis is that it cannot be extended to explain the consistency of triads in which the embedded names are rigid designators. Consider the following triad, derived from the discussion in Chapter 9:

---

[13] *Bel* is not related to the primitive, three-place belief relation discussed by Salmon. Remember, also, that in MIL, '$Bel(j, \hat{} \phi)$' is an abbreviation of '$[Bel(\hat{} \phi)](j)$.'

[14] The names 'm' and 'n' are not rigid, and so their intensions differ. Hence, so do the intensions of '$B(m)$' and '$B(n)$.' So $\hat{} B(m) \neq \hat{} B(n)$. Thus, they cannot be substituted for one another in (15) and (17).

[15] To see that (14) and (15) have distinct truth conditions, consider the way in which each is evaluated. Whereas (14) is about the individual in fact denoted by 'm,' (15) is about whoever m is as one moves from world to world. Refer again to the useful discussion on pp. 164–167 in [DWP].

(19) John believes Mark Twain is a writer.

(20) John doesn't believe Samuel Clemens is a writer.

(21) Mark Twain is Samuel Clemens.

If 'Twain' and 'Clemens' are represented as rigid designators, then the *de dicto* readings of (19) and (20) in MIL are not consistent with (21). To see this, consider the following representations, where (22) is the *de dicto* reading of (19), (23) is the *de dicto* reading of (20), and (24) represents (21):

(22) $Bel(j, {}^\wedge W(t))$

(23) $\sim Bel(j, {}^\wedge W(c))$

(24) $t = c$

Now if 't' and 'c' rigidly designate, then their intensions are identical, i.e., ${}^\wedge t = {}^\wedge c$. Meaning postulates in MIL guarantee the derivation of the identity of intensions from identity statements such as (24) when the names involved rigidly designate. But expressions with the same intension are substitutable everywhere in MIL. The following principle is valid: ${}^\wedge \alpha = {}^\wedge \beta \rightarrow [\phi \equiv \phi_\alpha^\beta]$ (see [DWP], p. 165). Consequently, the following is derivable from (22):

(25) $Bel(j, {}^\wedge W(c))$

Clearly, then, the contradiction between (23) and (25) suggests that the solution to the substitutivity problem in MIL does not square with the idea that names rigidly designate.

This much is described by Dowty *et al.* in their exposition of MIL (p. 171). They go on to point out that the problem is a bit more far reaching, because apparent failure of substitutivity affects property denoting expressions inside propositional attitude contexts as well. They cite as an example ([DWP], p. 171):

(26) John does not doubt that woodchucks are woodchucks.

(27) John does doubt that woodchucks are groundhogs.

(28) Being a woodchuck just is being a groundhog.

The problem here is that names of natural kinds such as 'woodchuck' and 'groundhog' rigidly designate as well. Yet if these expressions are represented as rigid designators in MIL, the consistency of the above triad is left unexplained.

By way of comparison, reconsider (11) – (13) from the standpoint of ILAO. The source of the apparent substitutivity failure is not located in the interaction between basic laws of logic and intensional contexts, but rather in a simple ambiguity of the English names and descriptions when they appear in belief reports. It is unclear exacly what kind of expression 'Miss America' is, since it has some of the features of descriptions and some of the features of names. One good reason for thinking that it functions more like a description is the fact that its sense does not vary from person to person as widely as the sense of a name does. Most of us associate the same conception with 'Miss America,' namely, being judged the most talented and beautiful woman in America in a certain annual and traditional competition. So we shall represent 'Miss America' as a description. Of course, there are data in which 'Miss America' appears to be used rigidly, and data in which it appears to be used non-rigidly. As far as (11) goes, however, 'Miss America' could be either rigid or non-rigid. What is of crucial importance is that it has a sense, and that its sense differs from the sense that 'Norma' has for John. Since we are trying to do without non-rigid terms, let us then represent 'Miss America' as the rigid description '$(\imath x)\phi$.'[16]

In the following symbolization, '$(\imath x)\phi$' denotes the sense of 'Miss America,' '$\underline{n}_j$' denotes the sense of 'Norma' for John, and 'B' denotes the relation representing belief, respectively. Moreover, (29) and (30) are readings of (11), (31) and (32) are readings of (12), and (33) is the reading of (13):

(29) $B(j,\ Bald((\imath x)\phi))$ (*re*)

(30) $B(j,\ Bald(\underline{(\imath x)\phi}))$ (*dicto*)

(31) $\sim B(j,\ Bald(n))$ (*re*)

(32) $\sim B(j,\ Bald(\underline{n}_j))$ (*dicto*)

(33) $(\imath x)\phi =_E n$

Our work in Chapters 9 – 11 should have left us with a good understanding of the truth conditions that these readings attribute to the English sentences. The apparent consistency of the English triad is explained by the fact that (30) and (32) are consistent with the identity (33).

---

[16]For those contexts in which 'Miss America' appears to be non-rigid, the system could be adjusted to include non-rigid descriptions. Such non-rigid descriptions would also have a sense, and their sense would still play a role in the analysis of the present case. But as we noted in Chapter 5, there are new ways of representing what appear to be non-rigid English descriptions by using just rigid descriptions and the logic of encoding. We'll see another example of this in the final section of this chapter.

Both readings of (11) and (12) preserve the apparent logical form of the English.[17]

In general, our method of analyzing the attitudes is consistent with the results of the theory of direct reference. Every name or description of type t has a sense that is an A-object of type t. In attitude contexts, such terms signify their senses when they are in *de dicto* position. No problems are encountered when building up the intermediate proposition signified by embedded sentences containing such terms, since the sense and the denotation of the term are of same type. Given our work in Chapters 9 – 11, the Twain/Clemens case and the woodchuck/groundhog case do not present special puzzles. Their representations are consistent with the view that the names in question are rigid.

12.4   Modality, Descriptions, and Intensionality

The main goal of this section is to criticize the analysis of the Morning Star/Evening Star case in MIL, as it is presented by Dowty *et al.* However, before we do so, it is necessary to review, and revise slightly, our analysis of certain puzzles about the interaction of definite descriptions and modal operators. In [1983], we examined the following group of sentences:[18]

(34) Necessarily, the teacher of Alexander is a teacher.

(35) Aristotle is the teacher of Alexander.

(36) Necessarily, Aristotle is a teacher.

These sentences may be viewed as an argument, in which (36) appears to validly follow from (34) by a substitution based on the identity (35). However, it appears that the premises are true and the conclusion false. Since valid arguments can't have true premises and a false conclusion, these sentences present a puzzle.

There are two classic ways of analyzing the problem. Russell's method is to find an ambiguity in (34) that can be resolved once the description is eliminated according to the theory of descriptions. Two readings

---

[17]It is *not* a restriction on identity substitution that prevents the substitution of 'n' for '$(\imath x)\phi$' in (30). That's because 'n' and '$(\imath x)\phi$' are not semantically significant parts of the special terms '$\underline{n}_j$' and '$\underline{(\imath x)\phi}$'. The denotations of these latter two complex terms are not defined in terms of the denotations of 'n' and '$(\imath x)\phi$.' Consequently, no restrictions need be placed on identity substitution in order to invalidate '$(\imath x)\phi = n \rightarrow [B(j, Bald(\underline{(\imath x)\phi})) \equiv B(j, Bald(\underline{n}_j))]$.' This sentence just fails to be an instance of identity substitution.

[18]See [1983], pp. 100–106.

of (34) result, one in which the existence and uniqueness claims embedded in the description appear outside the scope of the modal operator (so the description has wide scope), and the other in which these claims appear inside the scope of the modal operator (so the description has narrow scope). In addition, (35) is no longer analysed as a simple identity claim, but rather as the claim: there is an x such that x is a unique teacher of Alexander and such that Aristotle is identical with x. With this analysis of the English, it is straightforward to show that there is no valid argument with true premises and a false conclusion. There is a valid argument with a false premise: the wide scope reading of (34) is false, but together with the Russellian reading of (35), it does imply (36). And there is an invalid argument with true premises and a false conclusion: the narrow scope reading of (34) is true, but together with the reading of (35), it does not imply the false sentence (36). Though Russell's analysis works, it does not preserve the intuitions that some of us have, namely, that the sentence following the adverb 'necessarily' in (34) is atomic (with a complex subject term), and that (35) is a simple identity claim with a complex term on the right flank of the identity sign.

The other classic analysis of this argument, however, preserves these intuitions. This analysis employs primitive, non-rigid definite descriptions to read the English. (34) becomes a modalized, atomic formula with a complex subject term. (35) is a simple identity statement involving a name and a primitive description. To prevent the derivation of (36), this analysis requires that the principle of substitutivity be restricted. The terms of a contingent identity such as (35) cannot be validly substituted for one another inside modal contexts such as (34). So what appears to be a valid argument with true premises and a false conclusion turns out to be an invalid argument. This solves the puzzle, though it requires non-rigid descriptions and restrictions on the principle of substitutivity.

Note that if primitive descriptions are employed in the analysis of (34), then it seems that we have to use non-rigid descriptions. For if 'the teacher of Alexander' rigidly denotes Aristotle, then (34) would be true iff necessarily, Aristotle is a teacher. So if rigid descriptions are the only analytical tool available, how do we preserve the truth of (34)?

An answer is found in the logic of encoding. In [1983], we offered a second reading of 'the teacher of Alexander' by using the following formal description: $(\imath x)(\forall F)(xF \equiv ([\lambda y\ Tya_1] \Rightarrow F))$. This description denotes the A-object that encodes just the properties implied by the property of being a teacher of Alexander. For simplicity, let us abbreviate this description as: $(\imath x)\psi$. Note that $(\imath x)\psi$ encodes the property of being a teacher, since being a teacher of Alexander implies being a teacher.

This fact is crucial, for on the hypothesis that the copula 'is' in (34) is ambiguous, we get the following true reading of (34) using a rigid description:

(37) $\Box(\imath x)\psi T$

Since the atomic encoding formula is true, so is (37), by the rigidity of encoding.[19]

So in our system, (34) gets two readings, an exemplification reading and an encoding reading. Both readings employ rigid descriptions. The exemplification reading is: $\Box T(\imath x)Txa_1$. This is false, because Aristotle isn't necessarily a teacher. But together with the reading of (35) ($a_2=_E$ $(\imath x)Txa_1$), it does imply the reading of (36) ($\Box Ta_2$). So there is a valid argument here, except that it has a false premise. The encoding reading of (34), namely (37), is true, but together with the reading of (35), it doesn't imply the reading of (36). On this analysis, both readings of (34) preserve the apparent logical form of the English as a modalized atomic formula with a complex subject term. (35) is resolved as a simple identity statement with a complex term. Moreover, no restrictions are placed on the principle of substitution, since only rigidly designating terms are involved.

The success of this analysis is not a lucky coincidence. It proves to be successful in another infamous case due to Quine. Consider the following example from his [1961]:

(38) Necessarily, nine is greater than seven.

(39) Nine is the number of planets.

(40) Necessarily, the number of planets is greater than seven.

Again, it appears that (40) validly follows from (38) and (39), though the latter are true and the former is false. Both of the classic ways of analyzing the puzzle leave at least one intuition about the case unexplained. But the analysis that uses rigid descriptions and the logic of encoding preserves all of the intuitions. In this case, the encoding reading of (40) preserves the intuition that this sentence says something *false*.[20]

The main idea behind our analyses of these cases is that sometimes, the definite description 'the so and so,' instead of denoting the object

---

[19]Note that the A-object denoted by '$(\imath x)Txa_1$' would not have been useful, for it does not encode the property of being a teacher. An A-object that captures more information is required.

[20]For further details, the reader should consult [1983], pp. 100–106.

that uniquely exemplifies being so and so, denotes a certain conception of being so and so.[21] We've objectified this conception as a certain A-object. Intuitively, the conception connected with 'the teacher of Alexander' in this context carries with it the information of being a teacher, and necessarily so. That's basically why (34) is true. The conception connected with 'the number that numbers the planets' does not carry with it the information of being greater than seven, and necessarily so. That's basically why (40) is false.

The only problem with this view is that too much information may have been packed into the A-objects that objectify these conceptions. By encoding all of the properties implied by being so and so, all sorts of properties unrelated to being so and so get packed into the A-object that embodies the conception connected with 'the so and so.' For example, the property of being F or not F, for each property F, would be encoded by the A-object associated with 'the teacher of Alexander.' It seems reasonable to think that for many choices of F, the property of being F or not F is not a part of the conception associated with this description.

If this is true, then we need to utilize A-objects that encode only the relevant information associated with a description. The fact is, however, this information may vary from context to context. Just what conception a particular use of a description expresses depends on factors connected with the context of the utterance. Consequently, it is important to be flexible when deciding which A-object is the appropriate objectification of the conception expressed by a particular use of a description. Unfortunately, the more flexibility we retain in our choice of A-object, the less precise the account becomes. Probably the best way to proceed is to appeal to the somewhat imprecise notion of relevant entailment ($\overset{R}{\Rightarrow}$). If '$(\imath x)\phi$' is the exemplification reading of 'the so and so,' then the secondary reading of the English description may be captured by the following formal description: $(\imath x)(\forall F)(xF \equiv [\lambda y\ \phi_x^y] \overset{R}{\Rightarrow} F)$. Such an analysis should weed out the undesired information, yet retain the necessary information. For example, most of us would agree that, in ordinary contexts, the property of being a teacher is relevantly entailed by the property of being a teacher of Alexander, and that the property of being greater than seven is not relevantly entailed by being a number

---

[21]There are lots of conceptions that could be associated with 'the so and so'. We used a different one to analyze belief, namely, the A-object that encodes just the property of being the so and so. But this is not the conception that is involved with this kind of data, for the reasons noted above in footnote 19. Definite descriptions are used in a variety of ways, and the conception they embody varies from context to context. We need flexibility to handle the variety. That's why another reading of descriptions is now being offered.

that numbers the planets. So our (appropriately adjusted) readings of (34) and (40) still do the job they are supposed to do.

As our final piece of analysis, let us apply these ideas to the infamous Morning Star/Evening Star example. This is a genuine case of intensionality caused by the apparent failure of the principle of substitution. However, many philosophers treat this case as another example of the intensionality that is inherent in modal contexts. Since our system shows that modal contexts are not inherently intensional, let us try to track down the real source of the apparent substitution failure.

Here are the two sentences that are basic to the case:

(41) Necessarily, the Morning Star is the Morning Star.

(42) Necessarily, the Morning Star is the Evening Star.

Consider how Dowty *et al.* describe the puzzle about these sentences:[22]

> Sentence (41) is true because 'The Morning Star is the Morning Star' is a logically true sentence, an instance of the axiom $a = a$ (for any name a) in predicate logic with identity... . However, (42) is not true according to Frege, since it is a matter of contingent fact that the Morning Star is the same as the Evening Star, not a matter of logical necessity. Yet the truth of (42) should follow from the truth of (41) by Leibniz's Law, since (42) apparently substitutes for a name in (41) another name denoting the same individual. Apparently, the operator □ produces another case where the denotation of the whole expression is not strictly a function of the denotation of the parts. ([DWP], p. 142)

These authors now go on to describe a solution to the puzzle (p. 165).

They suggest that Montague would represent 'the Morning Star' and 'the Evening Star' as non-rigid names, with the following representations for (41) and (42):

(43) $\Box m = m$

(44) $\Box m = e$

The identity statement '$m = m$' is true at every world, even though the denotation of 'm' varies from world to world. So (43) is true. But (44) is false, since there are worlds where the non-rigid names 'm' and 'e' denote distinct objects. Moreover, the principle of substitution may not be applied to non-rigid names inside modal contexts. So we cannot use the contingent fact that $m = e$ to deduce (44) from (43).

---

[22]The numberings have been changed to square with our own.

The analysis in ILAO doesn't require "non-rigid names." 'The Morning Star' and 'the Evening Star' seem to be of mixed character—part name and part description. They are not simple names, however, for otherwise the truth value of (42) would be the same as that of (45):

(45) Necessarily, Hesperus is Phosphorus.

(45) is true—it may be epistemically possible that Hesperus is not Phosphorus, but it is not metaphysically possible.[23] So 'the Morning Star' and 'the Evening Star' are more like complex names, with a descriptional aspect. If their name-like character is emphasized, (42) will appear to be true (if they both just name Venus, then since Venus is necessarily self-identical, (42) is true). If their descriptional character is emphasized, (42) will appear to be false. But the false reading need not be traced back to the non-rigidity of 'the Morning Star' and 'the Evening Star'. Rather, it can be traced to the fact that the conception connected with 'the Morning Star' does not involve the property of being an Evening Star (in ordinary contexts).

Consider an analogous case:

(46) Necessarily, the last heavenly body to disappear in the morning is the last heavenly body to disappear in the morning.

(47) The last heavenly body to disappear in the morning is the first heavenly body to appear in the evening.

(48) Necessarily, the last heavenly body to disappear in the morning is the first heavenly body to appear in the evening.

Let us indulge in the astronomical fiction that Venus is, at one and the same time, not only the last heavenly body to disappear in the morning but also the first heavenly body to appear in the evening. Then consider what happens if we represent these claims using rigid definite descriptions. Let '$(\imath x)\chi$' and '$(\imath x)\theta$' be definite descriptions of ILAO that contain only exemplification subformulas and that represent 'the last heavenly body to disappear in the morning' and 'the first heavenly body to appear in the evening,' respectively (i.e., let $\chi = $ 'x exemplifies being a heavenly body & x disappears in the morning & $\sim(\exists y)(y$ exemplifies being a heavenly body & y disappears after $x)$'; and similarly for θ). So both $(\imath x)\chi$ and $(\imath x)\theta$ rigidly denote Venus. (46) – (48) may then be represented as:

(49) $\Box(\imath x)\chi = (\imath x)\chi$

---

[23] A proposition p is epistemically possible for person S just in case S would accept "For all I know, p."

(50) $(\imath x)\chi = (\imath x)\theta$

(51) $\Box(\imath x)\chi = (\imath x)\theta$

(49) and (50) are true, and since the descriptions are rigid, (51) is true as well. But this is not like the Hesperus/Phosphorus case. Whereas it seems plausible to argue that Hesperus is necessarily Phosphorus, it doesn't seem plausible to argue that the last heavenly body to disappear in the morning is necessarily the first heavenly body to appear in the evening. That is, even though (51) represents (48) as a truth, there seems to be another reading of (48) on which it is false. On this reading, the descriptions in (48) could not rigidly denote Venus.

In ILAO, there is a alternative reading of (48) that is indeed false. The description 'the last heavenly body to disappear in the morning' has a second reading, on which it denotes a certain conception. This conception is objectified by the A-object that encodes just the properties relevantly entailed by being the last heavenly body to disappear in the morning. In ordinary contexts, such properties include: being a heavenly body, disappearing in the morning, disappearing after all other heavenly bodies, etc. But being the first heavenly body to appear in the evening is not relevantly implied. Consequently, the following reading of (48) shows why it seems to be false:

(52) $\Box(\imath x)(\forall F)(xF \equiv [\lambda y\ \chi_x^y] \stackrel{R}{\Rightarrow} F)[\lambda z\ \theta_x^z]$

So on this reading, (48) is true iff necessarily, the A-object that encodes the properties relevantly implied by being the last heavenly body to disappear in the morning encodes the property of being the first heavenly body to appear in the evening. These conditions do not obtain.

Though (51) follows from (49) and (50) by the law of substitution, the premises and conclusion are true. The false (52) is not validly inferred from (49) and (50) by substitution. So the puzzle about the English sentences (46) – (48) is solved by appealing to an ambiguity in (48). The same goes for (41) and (42). These two sentences seem best understood as variations on (46) and (48). Like the description in (46), 'the Morning Star' has a reading on which it denotes Venus, and a reading on which it denotes the A-object that encodes all of the relevant information implied by being a Morning Star. In ordinary contexts, the properties relevantly implied are the same: being a heavenly body, disappearing in the morning, being the last heavenly body to disappear in the morning, etc. At least, these are the properties typically connected with 'the Morning Star.' The property of being an Evening Star is not typically connected, however (at least not until we discover that the two are the same).

In ILAO, the infamous Morning Star/Evening Star case is a genuine case of intensionality that results from the apparent failure of the law of substitutivity. It is not to be thought of as simply another example of the intensionality inherent in modal contexts. Such contexts are not inherently intensional when every term rigidly designates. Rather, it is the special interaction of modality and descriptions in natural language that causes the intensional behavior. Though such descriptions acquire their ordinary denotation by way of their conditions of satisfaction, they also signify a certain conception of the objects they purport to denote. The way to analyze this conception is by postulating a metaphysics of abstract, intentional objects, for this is the key to the logic of intensionality.

Appendix

The Formal Intensional Logic

In this appendix, we define the typed intensional logic. The system includes modality and tense operators, propositional attitude constructions, and indexicals. It is described in four sections: The Language, The Semantics, The Logic, and The Proper Axioms. We are not simply interested in the language and its interpretations, but also in the metaphysical theory expressible in the language, and in the logical apparatus that governs inference. Some of the formal definitions that follow are just sketched, since they can be found elsewhere in the literature.[1]

The system is governed by the following type construction. The types categorize not only the entities that inhabit the domains of quantification, but also the terms of the language that denote these entities. The set TYPE is the smallest set such that:

1. 'i' $\in$ TYPE

2. Whenever $t_1, \ldots, t_n \in$ TYPE, '$\langle t_1, \ldots, t_n \rangle$' $\in$ TYPE $(n \geq 0)$

The type 'i' is the type for *individuals*. The type '$\langle t_1, \ldots, t_n \rangle$' is the type for n-place relations the arguments of which have types $t_1, \ldots, t_n$, respectively. In Clause 2, we allow n to be 0, and so '$\langle \ \rangle$' is a type. This is the type for propositions (they have no arguments), and in what follows, we use 'p' to denote this type. Types may be thought of as symbols that categorize both pieces of language and pieces of the world,

---

[1] Compared with the system of Chapter V of [1983], the present system has some important new features. Besides the addition of tense operators, the language incorporates indexicals. To interpret the latter, the semantics includes a set of contexts relative to each interpretation. Context relative denotations are assigned to the indexicals. Also, the senses of names and indexicals are allowed to vary with context. These features are essential to the formalization of some of the ideas expressed in the previous chapters.

but in what follows, we omit the single quote marks when referring to them.

A.1   The Language

A.1.1   Primitive Symbols

The *primitive terms* of the language consist of the non-context-dependent names, the variables, and the context-dependent names.

Non-Context-Dependent Names: The symbols a_1^t, a_2^t, ..., for every type t, serve as the non-context-dependent names of the language. Informally, any lower or upper case letter may be used. For example, 'B' might serve as a name of a relation of type $\langle i, p \rangle$. The following are distinguished names: '$E!^{\langle t \rangle}$' is the existence predicate, for every t; '$=_{E^t}$' is the identity predicate, for every t; 'Ex' is the exemplification predicate having type $\langle \langle t_1, \ldots, t_n \rangle, t_1, \ldots, t_n \rangle$, where $t_1, \ldots, t_n$ are any types; and '$Tr^{\langle p \rangle}$' will serve as the explicit truth predicate for propositions.

Variables: The symbols x_1^t, x_2^t, ..., for every type t, serve as the variables of the language. Again, other lower and upper case letters may be used. For example, 'y' may be a variable of type i, and 'G' may be a variable of type $\langle i, i \rangle$.

Context-Dependent Names: For simplicity, we use only the indexicals 'I,' 'you,' and 'he,' which are all of type i. Without much modification, however, the system could accommodate other indexicals and demonstratives such as 'she', 'it', '$here$', and 'now'.

Other Primitive Symbols: The following primitive symbols have all appeared elsewhere in the text and should be familiar: $\sim$, $\rightarrow$, $\forall$, $\Box$, $\mathcal{H}$, $\mathcal{G}$, $\imath$, and λ. The symbols &, $\vee$, $\equiv$, $\exists$, $\Diamond$, $\mathcal{P}$, and $\mathcal{F}$ are all defined in the usual way.

A.1.2   Terms and (Propositional) Formulas

The terms and (propositional) formulas may be defined simultaneously by recursion.

1. Atomic terms: All primitive terms of type t are terms of type t.

2. Atomic formulas: If τ is a term of type p, then τ is a (propositional) formula.

3. Atomic formulas: If ρ is a term of type $\langle t_1, \ldots, t_n \rangle$, and $\tau_1, \ldots,$ τ_n are terms of type $t_1, \ldots, t_n$, respectively, then $\rho \tau_1 \ldots \tau_n$ is a (propositional) formula.

It will be convenient to call the first term in atomic propositional formulas the *initial term*, any other terms being the *argument terms* of the formula. So if 'P' and 'Qxy' are atomic propositional formulas, 'P' and 'Q' are initial terms. An *initial variable* is simply a variable that is an initial term. Sometimes, it is more perspicuous to separate the argument terms by commas and place parentheses around the arguments. So, for example, a formula involving the propositional attitude predicate 'B' of type $\langle i, p \rangle$ might be written: $B(x^i, y^p)$.

4. Atomic formulas: If ρ is a term of type $\langle t \rangle$ and τ is a term of type t, then $\tau\rho$ is a formula.

The formulas just defined are the atomic encoding formulas. These formulas are not propositional. The propositional formulas will ultimately consist of any (complex) formula having only atomic propositional formulas as proper parts. Only these formulas will be complex terms of type p and denote propositions.

5. Complex formulas: If ϕ and ψ are any (propositional) formulas and α is any variable (that is not an initial variable somewhere in ϕ) then $(\sim \phi)$, $(\phi \rightarrow \psi)$, $(\forall \alpha)\phi$, $(\Box \phi)$, $(\mathcal{H}\phi)$, and $(\mathcal{G}\phi)$ are (propositional) formulas.

We shall define the notion of *subformula* as follows: (a) every formula is a subformula of itself, (b) if ϕ is $\sim\psi$, $\psi \rightarrow \theta$, $(\forall \alpha)\psi$, $\Box\psi$, $\mathcal{H}\psi$, or $\mathcal{G}\psi$, then ψ is a subformula of ϕ, and (c) if θ is a subformula of ψ, and ψ is a subformula of ϕ, then θ is a subformula of ϕ.

By including all of the parenthetical remarks when reading the clauses (1) – (5), we get a definition of *propositional formula*. This is the only kind of formula that can be used to construct terms that denote complex properties, relations, and propositions. The propositional formulas meet two restrictions: (a) they must have no encoding subformulas, and (b) they must have no quantified subformulas $(\forall \alpha)\phi$ in which α is is an initial term somewhere in ϕ. The first restriction entails that no new relations are constructed out of encoding predications. Such relations sometimes engender paradox in the presence of the axiom that generates abstract objects, and so, in general, they are not routinely generated. The reason for the second restriction is that there is no simple way, using the logical functions like **PLUG**, etc., to produce denotations for formulas like '$(\forall F)Fa$' and '$(\forall G^p)(G^p \vee \sim G^p)$'. However, we may think of such formulas as abbreviations for '$(\forall F)ExFa$' and '$(\forall G^p)(TrG^p \vee$

$\sim TrG^p$),' respectively. By using the exemplification and truth predicates, the initial variables can be moved into argument position. Since an alternative means of expression are available, the second restriction on propositional formulas is not very significant.

Only propositional formulas may be used in the complex relation terms that are constructed in the next clause:

6. Complex terms: If ϕ is any propositional formula and $\alpha_1, \ldots, \alpha_n$ are any variables with types $t_1, \ldots, t_n$, respectively, such that none of the α_i's are initial variables somewhere in ϕ, then $[\lambda \alpha_1 \ldots \alpha_n \; \phi]$ is a term of type $\langle t_1, \ldots, t_n \rangle$.

In this clause, n may be 0, and so $[\lambda \; \phi]$ ("that-ϕ") is a term of type p. It is sometimes convenient to abbreviate '$[\lambda \; \phi]$' as 'ϕ.' For example, if 'B' is a propositional attitude predicate of type $\langle i, p \rangle$, and k is a term of type i, we often write '$B(k, \phi)$' instead of '$B(k, [\lambda \; \phi])$.'

Note that variables bound by the λ must not appear as initial variables somewhere in ϕ. Again, the reason is that there is no convenient way to interpret terms such as '$[\lambda F \; Fa]$' and '$[\lambda G^p \; G^p \vee \sim G^p]$.' But these terms may be used to abbreviate such terms as '$[\lambda F \; ExFa]$' and '$[\lambda G^p \; TrG^p \vee \sim TrG^p]$,' respectively. So little expressive power is lost through this restriction.

The next clause yields definite descriptions:

7. Complex terms: If ϕ is any formula and α^t any variable of type t, then $(\imath \alpha)\phi$ is a term of type t.

Note that definite descriptions containing encoding formulas may appear in propositional formulas. For example, the formula '$Ra(\imath y)yQ$' is propositional despite the presence of the encoding formula 'yQ.' The reason is that 'yQ' is not a subformula of the whole. Since the whole is propositional, it will denote a proposition as long as the description has a denotation. Furthermore, the λ-expression '$[\lambda x \; Rx(\imath y)yQ]$' is well formed. It will denote a property if the description denotes.

Finally, we form some special terms for denoting the senses of English terms:

8. Complex terms (Sense terms): If κ^t is any primitive or context-dependent name of type t, and σ is any primitive term of type i, then $\underline{\kappa}_\sigma$ is a term of type t.

9. Complex terms (Sense descriptions): If ϕ is any propositional formula, and α^t is any variable of type t, then $\underline{(\imath \alpha)\phi}$ is a term of type t.

These last two clauses formalize the underline and subscript notation used to denote the senses of English terms. If 'c' abbreviates 'Clemens' (type i) and 'a' denotes Anna, then '$\underline{c}_a$' is a name (type i) of the A-object that serves as the sense of 'Twain' for Anna. '$\underline{I}_a$' denotes the A-object that serves as the sense of the English word 'I' for Anna. If 'G' (type $\langle i \rangle$) abbreviates 'is a groundhog,' then '$\underline{G}_a$' is a name (type $\langle i \rangle$) of the A-property that serves as the sense of 'is a groundhog' for Anna. We should mention here that these special sense terms will not be entirely compositional—the underlined name is not a semantically significant part of the whole. The denotation of '$\underline{\kappa}_a$' is not constructed out of the denotations of 'κ' and 'a'. Rather, 'a' is the only semantically significant part of the term. Relative to each ordinary individual $o \in \mathbf{D}_i$, an indexed semantical function, $\mathbf{sen_o}$, maps every pair $\langle \kappa, \mathbf{c} \rangle$ consisting of a name κ of type t and a context $\mathbf{c}$, to an abstract object of type t that serves as the sense of κ for o in $\mathbf{c}$. So where o is the denotation of x, the denotation of '$\underline{\kappa}_x$' relative to a context $\mathbf{c}$ is $\mathbf{sen_o}(\kappa, \mathbf{c})$.

Note that the subscript on these special sense terms may be a variable. A sense term of the form '$\underline{\kappa}_x$' will receive a denotation relative to each assignment to the variables. Sense terms with variable subscripts are used in the reply to Kripke's objection concerning the sentence "Some people are unaware that Cicero is Tully" (Chapter 10). Note also that no primitive variable has a sense.

A sense description '$(\imath x^t)\phi$' will denote the A-object of type t that encodes just the property of being the unique ϕ, that is, just the property $[\lambda y^t\ (\forall z^t)(\phi_y^z \equiv z =_{E^t} y)]$. Note that ϕ must be a propositional formula (otherwise, it couldn't appear in the λ-predicate). There is no need for sense descriptions '$(\imath x)\phi$' in which ϕ contains an encoding subformula. That's because the descriptions of natural language do not contain encoding formulas. The sense of an English description 'the so and so' will always be understood as encoding the information associated with the *exemplification* reading of 'so and so.' Moreover, there is no need to represent the senses of formal descriptions because they do not have a sense. There are no substitutivity failures involving formal descriptions, since formal expressions are not part of the data.

The sense of an English term of type t is always identified as an entity of that same logical type. It is therefore logically coherent to build up the proposition signified by an English sentence by using either the denotations or the senses of the terms of the sentence. The result will still be a proposition. This is vastly unlike the theory of senses (or intensions) found in Church [1951] and in Montague [1974]. In their work, the sense (or intension) of an English term is always of a higher type than the denotation of the term.

A.2   The Semantics

A.2.1   Interpretations

An interpretation $\mathbf{I}$ of the above language is represented by any 9-tuple of the form $\langle\mathbf{D},(\mathbf{W},\mathbf{w}_0),(\mathbf{T},\mathbf{t},<),\mathbf{ext}_{\mathbf{w},\mathbf{t}},\mathbf{L},\mathbf{ext}_A,\mathbf{C},\mathbf{F},\mathbf{sen}\rangle$, the members of which are as follows:

1. $\mathbf{D}$ is the union of a collection of nonempty sets $\mathbf{D}_t$, $t \in$ TYPE. $\mathbf{D}_i$ is the domain of *individuals*. $\mathbf{D}_p$ is the domain of *propositions*. $\mathbf{D}_{\langle t_1,\ldots,t_n\rangle}$ is the domain of *relations* with arguments of type $t_1,\ldots,t_n$, respectively. As a subset of $\mathbf{D}$, we distinguish $\mathbf{R}$, the set of higher order objects. That is, $\mathbf{R}$ is the union of the sets $\mathbf{D}_t$, $t \neq i$. We use the metavariable 'o' to range over the members of $\mathbf{D}$, and the metavariable 'r' to range over the members of $\mathbf{R}$.

Within each set $\mathbf{D}_t$, we may distinguish the set of abstract objects of type t, $\mathbf{A}_t$, as follows: $\mathbf{A}_t = \{\mathbf{o}^t | (\forall \mathbf{w})(\forall \mathbf{t})(\mathbf{o}^t \notin \mathbf{ext}_{\mathbf{w},\mathbf{t}}(\mathbf{F}(E!)))\}$, where 'w' and 't' range over the members of $\mathbf{W}$ and $\mathbf{T}$, respectively, with $\mathbf{W}$, $\mathbf{T}$, $\mathbf{ext}_{\mathbf{w},\mathbf{t}}$, and $\mathbf{F}$ defined below.

2. $\mathbf{W}$ is the set of possible worlds, and $\mathbf{w}_0$ is a distinguished member of this set.

3. $\mathbf{T}$ is a nonempty set of times, and $\mathbf{t}_0$ is a distinguished member of this set. $<$ is a binary relation on $\mathbf{T}$.

4. $\mathbf{ext}_{\mathbf{w},\mathbf{t}}$ is a doubly indexed function that maps each member of $\mathbf{R}$ to an exemplification extension at each world-time pair $\langle\mathbf{w},\mathbf{t}\rangle$. If $\mathbf{r} \in \mathbf{R}_{\langle t_1,\ldots,t_n\rangle}$, then $\mathbf{ext}_{\mathbf{w},\mathbf{t}}(\mathbf{r})$ is a subset of the power set of $\mathbf{D}_{t_1} \times \ldots \times \mathbf{D}_{t_n}$. If $\mathbf{r} \in \mathbf{R}_p$, then $\mathbf{ext}_{\mathbf{w},\mathbf{t}}(\mathbf{r})$ is a member of $\{T, F\}$.

5. $\mathbf{L}$ is the set of logical functions that includes: $\mathbf{PLUG}_j$, $\mathbf{NEG}$, $\mathbf{UNIV}_j$, $\mathbf{CONV}_{j,k}$, $\mathbf{REFL}_{j,k}$, $\mathbf{VAC}_{j,t'}$, $\mathbf{COND}$, $\mathbf{NEC}$, $\mathbf{WAS}$, and $\mathbf{WILL}$. These are defined as follows:

   a. $\mathbf{PLUG}_j$ is a function from $(\bigcup_{1 \leq j \leq n}\mathbf{R}_{\langle t_1,\ldots,t_j,\ldots,t_n\rangle}) \times \mathbf{D}_{t_j}$ into $(\bigcup_{1 \leq j \leq n}\mathbf{R}_{\langle t_1,\ldots,t_{j-1},t_{j+1},\ldots,t_n\rangle}) \cup \mathbf{R}_p$ subject to the following conditions:

       i. for $n > 1$, $\mathbf{ext}_{\mathbf{w},\mathbf{t}}(\mathbf{PLUG}_j(\mathbf{r}^{\langle t_1,\ldots,t_n\rangle},\mathbf{o}^{t_j})) =$
   $$\{\langle\mathbf{o}^{t_1},\ldots,\mathbf{o}^{t_{j-1}},\mathbf{o}^{t_{j+1}},\ldots,\mathbf{o}^{t_n}\rangle|$$
   $$\langle\mathbf{o}^{t_1},\ldots,\mathbf{o}^{t_{j-1}},\mathbf{o}^{t_j},\mathbf{o}^{t_{j+1}},\ldots,\mathbf{o}^{t_n}\rangle \in \mathbf{ext}_{\mathbf{w},\mathbf{t}}(\mathbf{r}^{\langle t_1,\ldots,t_n\rangle})\}$$

       ii. for $n = 1$,

   $$\mathbf{ext}_{\mathbf{w},\mathbf{t}}(\mathbf{PLUG}_j(\mathbf{r}^{\langle t_1\rangle},\mathbf{o}^{t_1})) = \begin{cases} T \text{ iff } \mathbf{o}^{t_1} \in \mathbf{ext}_{\mathbf{w},\mathbf{t}}(\mathbf{r}^{\langle t_1\rangle}) \\ F \text{ otherwise} \end{cases}$$

b. **NEG** is a function from **R** into **R** subject to the following conditions:

    i. if $t = \langle t_1, \ldots, t_n \rangle$, then $\mathbf{ext_{w,t}}(\mathbf{NEG}(\mathbf{r}^t)) =$
$\{\langle \mathbf{o}^{t_1}, \ldots, \mathbf{o}^{t_n} \rangle | \langle \mathbf{o}^{t_1}, \ldots, \mathbf{o}^{t_n} \rangle \notin \mathbf{ext_{w,t}}(\mathbf{r}^t)\}$

    ii. if $t = p$, then

$$\mathbf{ext_{w,t}}(\mathbf{NEG}(\mathbf{r}^p)) = \begin{cases} T \text{ iff } \mathbf{ext_{w,t}}(\mathbf{r}^p) = F \\ F \text{ otherwise} \end{cases}$$

c. ... (etc., for $\mathbf{UNIV}_j$ (universalization), $\mathbf{CONV}_{j,k}$ (conversion), $\mathbf{REFL}_{j,k}$ (reflexivization), $\mathbf{VAC}_{j,t'}$ (vacuous expansion), $\mathbf{COND}$ (conditionalization), **NEC** (necessitation), **WAS** (past omnitemporalization), and **WILL** (future omnitemporalization)).[2]

Note that the function $\mathbf{ext_{w,t}}$ is constrained in such a way that the extension of a complex relation produced by the logical functions coheres naturally with the extensions of the simpler relations it may have as parts.

6. $\mathbf{ext}_A$ is a function that maps each member of $\mathbf{R}_{\langle t \rangle}$ to a subset of $\mathbf{D}_t$. Intuitively, it maps each property of type t objects to an encoding extension among those objects.

7. **C** is a non-empty set of contexts. There are three associated functions with domain **C** and range $\mathbf{D}_i$: g_I, g_{you}, and g_{he}. g_I maps context **c** to the denotation of the indexical 'I' in **c**. g_{you} maps **c** to the denotation of the indexical '*you*' in **c**. And similarly for g_{he}.

8. **F** is a function defined on the primitive names of the language. It assigns them elements of the appropriate domains. For each name κ^t, $\mathbf{F}(\kappa^t) \in \mathbf{D}_t$. In addition, **F** is constrained so that it assigns a relation with the appropriate extension to the distinguished predicates 'Ex' and 'Tr'.[3]

9. Finally, **sen** is a function that is defined as follows. Let $\mathbf{N}_t$ be the set of primitive and context-dependent names of type t. Then the domain of **sen** is $\mathbf{D}_i \times \mathbf{N}_t \times \mathbf{C}$, and its range is $\mathbf{A}_t$. This function identifies, for individual **o**, the A-object of type t that serves as the sense of name κ (of type t) in context **c**. It is convenient to index **sen** to its first argument.

---

[2] See our [1983], pp. 114–116, for the definitions of these functions in a modal type theory. However, **WAS** and **WILL** are new, but given the discussion of these functions in Chapter 3, it should be easy to define their type-theoretic counterparts.
[3] That is, $\mathbf{ext_{w,t}}(\mathbf{F}(Ex)) = \{\langle \mathbf{r}, \mathbf{o}^{t_1}, \ldots, \mathbf{o}^{t_n} \rangle | \langle \mathbf{o}^{t_1}, \ldots, \mathbf{o}^{t_n} \rangle \in \mathbf{ext_{w,t}}(\mathbf{r})\}$. Also, $\mathbf{ext_{w,t}}(\mathbf{F}(Tr)) = \{\mathbf{r}^p | \mathbf{ext_{w,t}}(\mathbf{r}^p) = T\}$.

A.2.2   Assignments

If given an interpretation **I**, an **I**-assignment will be any function, $\mathbf{f_I}$, defined on the primitive variables such that if α is a variable of type t, $\mathbf{f}(\alpha) \in \mathbf{D}_t$. In what follows, we suppress the subscript on the name of the function, with the understanding that all assignments are relativized to an interpretation.

A.2.3   Denotation and Satisfaction

These two notions will be defined simultaneously, though it will appear that denotation is defined first. The definition presupposes that the λ-expressions of the language have been uniquely classified by one of the following syntactic categories, for λ-expressions μ, ξ, and ζ: μ is *elementary*, μ is the jth-*plugging* of ξ by term τ, μ is the *negation* ξ, μ is the jth-*universalization* of ξ, μ is the j, k^{th}-*conversion* of ξ, μ is the j, k^{th}-*reflexivization* of ξ, μ is the j, t'-*vacuous expansion* of ξ, μ is the *conditionalization* of ξ and ζ, μ is the *necessitation* of ξ, μ is the *past omnitemporalization* of ξ, and μ is the *future omnitemporalization* of ξ. The definition constructing these syntactic categories (with the exception of the last two, which may be added in routine fashion) may be found in [1983] (pp. 117–118), and the reader may look there for the details.

Denotation: If given an interpretation **I**, an assignment **f**, and context **c**, we define the denotation of term τ with respect to **I**, **c**, and **f** ("$\mathbf{d_{I,c,f}}(\tau)$") as follows:

1. where κ is primitive name or a sense name, $\mathbf{d_{I,c,f}}(\kappa) = \mathbf{F}(\kappa)$

2. where α is any primitive variable, $\mathbf{d_{I,c,f}}(\alpha) = \mathbf{f}(\alpha)$

3. where κ is a context-dependent name, $\mathbf{d_{I,c,f}}(\kappa) = g_\kappa(\mathbf{c})$

4. where μ is an elementary λ-expression $[\lambda\alpha_1 \dots \alpha_n \, \rho\alpha_1 \dots \alpha_n]$, $\mathbf{d_{I,c,f}}(\mu) = \mathbf{d_{I,c,f}}(\rho)$

5. where μ is the jth-plugging of ξ by τ, $\mathbf{d_{I,c,f}}(\mu) = \mathbf{PLUG}_j(\mathbf{d_{I,c,f}}(\xi), \mathbf{d_{I,c,f}}(\tau))$

6. where μ is the negation of ξ, $\mathbf{d_{I,c,f}}(\mu) = \mathbf{NEG}(\mathbf{d_{I,c,f}}(\xi))$

7. ... (and so on, for $\mathbf{UNIV}_j, \mathbf{CONV}_{j,k}, \mathbf{REFL}_{j,k}, \mathbf{VAC}_{j,t'}$, **COND**, **NEC**, **WAS**, and **WILL**)

8. where μ is any λ-expression $[\lambda \, \phi]$, then

(a) if ϕ is a primitive term of type p, $\mathbf{d_{I,c,f}}([\lambda\ \phi]) = \mathbf{d_{I,c,f}}(\phi)$

(b) if $\phi = \rho\tau_1\ldots\tau_n$, $\mathbf{d_{I,c,f}}([\lambda\ \phi]) =$
$\mathbf{PLUG}_1(\ldots(\mathbf{PLUG}_n(\mathbf{d_{I,c,f}}(\rho),\mathbf{d_{I,c,f}}(\tau_n)),\ldots),\mathbf{d_{I,c,f}}(\tau_1))$

(c) if $\phi = (\sim\psi)$, $\mathbf{d_{I,c,f}}([\lambda\ \phi]) = \mathbf{NEG}(\mathbf{d_{I,c,f}}(\psi))$

(d) $\ldots$ (and so on, for $(\psi \to \chi)$, $(\forall\alpha)\psi)$, $(\Box\psi)$, $(\mathcal{H}\psi)$, and $(\mathcal{G}\psi)$)

9. where τ is any description $(\imath\alpha^t)\phi$, then

$$\mathbf{d_{I,c,f}}(\tau) = \begin{cases} \mathbf{o}^t \text{ iff } (\exists\mathbf{f'})(\mathbf{f'}\overset{\alpha}{=}\mathbf{f}\ \&\ \mathbf{f'}(x)=\mathbf{o}\ \&\ \mathbf{f'}\text{ satisfies}_{\mathbf{I,c}}\ \phi \\ \quad \text{at } \langle\mathbf{w}_0,\mathbf{t}_0\rangle\ \&\ (\forall\mathbf{f''})(\mathbf{f''}\overset{x}{=}\mathbf{f'}\ \&\ \mathbf{f''}\text{ satisfies}_{\mathbf{I,c}} \\ \quad \phi \text{ at } \langle\mathbf{w}_0,\mathbf{t}_0\rangle \to \mathbf{f''}=\mathbf{f'})) \\ \text{undefined, otherwise} \end{cases}$$

10. where $\underline{\kappa}^t_\sigma$ is any sense term, $\mathbf{d_{I,c,f}}(\underline{\kappa}^t_\sigma) = \mathbf{sen}_{\mathbf{d_{I,c,f}}(\sigma)}(\kappa^t,\mathbf{c})$

11. where τ is any sense description $(\underline{\imath x^t})\phi$, $\mathbf{d_{I,c,f}}(\tau) =$

$$\mathbf{d_{I,c,f}}((\imath z^t)(\forall F)(zF \equiv F = [\lambda x\ (\forall y^t)(\phi^y_x \equiv y =_{E^t} x)]))$$

Satisfaction: If given interpretation $\mathbf{I}$, assignment $\mathbf{f}$, and context $\mathbf{c}$, we may define $\mathbf{f}$ satisfies$_{\mathbf{I,c}}$ ϕ at world-time pair $\langle\mathbf{w,t}\rangle$ as follows:

1. If ϕ is a primitive term of type p, $\mathbf{f}$ satisfies$_{\mathbf{I,c}}$ ϕ at $\langle\mathbf{w,t}\rangle$ iff $\mathbf{ext_{w,t}}(\mathbf{d_{I,c,f}}(\phi)) = T$

2. If $\phi = \rho\tau_1\ldots\tau_n$, $\mathbf{f}$ satisfies$_{\mathbf{I,c}}$ ϕ at $\langle\mathbf{w,t}\rangle$ iff $(\exists\mathbf{o}_1)\ldots(\exists\mathbf{o}_n)(\exists\mathbf{r})(\mathbf{o}_1 = \mathbf{d_{I,c,f}}(\tau_1)\ \&\ldots\&\ \mathbf{o}_n = \mathbf{d_{I,c,f}}(\tau_n)\ \&\ \mathbf{r} = \mathbf{d_{I,c,f}}(\rho)\ \&\ \langle\mathbf{o}_1,\ldots,\mathbf{o}_n\rangle \in \mathbf{ext_{w,t}}(\mathbf{r}))$

3. If $\phi = \tau\rho$, $\mathbf{f}$ satisfies$_{\mathbf{I,c}}$ ϕ at $\langle\mathbf{w,t}\rangle$ iff $(\exists\mathbf{o})(\exists\mathbf{r})(\mathbf{o} = \mathbf{d_{I,c,f}}(\tau)\ \&\ \mathbf{r} = \mathbf{d_{I,c,f}}(\rho)\ \&\ \mathbf{o} \in \mathbf{ext}_A(\mathbf{r}))$

4. If $\phi = (\sim\psi)$, then $\mathbf{f}$ satisfies$_{\mathbf{I,c}}$ ϕ at $\langle\mathbf{w,t}\rangle$ iff it is not the case that $\mathbf{f}$ satisfies$_{\mathbf{I,c}}$ ψ at $\langle\mathbf{w,t}\rangle$

5. $\ldots$ (and so on, for $(\psi \to \chi)$, $(\forall\alpha)\psi$, $(\Box\psi)$, $(\mathcal{H}\psi)$, and $(\mathcal{G}\psi)$)

A.2.4   Truth, Logical Truth, and Logical Consequence

ϕ is *true*$_\mathbf{I}$ in context $\mathbf{c}$ iff every assignment $\mathbf{f}$ satisfies$_{\mathbf{I,c}}$ at $\langle\mathbf{w}_0, \mathbf{t}_0\rangle$. ϕ is *logically true* iff for every $\mathbf{I}$ and $\mathbf{c}$, ϕ is true$_\mathbf{I}$ in $\mathbf{c}$. ψ is a *logical consequence* of ϕ iff for every $\mathbf{I}$ and $\mathbf{c}$, if ϕ is true$_\mathbf{I}$ in $\mathbf{c}$, then ψ is true$_\mathbf{I}$ in $\mathbf{c}$.

A.3   The Logic

A.3.1   *The Logical Axioms*

The logical axioms of the system are to include all of the modal and tense closures of the following schemata, with the exception of Axiom (20) governing the ordinary descriptions. The unmodalized and untensed instances of the latter are axioms however.

Propositional Axioms:

1. $\phi \rightarrow (\psi \rightarrow \phi)$

2. $(\phi \rightarrow (\psi \rightarrow \chi)) \rightarrow ((\phi \rightarrow \psi) \rightarrow (\phi \rightarrow \chi))$

3. $(\sim\phi \rightarrow \sim\psi) \rightarrow ((\sim\phi \rightarrow \psi) \rightarrow \phi)$

Quantificational Axioms:

4a. $(\forall \alpha^t)\phi \rightarrow \phi_\alpha^\tau$, where τ contains no ordinary descriptions and is substitutable for α

4b. $(\forall \alpha^t)\phi \rightarrow (\psi_\beta^\tau \rightarrow \phi_\alpha^\tau)$, where ψ is any atomic formula, and τ both contains an ordinary description and is substitutable for both α and β

5. $(\forall \alpha^t)(\phi \rightarrow \psi) \rightarrow (\phi \rightarrow (\forall \alpha)\psi)$, provided α is not free in ϕ

Modal Axioms:

6. $\Box\phi \rightarrow \phi$

7. $\Box(\phi \rightarrow \psi) \rightarrow (\Box\phi \rightarrow \Box\psi)$

8. $\Diamond\phi \rightarrow \Box\Diamond\phi$

9. $\Box(\forall \alpha^t)\phi \equiv (\forall \alpha^t)\Box\phi$

Tense Axioms:[4]

10. $\phi \rightarrow \mathcal{HF}\phi$

11. $\phi \rightarrow \mathcal{GP}\phi$

12. $\mathcal{H}(\phi \rightarrow \psi) \rightarrow (\mathcal{H}\phi \rightarrow \mathcal{H}\psi)$

13. $\mathcal{G}(\phi \rightarrow \psi) \rightarrow (\mathcal{G}\phi \rightarrow \mathcal{G}\psi)$

---

[4] '$\mathcal{P}$' and '$\mathcal{F}$' are defined in the usual way.

14. $\mathcal{H}(\forall \alpha^t)\phi \equiv (\forall \alpha^t)\mathcal{H}\phi$

15. $\mathcal{G}(\forall \alpha^t)\phi \equiv (\forall \alpha^t)\mathcal{G}\phi$

Axiom of Encoding:[5]

16. $(\forall x^t)(\forall F^{\langle t \rangle}(\Diamond\blacklozenge xF \to \Box\blacksquare xF)$

λ-Axioms:

17. *λ-Equivalence*: Where ϕ is any propositional formula with no ordinary descriptions, and $x^{t_1}, \ldots, x^{t_n}$ are substitutable for $\alpha^{t_1}, \ldots, \alpha^{t_n}$, the following is an axiom:

$$(\forall x^{t_1})\ldots(\forall x^{t_n})([\lambda\alpha^{t_1}\ldots\alpha^{t_n}\ \phi]x^{t_1}\ldots x^{t_n} \equiv \phi^{x^{t_1},\ldots,x^{t_n}}_{\alpha^{t_1},\ldots,\alpha^{t_n}})$$

The second λ-schema is stated in terms of the definitions of relation identity. These are the type-theoretic formulations of the definitions described in Chapters 3 and 4.

Df: $F^{\langle t \rangle} = G^{\langle t \rangle} =_{df} \Box\blacksquare(\forall x^t)(xF \equiv xG)$

Df: $F^{\langle t_1,\ldots,t_n \rangle} = G^{\langle t_1,\ldots,t_n \rangle} =_{df}$ (where $n > 1$)
$(\forall x^{t_2})\ldots(\forall x^{t_n})([\lambda y^{t_1}\ Fyx^{t_2}\ldots x^{t_n}] = [\lambda y^{t_1}\ Gyx^{t_2}\ldots x^{t_n}])$ &
$(\forall x^{t_1})(\forall x^{t_3})\ldots(\forall x^{t_n})([\lambda y^{t_2}\ Fx^{t_1}yx^{t_3}\ldots x^{t_n}] =$
$\qquad [\lambda y^{t_2}\ Gx^{t_1}yx^{t_3}\ldots x^{t_n}])$ & $\ldots$ &
$(\forall x^{t_1})\ldots(\forall x^{t_{n-1}})([\lambda y^{t_n}\ Fx^{t_1}\ldots x^{t_{n-1}}y] = [\lambda y^{t_n}\ Gx^{t_1}\ldots x^{t_{n-1}}y])$

Df: $F^p = G^p =_{df} [\lambda y^i\ F^p] = [\lambda y^i\ G^p]$

In terms of these definitions, we have the following two axioms:

18. *λ-Identity₁*: Where ρ is any term of type $\langle t_1,\ldots,t_n \rangle$, the following is an axiom:

$$[\lambda\alpha^{t_1}\ldots\alpha^{t_n}\ \rho\alpha^{t_1}\ldots\alpha^{t_n}] = \rho$$

19. *λ-Identity₂*: Where $\beta_1, \ldots, \beta_n$ are any variables distinct from, but substitutable for $\alpha^{t_1}, \ldots, \alpha^{t_n}$, respectively, and ϕ' is the result of substituting all of the β's for the α's in ϕ, respectively, then the following is an axiom:

$$[\lambda\alpha^{t_1}\ldots\alpha^{t_n}\ \phi] = [\lambda\beta_1\ldots\beta_n\ \phi']$$

Axiom (18) reflects the fact that the denotation of an elementary λ-predicate is the same as the denotation of its relation term. Axiom (19) reflects the fact that λ-expressions that are alphabetic variants of one another have the same denotation.

---

[5]'$\blacksquare$' and '$\blacklozenge$' are defined in Chapter 2.

Description Axiom: The schema governing descriptions is stated in terms of the following defined notation:

Df: $O!^{\langle t \rangle} =_{df} [\lambda y^t \; \Diamond\blacklozenge E!^{\langle t \rangle} y^t]$

Df: $A!^{\langle t \rangle} =_{df} [\lambda y^t \; \Box\blacksquare \sim E!^{\langle t \rangle} y^t]$

Df: $x^i = y^i =_{df}$

$$(O!x \& O!y \& \Box\blacksquare(\forall F)(Fx \equiv Fy)) \lor (A!x \& A!y \& \Box\blacksquare(\forall F)(xF \equiv yF))$$

Df: $(\exists!\alpha^t)\phi =_{df} (\exists\alpha^t)(\forall\beta^t)(\phi_\alpha^\beta \equiv \beta = \alpha)$

The first definition identifies the "ordinary" objects of a given type. The second identifies the "abstract" objects of a given type. The third places identity conditions on individuals (ordinary individuals are identical iff they necessarily, always exemplify the same properties, whereas abstract individuals are identical iff they necessarily, always encode the same properties). The third definition, together with the definitions for relation and proposition identity, give us a complete set of identity conditions. Identity is now defined for objects of every type. The fourth definition is a schema for "uniqueness." It says different things depending on the type of object that uniquely satisfies the formula ϕ. Uniqueness claims are crucial to the following logical axiom schema that governs descriptions:

20. *Descriptions$_{LR}$*: Where $\psi_{\beta^t}^{(\iota\alpha^t)\phi}$ is any atomic or (defined) identity formula (or conjunction of such formulas) in which the description '$(\iota\alpha^t)\phi$' replaces the variable 'β^t' in ψ, the following is an axiom:

$$\psi_{\beta^t}^{(\iota\alpha^t)\phi} \rightarrow (\exists!\beta^t)\phi_\alpha^\beta \;\&\; (\exists\beta^t)(\phi_\alpha^\beta \;\&\; \psi)$$

The subscript on the name of this axiom indicates that this is the "left-to-right" version of a more general principle. Only the left-to-right version is logically true. The right-to-left version will be a proper axiom.

Axioms for the Special Terms:

21. $(\forall F^{\langle t_1,\ldots,t_n \rangle})(\forall x^{t_1})\ldots(\forall x^{t_n})(ExFx^{t_1}\ldots x^{t_n} \equiv Fx^{t_1}\ldots x^{t_n})$

22. $(\forall F^p)(TrF^p \equiv F^p)$

23. $A!^{\langle t \rangle}\underline{\kappa}_\sigma^t$

24. $\underline{(\iota x^t)\phi} = (\iota z^t)(\forall F^{\langle t \rangle})(zF \equiv F = [\lambda x^t \; (\forall y^t)(\phi_x^y \equiv y =_{E^t} x)])$

Axioms (21) and (22) reflect the constraints placed on the function $\mathbf{F}$ of interpretations. Axiom schema (23) reflects the fact that the function **sen** requires the sense of a name of type t to be an abstract object of type t. Axiom schema (24) reflects the clause assigning a denotation to the special sense descriptions.

A.3.2   The Rules of Inference

There are only two rules of inference: Modus Ponens and Generalization. The rule of necessitation and the rules of past and future omnitemporalization are derivable, subject to the restriction that they may not be applied to any line of proof that depends on an instance of $Descriptions_{LR}$ (Axiom 20).[6] The other standard rules of inference are derivable in the usual way. It is important to remember that the formal rule of Existential Generalization has two formulations, one derived from Axiom 4a, the other derived from Axiom 4b. Existential Generalization may not be applied to any formula containing a non-denoting description.

These rules permit the derivation of typed abstraction schemata asserting that there is a wide variety of relations (of every type $\langle t_1, \ldots, t_n \rangle$) and propositions (of type p). The derivations are routine, and they yield schemata that are the type-theoretic counterparts of the *Relations* and *Propositions* schemata described in Chapters 3 and 4, respectively. These schemata, together with the definitions for relation and proposition identity, offer a comprehensive modal and tensed theory of relations and propositions.

A.4   The Proper Axioms

The modal and tense closures of the following sentences and schemata constitute the proper axioms of the system, with the exception of the instances of Axiom 5 ($Descriptions_{RL}$), the unmodalized and untensed instances of which are proper axioms:

1. $(\forall x^t)(O!^{\langle t \rangle} x \rightarrow \Box\blacksquare\sim(\exists F^{\langle t \rangle})xF)$

2. $(\forall x^t)(\forall y^t)(x =_{E^t} y \equiv O!^{\langle t \rangle}x \ \& \ O!y \ \& \ \Box\blacksquare(\forall F^{\langle t \rangle})(Fx \equiv Fy))$

3. $\alpha^t = \beta^t \rightarrow (\phi(\alpha^t, \alpha^t) \equiv \phi(\alpha^t, \beta^t))$, where $\phi(\alpha^t, \beta^t)$ is the result of replacing some, but not necesarily all, free occurrences of α^t by β^t in $\phi(\alpha^t, \alpha^t)$, provided β^t is substitutable for α^t in the occurrences of α^t it replaces.

---

[6]The reason has to do with the fact that $Descriptions_{LR}$ is a logical truth that is not necessary. Refer to the end of Chapter 5, Section 4.

4. $(\exists x^t)(A!^{\langle t \rangle} x \And (\forall F^{\langle t \rangle})(xF \equiv \phi))$, where ϕ is any formula in which x^t is not free

5. $[(\exists! \beta^t)\phi_\alpha^\beta \And (\exists \beta)(\phi_\alpha^\beta \And \psi)] \rightarrow \psi_\beta^{(\iota \alpha^t)\phi}$, where ψ is any atomic or (defined) identity formula (or conjunction of such formulas) in which β is free

6. $(\forall x^t)(O!^{\langle t \rangle} x \rightarrow \Box \blacksquare E!^{\langle t \rangle} x)$, for any type t, $t \neq i$

These axioms have been discussed in the text, with the exception of Axiom 6. It simply asserts that any relational type object that exists at some world and time necessarily, always exists. Thus, all relational type objects either exist necessarily and always (in virtue of being ordinary) or they necessarily and always fail to exist (in virtue of being abstract).[7]

---

[7]Note that Axiom 3, the Principle of Substitutivity, is a proper rather than a logical axiom schema. The reason is that identity is not a primitive logical notion. The system offers an *theory* of identity, and Axioms 3 constitute an important part of the theory.

Bibliography

Adams, R. M.
[1974] "Theories of Actuality," *Nous* **8**: 211–231
[1986] "Time and Thisness," *Midwest Studies in Philosophy*, Volume XI: Studies in Essentialism, P. French, T. Uehling, and H. Wettstein (eds.), Minneapolis: University of Minnesota Press, 1986, 315–330

Barwise, Jon and Perry, John
[1983] *Situations and Attitudes*, Cambridge: MIT Press

Barwise, Jon
[1985] "The Situation in Logic–III: Situations, Sets, and the Axiom of Foundation," Center for the Study of Language and Information, Technical Report No. CSLI–85–26, Stanford University (June)

Bealer, George
[1982] *Quality and Concept*, Oxford: Clarendon

van Benthem, J. F. A. K.
[1985] *A Manual of Intensional Logic*, Center for the Study of Language and Information, Lecture Notes Number 1, Stanford University

Burge, Tyler
[1977] "Belief *De Re*," *Journal of Philosophy* **74** (June): 338–362

Brentano, Franz
[1874] *Psychologie vom empirischen Standpunkt*, in *Philosophische Bibliothek*, Hamburg: Meiner

Carnap, Rudolf
[1947] *Meaning and Necessity*, Chicago: University of Chicago Press

Castañeda, Hector-Neri
[1966] "'He': A Study in the Logic of Self-Consciousness," *Ratio* **8**: 130–157

[1967] "Indicators and Quasi-Indicators," *American Philosophical Quarterly* **4**: 85–100

Chierchia, Gennaro
[1984] *Topics in the Syntax and Semantics of Infinitives and Gerunds*, Ph.D. dissertation, Department of Linguistics, University of Massachusetts/Amherst

Chierchia, G., and Turner, R.
[1985] "Semantics and Property Theory," forthcoming, *Linguistics and Philosophy*, 1988

Chisholm, Roderick
[1960] *Realism and the Background of Phenomenology* (ed.), Glencoe: The Free Press

[1973] "Beyond Being and Nonbeing," *Philosophical Studies* **24** (1973): 245–257

[1976] *Person and Object*, La Salle: Open Court

Church, Alonzo
[1951] "A Formulation of the Logic of Sense and Denotation," *Structure, Method, and Meaning* New York: The Liberal Arts Press

Cocchiarella, Nino
[1978] "On the Logic of Nominalized Predicates and its Philosophical Interpretations," *Erkenntniss* **13**: 339–369

Dowty, D., Wall, F., and Peters, S.
[1981] *An Introduction to Montague Semantics*, Dordrecht: D. Reidel

Dreyfus, Hubert
[1982] *Husserl: Intentionality and Cognitive Science*, Cambridge: Bradford Books/The MIT Press

Donnellan, Keith
[1972] "Proper Names and Identifying Descriptions," in D. Davidson and G. Harman (eds.), *Semantics of Natural Language*, Dordrecht: D. Reidel, 356–379

Findlay, J. N
[1933] *Meinong's Theory of Objects and Values*, Oxford: Clarendon Press

Fine, Kit
[1977] "Postscript" to Prior [1977], *op. cit.*

Føllesdal, Dagfinn
[1982a] "Brentano and Husserl on Intentional Objects and Perception" in Dreyfus [1982], *op. cit.*

[1982b] "Husserl's Notion of Noema," in Dreyfus [1982], op. cit.

Forbes, Graeme
[1987] "Indexicals and Intensionality: A Fregean Perspective," *The Philosophical Review* XCVI/1 (January): 3–31

Frege, Gottlob
[1892] "On Sense and Reference," in *Translations from the Philosophical Writings of Gottlob Frege*, P. Geach and M. Black (eds.), Oxford: Basil Blackwell, 1970, 56–78

[1884] *Die Grundlagen der Arithmetik*, Breslau: Koebner; in English translation, *The Foundations of Arithmetic*, J. L. Austin (trans.), Oxford: Basil Blackwell, 2nd rev. ed., 1953

Husserl, Edmund
[1913] *Ideen zu einer reinen Phänomenologie und phänomenologischen Philosophie*, Halle: Niemeyer

van Inwagen, Peter
[1977] "Creatures of Fiction," *American Philosophical Quarterly* **14**: 299–308

Kaplan, David
[1977] "Demonstratives," Draft # 2, UCLA Monograph/Philosophy Department; forthcoming in *Themes from Kaplan*, J. Almog *et al.* (eds.), Oxford: Oxford University Press, 1988

Kripke, Saul
[1963] "Semantical Considerations on Modal Logic," *Acta Philosophica Fennica* **16**: 83–94

[1972] "Naming and Necessity," in D. Davidson and G. Harman (eds.), *Semantics of Natural Language*, Dordrecht: D. Reidel, 253–354

[1979] "A Puzzle About Belief," in *Meaning and Use*, A. Margalit (ed.), Dordrecht: D. Reidel, 239–283

Lakatos, Imre
[1973] "Science and Pseudoscience," in *The Methodology of Scientific Research Programmes*, Cambridge: Cambridge University Press

Lambert, Karel
[1983] *Meinong and the Principle of Independence*, Cambridge: Cambridge University Press

Lewis, David
[1986] *On the Plurality of Worlds*, Oxford: Blackwell

[1979] "Attitudes De Dicto and De Se," *Philosophical Review* **88**: 513–543

[1978] "Truth in Fiction," *American Philosophical Quarterly* **15**/1 (January): 37–46

Lockwood, Michael
[1971] "Identity and Reference," in *Identity and Individuation*, M. Munitz (ed.), New York: New York University Press, 199–211

Mally, Ernst
[1904] "Zur Gegenstandstheorie des Messens," in Meinong [1904b], *op. cit.*
[1912] *Gegenstandstheoretische Grundlagen der Logik und Logistik*, Leipzig: Barth

Meinong, Alexius
[1904a] "Über Gegenstandstheorie," in Meinong [1904b], *op. cit.*; English translation, "On the Theory of Objects," in Chisholm [1960], *op. cit.*, 76–117
[1904b] *Untersuchungen zur Gegenstandstheorie und Psychologie*, Leipzig: Barth

Menzel, Chris
[1986] "A Complete, Type-Free Second Order Logic of Properties, Relations, and Propositions, Center for the Study of Language and Information, Technical Report #CSLI–86–40, Stanford University

McMichael, Alan
[1983a] "A Problem for Actualism About Possible Worlds," *The Philosophical Review* LIXII (January): 49–66
[1983b] "A New Actualist Modal Semantics," *Journal of Philosophical Logic* **12**: 73–99

Montague, Richard
[1974] "The Proper Treatment of Quantification in Ordinary English," in *Formal Philosophy: Selected Papers of Richard Montague*, Richmond Thomason (ed.), New Haven: Yale University Press

Parsons, Terence
[1982] "Are There Nonexistent Objects," *American Philosophical Quarterly* **19**/4 (October): 365–371
[1980] *Nonexistent Objects*, New Haven: Yale University Press
[1979] "Referring to Nonexistent Objects," *Theory and Decision*, Dordrecht: D. Reidel, 95–110

Partee, Barbara
[1975] "Montague Grammar and Transformational Grammar," *Linguistic Inquiry* **6**: 203–300

Peacocke, Christopher
[1983] *Sense and Content,* Oxford: Oxford University Press, 1983

Perry, John
[1977] "Frege on Demonstratives," *The Philosophical Review,* LXXXVI/4 (October): 474–497

[1979] "The Problem of the Essential Indexical," *Nous* **13**: 3–21

[1980a] "Problem of Continued Belief," *Pacific Philosophical Quarterly* **61**: 317–332

[1980b] "Belief and Acceptance," in *Midwestern Studies in Philosophy,* Volume V, P. French *et al.* (eds.), Minneapolis: University of Minnesota Press, 1980

Plantinga, Alvin
[1976] "Actualism and Possble Worlds," *Theoria* **42**: 139–160

Pollock, John
[1984] *The Foundations of Philosophical Semantics,* Princeton: Princeton University Press

Prior, Arthur N.
[1977] *Worlds, Times and Selves,* Amherst: University of Massachusetts Press

Putnam, Hilary
[1973] "Meaning and Reference," *Journal of Philosophy* **70** (November): 699–711

Quine, W. V. O.
[1948] "On What There Is," in *From a Logical Point of View,* New York: Harper, 1953, 1–19

[1956] "Quantifiers and Propositional Attitudes," reprinted in *Reference and Modality,* L. Linsky (ed.), London: Oxford University Press, 1971, 101–111

[1960] "Variables Explained Away," in *Selected Logical Papers,* New York: Random House, 227–235

[1961] "Reference and Modality," in his *From a Logical Point of View,* Cambridge: Harvard University Press, 139–157

Rapaport, William
[1978] "Meinongian Theories and a Russellian Paradox," *Nous* **12**: 153–180

Richard, Mark
[1983] "Direct Reference and Ascriptions of Belief," *Journal of Philosophical Logic* **12**: 425–452

Routley, Richard
[1980] *Exploring Meinong's Jungle and Beyond*, Departmental Monograph #3, Philosophy Department, Research School of Social Sciences, Australian National University, Canberra

Russell, Bertrand
[1903] *The Principles of Mathematics* (2nd ed.), New York: Norton, 1938
[1904] "Meinong's Theory of Complexes and Assumptions," *Mind* **13** (April, July, and October): 204–219, 336–354, 509–524
[1905a] "On Denoting," *Mind* **14** (October): 479–493
[1905b] "Review of: A. Meinong, *Untersuchungen zur Gegenstandstheorie und Psychologie*," *Mind* **14** (October): 530–538
[1907] "Review of: A. Meinong, *Über die Stellung der Gegenstandstheorie im System der Wissenschaften*," *Mind* **16**: 436–439

Salmon, Nathan
[1979] "Review of Linsky, 1977," *Journal of Philosophy* **76** (August): 436–452
[1981] *Reference and Essence*, Princeton: Princeton University Press
[1986] *Frege's Puzzle*, Cambridge: The MIT Press

Scales, Ronald
[1969] *Attribution and Existence*, University of Michigan Microfilms

Searle, John
[1983] *Intentionality: An Essay in the Philosophy of Mind*, Cambridge: Cambridge University Press
[1979] "Intentionality and the Use of Language," in *Meaning and Use*, A. Margalit (ed.), Dordrecht: D. Reidel, 181–197

Smith, David W.
[1981] "Indexical Sense and Reference," *Synthese* **49**: 101–127

Smith, Janet Farrell
[1985] "The Russell–Meinong Debate," *Philosophy and Phenomenological Research* XLV/3: 305–350

Soames, Scott
[1987] "Direct Reference, Propositional Attitudes, and Semantic Content," *Philosophical Topics* XV/1: 47–87
[1988] "Direct Reference and Propositional Attitudes," in *Themes From Kaplan*, J. Almog *et al.* (eds.), Oxford: Oxford University Press

Stalnaker, Robert
[1976] "Possible Worlds," *Nous* **10**: 65–75

[1981] "Indexical Belief," *Synthese* **49** (1981): 129–152

[1985] *Inquiry*, Cambridge: Bradford Books/MIT Press

Stalnaker, Robert, and Thomason, Richmond
[1968] "Attribution in First Order Modal Logic," *Theoria* **3**: 203–207

Thomason, Richmond
[1980] "A Model Theory for Propositional Attitudes," *Linguistics and Philosophy* **4**: 47–70

Turner, Ray
[1987] "A Theory of Properties," *Journal of Symbolic Logic* **52**/2 (June): 455–472

Zalta, Edward N.
[1988a] "Logical and Analytic Truths That Are Not Necessary," *The Journal of Philosophy* **85**/2 (February): 57–74

[1988b] "A Comparison of Two Intensional Logics," *Linguistics and Philosophy* **11**/1 (February): 59–89

[1988c] "Singular Propositions, Abstract Constituents, and Propositional Attitudes," in *Themes From Kaplan*, J. Almog *et al.* (eds.), Oxford: Oxford University Press (forthcoming), 444–467

[1987] "On the Structural Similarities Between Worlds and Times," *Philosophical Studies* **51**: 213–239

[1986] "Lambert, Mally, and the Principle of Independence," *Grazer Philosophische Studien* **25**/**26**: 447–459

[1983] *Abstract Objects: An Introduction to Axiomatic Metaphysics*, Dordrecht: D. Reidel

Index